Inside the East European Planned Economy

This book puts forward a new perspective on the planned economies of communist Eastern Europe, demonstrating in detail how economic practice in such countries was shaped by the interplay among planners, managers and Party apparatchiks. Based on extensive original research, including interviews with former employees of industrial enterprises, the book argues that shortages, chronic overcapacities and erroneous planning decisions were present from the very beginning, rather than the consequences of later plan mistakes. They were the natural outcome of a profound conflict between leaders' attempt to adapt the basic laws of economics to their ideology and interests, and the requirements for rational bureaucracy of an increasingly sophisticated economy. The book discusses the evolution of and debates about the planned economy, considers the practice of plan development and implementation, and provides very detailed examples of how the planned economy actually worked at the level of the factory, at the point where plans and managers interacted with workers and production.

Voicu Ion Sucală is a Senior Lecturer in Engineering Management at the University of Exeter.

BASEES/Routledge Series on Russian and East European Studies

For a full list of available titles please visit: www.routledge.com/BASEES-Routledge-Series-on-Russian-and-East-European-Studies/book-series/BASEES

This series is published on behalf of BASEES (the British Association for Slavonic and East European Studies). The series comprises original, high-quality, research-level work by both new and established scholars on all aspects of Russian, Soviet, post-Soviet and East European Studies in humanities and social science subjects.

Inside the East European Planned Economy

State Planning, Factory and Manager

Voicu Ion Sucală

Routledge
Taylor & Francis Group
LONDON AND NEW YORK

First published 2018
by Routledge
2 Park Square, Milton Park, Abingdon, Oxon OX14 4RN

and by Routledge
605 Third Avenue, New York, NY 10017

First issued in paperback 2021

Routledge is an imprint of the Taylor & Francis Group, an informa business

Publisher's Note
The publisher has gone to great lengths to ensure the quality of this reprint but points out that some imperfections in the original copies may be apparent.

British Library Cataloguing-in-Publication Data
A catalogue record for this book is available from the British Library

Library of Congress Cataloging-in-Publication Data
Names: Sucala, Voicu Ion, author.
Title: Inside the East European planned economy : state planning, factory and manager / Voicu Ion Sucala.
Description: First Edition. | New York : Routledge, 2018. |
Series: BASEES/Routledge series on Russian and East European studies ; 122 | Includes bibliographical references and index.
Identifiers: LCCN 2017054007| ISBN 9781138068681 (hardback) | ISBN 9781315157689 (ebook)
Subjects: LCSH: Romania–Economic policy–1945-1989. | Industrial management–Romania. | Romania–Politics and government–1944–1989.
Classification: LCC HC405 .S83 2018 | DDC 330.9498–dc23
LC record available at https://lccn.loc.gov/2017054007

Typeset in Times New Roman
by Wearset Ltd, Boldon, Tyne and Wear

ISBN 13: 978-1-138-06868-1 (hbk)
ISBN 13: 978-0-367-43856-2 (pbk)

Book DOI: 10.4324/9781315157689

To Felicia and Ioan Sucală

Contents

Illustrations

Figures

Tables

Acknowledgements

This book wouldn't have been possible without the work, time, effort and support of so many different people, a few of whom I would like to thank here. The book is based on research I carried out in the last decade, mostly as part of my doctoral studies at University of Glasgow.

First, I'd like to thank to Professors Terry Cox and Stephen White, both from University of Glasgow, for supporting me with their exceptional erudition, knowledge and advice. Their careful and always constructive feedback has been crucial.

Along time many other academics have kindly helped me with advices, comments, suggestions and sometimes with much needed criticism. They are too many to mention them all here. However, I feel that a few names should be mentioned: Kate Brown, Dan Cândea, Carmen Constantinescu, Cezar Mereuţă, David Moon, Petru Prunea, Neelu Rohmetra, Dan Stegăroiu and Neharika Vohra. Ioan Abrudan's idea to invite managers to discuss with students, and to record those meetings for further research has been proved seminal. Additionally, all the interviewees who allowed themselves to be questioned deserve my gratitude. Even if not all of them are quoted in this book, they all helped me to get a better understanding of the industrial activity on that period.

I also thank Peter Sowden and the staff at Routledge for the patience, support and assistance in the process of production of this book.

I'd finally like to thank all of my close friends and family for providing the support during this difficult and exciting endeavour. I cannot express my gratitude enough to my parents, without whom I wouldn't be here today. And to Dan and Tudor, my perpetual sources of inspiration.

1 Introduction

This book presents the results of research focused on the main organisational and social practices within the Romanian industrial enterprise in the period of communist rule. This includes the relation between the enterprises and the planning structures – mostly the industrial branch ministry, aspects of personnel relations with the enterprise, the processes of selection and promotion, and the relations between these processes and the ruling Communist Party's strategies, directives and plans. The research made use of documents identified in Romanian National Archives, of two enterprises' monographs, and of interviews with former employees of these and other organisations.

The research thus was focused on key aspects of Romanian society and economy under communism that have so far attracted very little attention from academic research. A more detailed and nuanced understanding of the specific Romanian experience of communist rule is important both for an appreciation of Europe's complex history and memory, and for an understanding of the historical legacies that have helped to shape the character of the Romanian transition and of contemporary post-communist Romania.

The research had drawn on recent thinking about post-communism that stresses the idea that Eastern Europe is not a homogenous region – historical legacies, the cultural context and communist influences have generated different paths of communist evolution as well of the transition from communism to capitalism. In the words of Gallagher (1998, p. 52), 'while it is still weighted down by the legacies of foreign rule, the strength of collectivist values, and the damaging effects of Stalinism, the upheavals of the post-1989 era have resulted in different outcomes'.

In the Western academic literature, compared with the amount of work on other former communist countries, there are very few research studies that have focused on Romania. Among the authors who have focused on Romania, the most investigated subjects have been the history of the Romanian Communist Party (PCR), the Securitate (the notorious political police) and the violent events of 1989 and 1990. A detailed history of the PCR and of the establishment of Soviet rule was written by Ionescu (1964), and King (1980) also focused on the history of the PCR. Other subjects discussed in the literature have included the works of Kenneth Jowitt on the relation between PCR and other communist parties (1970), on Romanian political culture (1974), on Romanian communist elite policy of inclusion (1975) and on Romanian development (1971, 1978). Michael Shafir (1985) focused on the political stagnation and simulated change, and Katherine Verdery (1991, 1996) undertook anthropological studies on communist and post-communist Romanian society. It is also important to note the observation of Holmes (1997, p. 83) that 'certainly, the nature of the legitimation crisis was different in Romania from the other countries ..., as were the balances between coercion and legitimation and between internal and external modes of legitimation'. Kideckel (2008, p. 38) noted the uniqueness of the 'cult of labour' (*cultul muncii*) – 'one of the most elaborated regimes of worker symbolism in the socialist world'. Lee (2009) has argued that the former communist elite dominated, to some extent, the Romanian post-communist political scene. Dennis Deletant (1999a, 1999b) contributed significantly to research on communist Romania but as well on the 1989 events and the first decade of transition.

A common feature of much writing on Romania has been its stress on the strongly totalitarian or authoritarian nature of communist rule. Mary Ellen Fischer (1996, p. 208) accurately formulates it as follows: that 'Romania was totalitarian for much of the Gheorghiu-Dej period, authoritarian during the 1960s and early 1970s, and totalitarian again by the 1980s'. A similar perspective on the Stalinist character of the last decades of communism was that of Nelson (1988, p. 1), arguing that 'the regime has been oppressive and inflexible in its relationship with the people'. This perspective is also supported by one of the latest and best documented works, *The Final Report of the Presidential Committee for the Analysis of the Communist Dictatorship in Romania* (Tismăneanu, Dobrincu and Vasile, 2007), which is based on extensive archival research and on comparisons with experiences from other former communist countries. The authors stress the unusual character of Romanian communism: 'taking into consideration the lack of de-Stalinisation and of real reforms, the amplitude of the personality cult, and the inception of a dynastic scenario, one can consider the Romanian exceptionalism' (Tismăneanu, Dobrincu and Vasile, 2007, p. 25). The authors also consider that except for Albania, in no other European communist country did the Stalinist system have such an intensity and longevity.

According to King (2007, p. 719) the book authored by Tismăneanu, Dobrincu and Vasile (2007) represents 'the most serious, in-depth, and far-reaching attempt to understand Romania's communist experience ever produced'. But Murgescu (2010, p. 327) considers that the report dedicated an extensive part to the repressive system but missed a proper economic analysis. There are arguments supporting this criticism, because the main aspects discussed extensively by Tismăneanu, Dobrincu and Vasile (2007) are nationalisation, the collectivisation of agriculture and the effects of the economic crises of 1980s. Nevertheless, the authors consider that the economic failure wasn't generated only by ideological factors such as the command economy and obsession for industrialisation, but also by a complex of conjunctures including external factors, such as the oil crises in the 70s, and internal factors such as the relations between political elite and intellectuals or the inadequate strategies in education.

Two other volumes edited by Berindei, Dobrincu and Goşu (2009, 2012) contain a selection of relevant documents regarding the history of communism in Romania. The first volume published in 2009 contains 193 documents, and the second volume includes 102 documents. Both volumes contain extremely useful documents – notes, reports, memos, verbatim records, autobiographies and statistics issued by local and central state institutions. The documents were selected from various sources such as National History Archives, the Archive of Romanian Intelligence Service (SRI) and the Army Archives.

The common understanding of the strongly totalitarian and authoritarian nature of Romanian communism has had implications for the dominant view of Romanian society: that it had a distinctly top-down nature of economic and social policy making, and that elite recruitment and circulation were shaped predominantly by strict insistence on following the leadership's party line. The top-down antagonistic character of Romanian politics is not an exclusive characteristic of the communism; it can be traced back into the traditional view on the relation between the regime and society (Jowitt, 1974, p. 1179). However, there is very little detailed research on topics that are central to such an understanding, such as the nature of communist elites, their social characteristics, the processes determining recruitment to elite positions or on the broader social and demographic evolution of Romanian society. Nelson's work (1981, 1988) must be mentioned as an exception due to his focus on three main areas – elite-mass relations, local politics and vertical control and Romanian defence and military policies during the communist regime. A strong reason for the general lack of study of social and demographic aspects could be the secrecy and inconsistency of the sources regarding Romanian communist society. As Mary Ellen Fischer (Fischer, 1980, p. 210) noted, 'information on the Romanian elite is consistent only in its inconsistency'. Shafir (1985, p. 65) suggested that this could be the reason why political scientists who concentrate on Romania have 'never quite matched the performances of their colleagues who specialise in the Soviet Union'.

This research presented here also drew on the scientific works of Romanian scholars who are less known to the Western scientific community. Most of these works were published after the demise of communism, and are based on the systematic historical investigation of Romanian and foreign sources. Authors such as Victor Frunzã (1999), Victor Axenciuc (1992–2000a, b, c, 1997), Stelian Tãnase (1998), Bogdan Murgescu (2010), Constantin Ionete (1993) and N.N. Constantinescu (1997, 2000) extensively investigated important subjects such as the history of the PCR or the economic development in the last two centuries. Their works include relevant information for the context on which this research has been focused. Other sources of information are recollections, memoirs and interviews with people involved in the system. Authors such as Silviu Brucan (1996, 2012) and Gaston Marin (2000), who held important positions in the communist system, bring relevant information regarding the research theme.

The broader context

An understanding of Romanian economic management and the character of the industrial enterprise needs to be located within its broader economic, political and geo-political contexts. The following sub-sections attempt to do this through a discussion first of the question of Romania's economic backwardness and its significance in the shaping of strategies for economic and industrial development, second of the specific characteristics of the ruling Romanian Communist Party for the character of industrial and the formation of its system of industrial management, and third, the influence of the Soviet Union in the formation of Romanian industrialisation and economic management.

The legacy of backwardness

The relation between Romania and Europe has been a subject of intense debates over the last two centuries. Europe has been 'the main reference element for Romanian society, the object of complex attitudes, from admiration and imitation to fear and rejection' (Murgescu, 2010, p. 15). The obsession with disparities between Romania and Europe has been the *leitmotif* of many academic works, mainly from economics and sociology. However, the general interest seems to be less oriented on the historical causes and mechanisms that generated the disparities, and more focused on paths or methods suggested to reduce them. The discrepancies between Romania and the Western countries was a subject of intense debate in the Romanian elite. The problem of modernisation has been the key issue for the Romanian elites from the fourth decade of the nineteenth century until today (Tănase, 1998, p. 7). For Romanian elites, regardless of their nature or origin, the objective of modernisation has been essential. This objective has been defined either in negative terms – a liquidation of the disparities in comparison with the Western world, or in positive terms – a process of building a Western society. In spite of this objective's centrality, in the same period the gap has widened, even in comparison with Central and Eastern European countries, in terms of economic and social development. The internal and external factors that contributed to this evolution are presented here through a review of the existing literature.

The obsession with backwardness was not intensely debated only in Romanian society. For example, Bertram D. Wolfe (1967) has presented the history of political thought on backwardness in Russia. A book authored by Alexander Gerschenkron (1962) comprises a collection of essays previously published between 1951 and 1961 in various journals and delivered at conferences. The author focused mostly on the case of Soviet industrialisation, but also on the cases of Italy and Bulgaria. For Gerschenkron (1962, p. 1), the underlying hypothesis of all his essays was that 'very significant interspatial variations in the process of industrialization are functionally related to the degree of economic backwardness that prevailed in the countries concerned on the eve of their "great spurts" of industrial growth'. The author argues that neither the socialist characteristic, nor the high rate of growth help to understand the Soviet economy.

Andrew C. Janos focused on the problem of backwardness in the case of Hungary. His book *The Politics of Backwardness in Hungary 1825–1945* was published in 1982, and it analysed the modern period up to World War II. According to Janos, one of the main reasons for the backwardness could be related to the progress generated by the epochal innovations in production and transportation in the Western countries. In this area, technological innovations generated a new social configuration and finally led to the modern nation state. In the periphery, the phases of development were reversed, and the modern state took shape through a process of diffusion before the modern economy. Moreover, the modern state was supposed to be 'a potential instrument of social change' (Janos, 1982, p. 314), not a result of the technologic and economic development. This reversal had some important consequences for the social structure but also for public attitudes. At the social level a progressive narrowing of the political regimes, a gradual increase in *etatism* and a political class looting the state had been encountered instead of a gradual democratisation, the development of a capitalist economy and of a bourgeois society. In the Hungarian case, Janos (1982) argued that because expectations were disseminated faster than the means of material improvement, a deep sense of frustration, of relative deprivation had been generated. In a long run the masses' pent-up frustrations acted 'as the single most important destabilising factor in peripheral politics' (Janos, 1982, p. 315). This sense of frustration affected the whole society, including the members of the political elites because from an international perspective their identity was 'stamped with poverty and backwardness of their country of origin' (Janos, 1982, p. 316). However, it is not very simple to identify the causes of the backwardness of Hungary and, broadly speaking, of other countries in Eastern Europe. The most popular hypothesis considers the dependence of the backward nations on the more advanced one. But as Janos (1982) argued this is not the case for Hungary, except for a few periods in its history. Another hypothesis considered regards the costs of maintaining a modern state apparatus while the supporting economic system is under-developed. Consequently, the state will become a drain on scarce resources and it will prevent the rise of a viable economy. Again, Janos (1982) argued this is not a situation significantly present in the case in Hungary. He also brought into discussion the issue of the culture as 'the injunctions of collective memories and religious heritage' (Janos, 1982, p. 323), suggesting that the attempt to link successful development to Western culture should be cautiously considered. Janos (1982, p. 323) concluded that 'a hospitable institutional and international environment' is the only context in which the social, economic and political change can succeed, in a close relation with culture as a necessary condition.

Since the problem of measuring economic and social differences is a complex one and it is not the objective of this study to approach the issue, in this section will be presented a brief outline of the historical evolution of the main social and economic disparities between Romania and the other European countries, as it is evidenced in the existing literature.

Usually, the disparity between Romania and Europe has been discussed in the Romanian literature from three main points of view – economic, political and cultural. Murgescu (2010) has made an extensive analysis of the economic disparities accumulated in the last five centuries. He has based his analysis on the works of Victor Axenciuc, Georgescu-Roegen, Paul Bairoch, Angus Maddison and Sydney Pollard, and on the statistical data available for the twentieth century. The increasing economic disparity between Romania, Europe and the world averages is synthetically represented by the GDP/capita index. Angus Maddison's works were used to illustrate the evolution of these economic disparities in the first half of twentieth century. Maddison was a British researcher on quantitative macroeconomic history and he focused his work mostly on the measurement and analysis of economic growth and development. He was professor at the University of Groningen from 1978 to 1997, and a founder of the Groningen Growth and Development Centre. After Maddison's death in 2010, the Maddison Project has been initiated by a group of close colleagues, with the aim of supporting effective cooperation between scholars to continue Maddison's work on measuring economic performance for different regions, time periods and subtopics. Some of Maddison's results are disputed, but mostly those regarding the period before 1900, and other regions than Europe and the USA. Maddison's results regarding communist countries are very useful because they offer a more realistic perspective on the economic performance of the command economy than provided by official statistics. Maddison's results are relevant on the one hand for an assessment of the efforts made by state propaganda to paint reality in brighter colours, and on the other hand to understand the limitations of the economic system to relate prices with real values. However, the comparison of the economic performance of communist countries with the performance of capitalist countries was not an easy task. In 1998 Angus Maddison published a paper focused on the analysis of Central Intelligence Agency (CIA) estimates of major economic indicators of the Soviet economy. According to Maddison (1998), there are major methodological and practical problems when one tries to compare capitalist and communist economies because in the communist official statistics 'coverage was narrow, they overstated growth, and understated inflation' (Maddison, 1998, p. 308). The problems were amplified by differences in statistical practice between communist and capitalist countries, and by a few characteristics of command economies. According to Maddison, one of the most relevant characteristics was the narrower scope of economic activity which relied only on material production and ignored non-material service activities because they were considered non-productive. Consequently, important sectors of the economy such as passenger transport, housing, health, education, entertainment, banking, insurance, government, party administration and the military had a much lower share in the GDP. Another important characteristic of communist statistical practices was the strong preference for measures of gross output rather than value added. Considering the planning system incentive for fulfilling plan objectives, it resulted in a universal tendency to understate inflation and exaggerate growth in the volume of output. Maddison concluded that CIA estimates regarding Soviet economy performance were 'the best documented and most reasonable' (Maddison, 1998, p. 314).

The results published mostly on the Maddison Project's website have been used in this study in order to create a realistic perspective on the performance of the Romanian communist economy. The figures in Table 1.1 are taken from Murgescu (2010), who compiled some of the results from Maddison's research. It clearly shows that at the beginning of the twentieth century Romania's economic performance was slightly better than the average of 7 East European countries (Albania, Yugoslavia, Bulgaria, Poland, Hungary, Romania and Czechoslovakia). But during the next four decades Romania lost ground, not only in comparison with Western countries but also in comparison with the East European average. The most important factors explaining this negative evolution are presented below.

According to Murgescu, around the 1500s the disparity between the Romanian principalities (Transylvania, Moldova and Muntenia) and Western Europe was relatively small. The development of the Romanian principalities during the sixteenth to eighteenth centuries was in line with the European average, keeping the disparity relatively small and constant. The situation then changed in the nineteenth and twentieth centuries, as Romania suffered from the lack of a coherent and consistent development strategy. The basic problem was that economic development was based on extensive exploitation of resources and population growth without a consistent change of economic structures.

There are few significant similarities between Hungary and Romania. The rural character and the industrial backwardness in comparison with West European countries represented important similarities; therefore, an important effort had been made during the communist regime in both countries for industrialisation. Table 1.2 presents the GDP (in equivalent units) of Romania and Hungary from 1870 to 1990, in comparison with the average of 7 East European countries (Albania, Bulgaria, Czechoslovakia, Hungary, Romania, Yugoslavia and Poland), and the average of 12 West European countries. The data indicate a divergent path of development followed by Romanian in contrast both with Hungary – in spite of a similar starting point at the end of nineteenth century, and in contrast with the European average.

Attempts at economic reform began after Romania gained self-government in 1859 when Alexandru Ioan Cuza was elected with French support as ruler both

Table 1.1 GDP/capita (international dollars Geary-Khamis, 1990)

	1913	*1929*	*1938*	*1950*
World average	1,525	1,806	–	2,111
Average of 12 Western countries	3,688	4,387	4,818	5,018
Average of 7 CEE countries	1,695	1,942	1,980	2,111
Russia/USSR	1,448	1,386	2,150	2,841
Romania	1,741	1,152	1,242	1,182

Source: Murgescu, 2010, p. 211.

Table 1.2 Hungary and Romania GDP evolution (in equivalent units)

	12 Western European countries	*Hungary*	*Romania*	*7 Eastern European countries*
1870	2,141	1,092	931	953
1890	2,703	1,473	1,246	1,276
1910	3,442	2,000	1,660	1,667
1929	4,452	2,476	1,152	1,982
1950	4,944	2,480	1,182	2,088
1960	7,498	3,649	1,844	3,058
1970	10,853	5,028	2,853	4,350
1980	13,958	6,306	4,135	5,829
1990	16,793	6,459	3,511	5,427

Source: Maddison project database, available at www.ggdc.net/maddison/maddison-project/home.htm.

in Moldavia and Wallachia. Many important reforms were introduced by Cuza in a period of six years, among which probably the most important was land reform. In 1866 however, after 'the only genuinely radical political interlude in Romania's history as a state' (Gallagher, 2005, p. 22), a coup removed Cuza and replaced him with a member of the German Hohenzollern family – Prince Carol. During his reign, although radical reform came to an end, Romania achieved independence in 1877 after an independence war in which Carol led combined Romanian and Russian forces against the Ottoman army, and it was internationally recognised as a state in 1881. Overall, according to Axenciuc (1997), the result of the period between 1859 and 1914 was positive. The transition from a feudal society towards a modern one, with an economy based more on trade than on self-sufficiency, with a new legal and institutional system, with an infrastructure and an industry in a development process were the most important achievements.

This period also witnessed the beginning of the Westernisation of the political elites who increasingly received a Western education and began to adopt the principles of a modern society. By the time of the interwar period, about 75 percent of the Romanian political elite were graduates from Western European universities (Gavrilovici and Iacob, 2006, p. 701). However, according to an article published by Titu Maiorescu in the newspaper *Convorbiri literare* in 1868, the changes that took place in this period can be best described as forms without content (*forme fără fond*), resulting from 'the lack of any solid foundation for the forms we are continuously receiving from outside'. This clearly describes a top-down modernisation process in which, as Janos (1982) argued, the ameliorations in living conditions did not reach people's expectations. Until World War I, in spite of consistent economic growth, the reform of the state lagged behind other developments. Moreover, the pace of modernisation was insufficient to significantly boost the economy and the gap relative to Western Europe increased in terms of economic development. Murgescu (2010, p. 204) concluded that

> the historical causes accumulated in time have had a decisive role in preserving Romania at the periphery of Europe, but on the other hand, the political elites have perceived the economic problems only partially and with a great delay, and their policies were undue, inadequate and inefficient.

According to Axenciuc (1997, p. 203) 'the time was short, the means of implementing the change were insufficient, the social and political resistance was strong and the economic and mentality backwardness were too strong to obtain better results in that fifty years'.

Once World War I ended, Romania faced new challenges: its territory and population more than doubled. According to 1930 census, the population of the Old Kingdom (*Vechiul Regat*) represented 48.6 per cent of the whole of Romania's population at the moment of the census (Direcţiunea Recensământului General al Populaţiunei, 1931a, p. 31). According to the same census, ethnic minorities represented more than 28 per cent of the total population (Direcţiunea Recensământului General al Populaţiunei, 1931b, p. xxiv). This significant increase in territory and population, and 'a happy ending to the long-fought struggle for national unity seemed a most auspicious foundation for Rumania's new postwar life', but it resulted only in a 'rather dismal history of interwar Rumania' (Brown, 1979, p. 456). The centralised policies of the government performed poorly in attempting to reconcile with the new status. In spite of a prevailing positive public appreciation of the economic development of the country in the interwar period, most historians agreed on the economic failure of this period. According to Murgescu (2010) there are three main causes of this failure: the economic cost of World War I, the agricultural conjuncture and the oil conjuncture. While the first cause represents a price consciously assumed by the political elite to achieve national unity, the other two causes were generated by inadequate government policies addressing internal and external situations.

The population deficit of Romania generated by World War I was 14 per cent, ranking the country third among European countries. Only Serbia (31.3 per cent) and Russia (18.5 per cent) recorded higher figures for this indicator (Murgescu, 2010, p. 222). Huge material losses were generated both by the wartime devastation and by the seizure of large quantities of oil, cereals, livestock and other goods by the German occupation (Axenciuc, 1997, p. 220). Besides the human losses, at the end of the World War I roughly 60 per cent of industry and 30 per cent of the railway system were destroyed and livestock was reduced by 50 per cent. The post-war inflation was aggravated by three additional factors: the gold reserve appropriated by the new Soviet government, the money supplied by the German occupying authorities in 1917–18 and the monetary unification required by the new territories acquired after the war. At the end of 1916 and the beginning of 1917, under the threat of German occupation, 105 tons of gold (Axenciuc, 1997, p. 200) and other valuable objects from the treasury of the Romanian National Bank were sent to Moscow to be kept safe by the Russian Empire. The new Soviet authorities seized the gold and this issue has remained a bilateral problem up to the present. After World War I roughly half of the circulating money in Romania was issued by the German occupation authorities (Kiriţescu, 1997, vol. II, p. 127). Finally, the monetary unification of the new territories cost Romania more than 73 per cent of the 1920/1921 state budget (Kiriţescu, 1997, vol. II, p. 288; Axenciuc, 1992–2000c, p. 621). As a result of all these causes, the devaluation of the Romanian currency lasted until 1925 and monetary stabilisation was not achieved until 1929 (Axenciuc, 1997, p. 305).

The country's poor industrialisation, concentrated in few areas mainly in Transylvania, Bucharest and Ploieşti County left the country with a mainly agricultural economy, with roughly 80 per cent of the population living in rural areas according to the official statistics (Direcţia Centralã de Statisticã, 1990). Roberts (1951, p. 83) argued that Romania's agricultural stagnation was generated by factors such as the demographic pressure that compensated for the effects of the agrarian reform in terms of average area owned by a household, the slump in the European cereals trade, disadvantageous agricultural policies, fragmented agricultural areas, the extensive system of exploitation and the archaic system of social relations. The decline of productivity in agriculture was significant relative not only to Western countries but also to other predominantly agricultural countries like Hungary, Poland or Bulgaria (Murgescu, 2010, p. 228). According to Korkut (2006, p. 133) 'during the interwar years the country was predominantly rural, and ethnic Romanians were still mostly serfs on lands owned by members of the numerous minorities'. This assertion might be less than accurate since through a significant agrarian reform (1919–21) 6.4 million hectares were distributed to 1.6 million peasant households (Axenciuc, 1997, p. 246). But Axenciuc (1992–2000b, p. 183) showed that after the reform more than three quarters of households owned less than 5 hectares, which was considered at that time the subsistence minimum limit for a family. Cereals accounted for a significant proportion of Romania's exports. Both internal and external contexts generated unfavourable results: when international prices were high Romania exported small quantities and when prices dropped Romania tripled exports (Murgescu, 2010, p. 234).

Oil had been one of the most important resources of Romania. Exploitation increased significantly after the Law of Mines was adopted in 1895. According to Axenciuc (1992–2000a, p. 291) crude oil extraction increased from 200 tonnes in 1857 to 247,000 tonnes in 1900 and to 1,848 million tonnes in 1913. The oil extraction industry attracted most of the foreign investment from the end of the nineteenth century to 1947. Because in the interwar period oil demand increased constantly, the only limit faced by Romanian oil exports was its production capacity. After the effects of World War I, Romania had reached the pre-war level of exports in 1926, and they constantly increased until 1936. But like cereals exports, oil exports experienced a similar situation: when oil prices were high (1923–26) Romanian exports were low, and when exports reached their peak (1936) international prices dropped (1931–36).

In the spirit of Maiorescu's 'forms without content', in the interwar period 'the practice of government was subject to patronage and to narrow sectional interests' (Deletant, 1999b, p. 12). This practice, combined with the 1930s economic recession, led to a decade of instability, right-wing movements and dictatorship. In addition to the internal problems faced by the Romanian state, relations with the neighbours were as problematic. After World War I, Transylvania 'was the most significant, and emotionally felt, loss' (King, 1980, p. 11) for Hungarians who considered it an important part of their homeland. The Soviet government refused to accept the union of Bessarabia with Romania and Bulgaria claimed the South of Dobruja. As King (1980, p. 11) has concluded, 'the Romanian governments during the interwar period were not terribly successful in dealing with the multiple challenges they faced'.

An important phase in the interwar economic evolution was the Economic Treaty (Wohltat-Bujoiu Accord) signed by Romania and Nazi Germany on 23 March 1939. Its main objective was to guarantee a dominant position for Germany in Eastern Europe and access to Romanian resources. The Romanian political elite's objective was to postpone as much as possible the implementation of the treaty, in the hope that France and United Kingdom would eventually manage to balance Germany's power (Banu, 2004, pp. 23–36). The Romanian Foreign Minister Grigore Gafencu noted on official documents on 26 March 1940 that 'we have to resist and to gain time. Germany must not win the economic war in East at our expense and sacrificing our independence, before Germany is defeated in West' (cited in Banu, 2004, p. 34). But France's capitulation on 22 June 1940 and the implementation of the Ribbentrop-Molotov treaty marked the total failure of Romanian foreign policy. After a disastrous 1940 in which Romania lost Bessarabia and Northern Bukovina to the USSR, Northern Transylvania to Hungary and Southern Dobruja to Bulgaria, Romania participated in the German attack on the Soviet Union in June 1941. During World War II German capital had increased its share in the Romanian economy through three methods: by taking over the Allies' assets, by taking over the properties of Jews, and, on a smaller scale, through direct investments. The German interest in Romania materialised in companies in different sectors such as oil and coal extraction, metallurgy, agriculture and forestry. Between January and August 1944 Romanian resistance to the German attempt to control the economy had significantly weakened. Most of the oil and metallurgical industries were controlled by German representatives. In addition, German companies attempted to monopolise other activities such as acquisitions of agricultural products or the insurance sector (Banu, 2004, pp. 45–56). The Axis defeat at Stalingrad in February 1943 provided the final impulse for the coup of 23 August 1944. After this moment communism took over in Romania with the support of the Soviet Army and of Soviet counsellors. Romanian society 'was demolished by an outside force, The Soviet Union' (Kornai, 1992, p. 30). After King Michael's abdication on 30 December 1947, the communists led the country without any kind of real opposition. The main instrument for the economic subordination to Soviet interests was the Armistice Convention signed on 12 September.

Once again, the issue of backwardness then came into the mainstream discourse, this time into the one of the communist leaders. The promise to eliminate backwardness was 'a major constituent of the official ideology' (Kornai, 1992,

p. 161), and it was based on a belief in the socialist system's superiority. The closing of this gap was an important topic in Romanian communist strategies and propaganda. Consequently, the leaders of the communist parties had to insist on fast growth 'because it will provide further evidence of that superiority' (Kornai, 1992, p. 161). The communist leadership's decision to transform Romania's agricultural and predominantly rural society into an industrial and urban one generated 'rapid and fundamental socioeconomic change in the 1960s and 1970s' (Nelson, 1988, p. 7). According to official statistics, economic growth throughout the 1960s and 1970s was among the highest in the world, and it was followed by the improvement of health and education systems, an increase in the percentage of the urban population, the lowering of infant mortality, the increasing of life expectancy and other improvements in living conditions (Direcţia Centrală de Statistică, 1972, 1979, 1980).

However, in spite of some irrefutable successes, for example the spectacular reduction of illiteracy from roughly 29 per cent of the total population older than seven in 1948 to 3–4 per cent (Constantinescu, 2000, pp. 321–340), Romania's economic failure was the most pronounced among the communist countries. The cost of these significant improvements was high, consisting in 'mounting hard-currency debt, trade imbalances and labour-based difficulties of the 1980s' (Nelson, 1988, p. 8). The reality had finally contradicted the Party's expectations. Furthermore, the case of Romania is significant from this point of view. At the end of the communist regime, the discrepancies between Romania and the Western countries had consistently increased, and so also did the discrepancies between Romania and the other European communist countries. Table 1.3 is adapted from Maddison (2003, p. 101) and it presents synthetically the evolution of GDP per capita for eight European communist countries in the last decade of communism. In that period only Romania and Poland recorded a negative GDP per capita evolution, but while in Poland the GDP per capita in 1989 was 99 per cent of 1980, in Romania it was 95.3 per cent.

According to Kornai (1992) the economic growth experienced by the communist states was forced, being generated not by society itself but by top-down

Table 1.3 The evolution of GDP/capita in eight communist countries between 1980 and 1989 (1980=100)

	1980	*1982*	*1987*	*1989*
Albania	100	101.1	104.1	105.5
Bulgaria	100	105.4	105.6	102.8
Czechoslovakia	100	100.8	106.9	109.8
Yugoslavia	100	101.4	106.6	103.0
Poland	100	92.1	99.0	99.0
Romania	100	98.5	99.4	95.3
Hungary	100	104.4	108.1	109.5
USSR	100	101.7	108.0	110.5

Source: Maddison, 2003, p. 101.

bureaucratic decision. This kind of growth is unsustainable, and sooner or later it will slow down. In the same manner, after initial steps to fulfil communism's basic promises, complete fulfilment 'never occurs and never can occur' (Kornai, 1992, p. 54). For Romania, the slowdown of economic growth came later than in other communist countries (Murgescu, 2010, p. 369). The most visible symptom of the economic failure was the fall in domestic consumption. An extensive analysis of this process was made by Ionete (1993). Initially requested by the first post-1989 government, Ionete's report contains a well-documented analysis of Romania's economic crises in its explosive phase.

According to Ionete (1993, p. 15) the crises took the shape of 'ruined production capabilities, exhausted material and human resources, economic isolation, biological degradation of the population and a threat to Romanian spirituality'. Consumption was affected in almost all areas, from basic food to public services. As an example, in 1989 the energy consumption of the population was smaller than the losses in the energy network because of the frequent black-outs of the private supply and of public lighting (Ionete, 1993, p. 79). Murgescu (2010, p. 372) estimated the reduction of the overall meat consumption from 1980 until 1989 at 200,000 tonnes. According to the calculations of Marvin Jackson cited in Siani-Davies (2005, p. 14) the greatest decline in living standards occurred between 1980 and 1983 when the overall domestic consumption fell by 17 percent. The reduction of private consumption was related to Ceaușescu's decision to pay back foreign debt by reducing imports and boosting the exports of consumer goods. But the systemic crisis of the Romanian economy in the last decade of the communism had multiple causes and aspects. It was generated by internal factors as well as by the evolution of the international conjuncture. Ionete (1993) had argued that in the Romanian command economy the decision-making system did not create the minimum conditions for proper observation and adjustment of economic imbalances. The stubborn refusal to adjust the economy to reality and to attenuate the social tensions, the focus on the preservation of the political system had altogether amplified the unfavourable internal and external contexts. The crisis was painfully perceived after three decades of apparent economic growth, with slow improvements in living standards. At the end of the communist regime Romania's place in the European economy had worsened in terms of absolute and relative economic indicators in comparison with 1938 (Ionete, 1993, p. 28).

The Romanian Communist Party – a short and obscure history

The 1944 coup transformed the PCR from a small faction-ridden group irrelevant to Romanian society into an influential factor in the political scene. The role played by the PCR before 1944 had little significance for Romanian society. The PCR's lack of influence in Romania's interwar politics can be attributed to three main factors: the government decision to outlaw it in April 1924, less than three years after it was founded; Soviet pressures on the PCR to consider Romania an imperialistic state, which considerably limited the PCR's appeal; and the reduced working class proportion in Romanian society. According to CIA (1944, p. 4) and Tismăneanu, Dobrincu and Vasile (2007, p. 56) the PCR had fewer than 1,000 members immediately after 23 August 1944.

In 1930 'less than 10 percent of the active population was engaged in industry' (King, 1980, p. 20), and the former Austro-Hungarian territories (Transylvania and Banat) comprised the largest part of it. Because these territories had a longer tradition of industrialisation, in 1929 the proportion of total union members of these two areas was 60 per cent, while they accounted for only 23 percent of the country's total population (King, 1980, p. 20). More than that, the Social Democratic movement had a longer history, having been founded in 1893 in the Kingdom of Romania. The first workers' organisation was the 'House for Insurance and Mutual Help of the Printers', founded on 24 August 1858, and in the former Austro-Hungarian territories the 'General Workers' Association of Self-Education' was publishing syndicalist literature in six languages, including Romanian, as early as 1866 (Ionescu, 1964, p. 1). Because the Social Democrats based their party largely on the trade unions, the PCR tried to seize the control of the trade unions but the confrontation between the two parties resulted in defeat for the PCR in 1923 (King, 1980, p. 21). During World War II there were three factions competing in the PCR: the underground Central Committee led by Ştefan Foriş, the prison centre led by Gheorghiu-Dej, and the Romanian emigre office in Moscow led by Ana Pauker. As a consequence of its lack of support in the working class, together with continuous internal fighting in the top leadership, the PCR was demoralised and lacked confidence. Its inferiority complex represented 'the only important psychological characteristic of the Party's elites, from the first Comintern generation until Gheorghiu-Dej and Nicolae Ceauşescu' (Tismăneanu, Dobrincu and Vasile, 2007, p. 63). In spite of the Party's claim that it represented the working class, it had stood for objectives and directives formulated outside Romania and very often in contradiction to political common sense or to the Party's interests. As Tismăneanu, Dobrincu and Vasile (2007) argued, the PCR lacked mass support, was fragmented, dominated by foreigners, politically helpless and disregarded by the Comintern. All these characteristics increased its 'castaway' psychology, and later on, generated anti-Soviet behaviour. The PCR had experienced success only in one out of three target groups – the ethnic minorities. According to King (1980, p. 33) 'in the parliamentary elections of 1926, 1927, and 1928, the party's strength clearly lay in areas with large non-Romanian ethnic populations'. There are a few factors that must be considered for an explanation. Among these were the large proportion of minorities in the working class, but also other appeals of communism among the minorities. Quoting classified Party statistics from 1933, Korkut (2006, p. 140) indicates the following ethnic structure of the PCR: 26.5 per cent of its members were of Hungarian origin, 22.6 per cent were of Romanian origin, and 18 per cent were Jews. According to Tănase (1998, p. 31) two ethnic categories had been attracted by communism: the 'rejected peoples' without a territorial base or a coherent ethnic identity, and the irredentists of the neighbouring states. The Jews were the main group in the first category. Between 1922 and 1944 not a single leader of the Romanian Communist Party was ethnic Romanian – Elek Koblos and Ştefan Foriş were Hungarians, Vitali Holostenko-Barbu was Ukrainian, Boris Stefanov was Bulgarian and Alexandru Stepanski-Gorn was Polish.

Stalin used the armistice signed on 13 September 1944 to create a 'legal framework for securing a dominant political and economic interest in Romania' (Deletant, 1999a, p. 35). Since the Soviet Union acted on behalf of the Allied Powers and it had a monopoly over interpretation of the Armistice Agreement, Stalin had two instruments for an efficient takeover of Romania: the Armistice Convention and the Communist Party. The total lack of public support for the PCR was a problem to be solved by destroying the support for monarchy and traditional parties. It took less than four years of terror and purges for the PCR and the Soviet Union to completely fulfil these objectives. The major opposition parties – the National Peasant Party and the National Liberal Party – were dissolved in the summer of 1947, and on 30 December 1947 King Michael signed an abdication statement. On the same day, the Romanian People's Republic was declared by a parliament that was itself the result of 'neither free nor fair elections', as the British under-secretary for foreign affairs had declared (cited in Deletant, 1999b, p. 78). From that moment, the communists – re-branded as the Romanian Workers' Party (Partidul Muncitoresc Romîn – PMR) formed from the merger between the PCR and the Social Democratic Party in February 1948 – led the country without any opposition. In 1965 Ceauşescu restored the original name of the Party, Partidul Comunist Român – PCR.

Because 'educated Romanians were considered by Soviet advisers to be unreliable and compromised' (Deletant, 1999a, p. 124), a new elite was established, 'copying in spirit and shape the Soviet elite, and approved by Moscow' (Gavrilovici and Iacob, 2006, p. 701). The practice of mass arrests and imprisonment without trial spread over the whole country once communist rule was imposed in Romania by the Soviet Union. By 1948 the number of Party members had increased from fewer than 1,000 to more than 1 million (Tănase, 1998, p. 48). But over the next seven years almost half of the members were purged, a phenomenon similar to the other communist parties in Eastern Europe. An education system within the Party was constructed at several levels – Party universities, workers' faculties, one-year courses, and six-months courses. The main objectives of the education system were to indoctrinate cadres with Marxist-Leninist ideology, to professionalise cadres because of their low level of education, and to provide a body of cadres loyal to the Party leadership.

According to Tănase (1998, pp. 22–27) the communist regime in Romania had been influenced by three important conditions. First, in Romania there was no communist revolution, and furthermore the Party was almost insignificant in the society before World War II. Djilas (1957, p. 13) considered that this condition was related to the tendency to replicate the Soviet model: 'the weaker the communism is, the more should it replicate even in form the Russian totalitarian communism of the "big brother"'. The CIA (1958, p. 7) reported that the PMR, 'though probably one of Eastern Europe weakest in numbers of faithful and capable personnel, is firmly in control, is supported by the presence of Soviet troops and is probably united behind party leader Gheorghiu-Dej'. Second, the totalitarian regimes' characteristics had to be moderated in the case of smaller countries such as Romania. As a consequence, the new East European communist regimes had to create alternative models, and in Romania's case, the model was called *modernisation* (Tãnase, 1998, p. 25). Third, before World War II the processes of modernisation and integration in Romanian society had developed simultaneously and had limited each other. Therefore, the PCR had placed itself on the side of less integrated social groups – peasants and workers. The communist elite was governing on behalf of marginal social groups and it tried to build a new society based on these groups.

The industrialisation process had given rise to a new social category with higher education and influential positions in the Romanian economy. The post-war technocracy usually had a peasant background with a traditionalist mentality, and strong nationalist values. This social category had perceived the industrialisation effort as a patriotic struggle to achieve independence from the USSR (Tãnase, 1998, p. 172). A bipolar relationship had developed between the political elite and the managerial elite. Adaptation and confrontation had been the two aspects of this relation. The core issue of the relation had been the distribution of power and of resources. According to Tãnase (1998, p. 174) adaptation became the main dimension of this relation between 1958 and 1962. The high priority on industrialisation and independence had united both elites, while they had been divided by the power monopoly held by the top leadership.

From 1965 Nicolae Ceauşescu was the communist party leader, the dictator of the country and 'the centre of a bizarre personality cult' (White, 2001, p. 56). As mentioned before, Mary Ellen Fischer (1996, p. 208) defined the communist regime during the 1980s as totalitarian. Siani-Davies (2005, p. 16) described it in a more detailed way as a highly personalised neo-Stalinist neo-patrimonial state in a partly modernised society. According to Snyder, 'neo-patrimonial states are "characterised by the chief executive's maintenance of state authority through an extensive network of personal patronage, rather than through ideology or impersonal law"' (Snyder, 1992, p. 379). Nepotism and favouritism were the main criteria used in promotion at the top level of party and state. Ceauşescu and his wife's families' members were promoted to prominent positions of the regime. The only European case of dynastic communism was synthesised in a popular joke, *socialism in a single family*. Or as Daniel Nelson (1988, p. xv) described this version of modern autocracy 'where the unbridled power of one ruler continues no matter how dubious his policies may be'. In addition to the Ceauşescu family networks, the country's elite members were 'anti-intellectual, xenophobic, isolationist, anti-technocratic, and hostile to change' (Georgescu, 1988, p. 81). All these aspects undermined Ceauşescu's regime 'by sapping its moral authority and giving ground for popular discontent' (Siani-Davies, 2005, p. 19). According to Siani-Davies (2005, p. 20), Ceauşescu had been able to concentrate power so successfully mainly because of two strategies he employed to prevent any rivals: 'divide and rule' and 'circulation of cadres'. The first strategy was based on the multiplication of structures competing one against another, while the second strategy was based on the arbitrary movement of officeholders from one position to another. Rather than offering opportunities for upward social mobility, the 'circulation of cadres' was meant to block any possible contender from creating their own power base. Ceauşescu's success in concentrating power in his hands was 'totally self-defeating' (Siani-Davies, 2005, p. 19), made him responsible for all decisions, created a rigid system of policy making and finally eliminated any corrective mechanism. Consequently, in the last decade of the communist regime the relations between the population and the ruling elite were 'fraught with mistrust and uncertainty' (Nelson, 1988, p. xvi).

Relations with the Soviet Union

In some important respects, the relation between Romania and the Soviet Union was the echo of a long history. In the nineteenth century, all three empires with strong interests in Eastern Europe – the Habsburg, the Ottoman and the Russian empires – were unfavourable to the union of the two Romanian principalities. Both the Habsburg and the Russian empires had feared that a unified Romanian would be attractive to the populations of provinces under their control, Bessarabia and Transylvania.

Relations with the Soviet Union were sensitive from the establishment of the communist state. These relations were affected from the very beginning by two delicate problems – Bessarabia and the Romanian treasure. There were also more marginal issues such as the legacy of the intervention of the Romanian Army in Hungary in August 1919 to help suppress the Hungarian Soviet Republic, and the establishment of the Moldavian Autonomous Soviet Socialist Republic in the Soviet Union in 1924. The Soviet Union had considered Romania as an outpost of imperialism, so its main objective was to weaken the country internally by inciting national unrest. Moreover, the problem of Bessarabia was an important issue in the official relations between Romania and the Soviet Union. However, in the interwar period, the PCR leadership had been divided over the self-determination problem.

After the establishment of communism in Romania, the relations between the two states varied from complete obedience to 'the three phases of the Romanian-Soviet cold war' as they were described by Frunză (1999). After 1964 the Romanian authorities took many decisions to reduce Russian influence in Romanian society. As examples, the status of the Russian language was modified from mandatory to optional in Romanian education, the Romanian-Russian Museum was abolished and the Russian Book Publishing House became the Universal Literature Publishing House. A CIA report considered that this

> intransigence was the product, primarily, of Gheorghiu-Dej's early opposition to de-Stalinisation, of longstanding economic grievances against the USSR and of increased confidence as a result of economic success.... An awakening nationalism, encouraged since 1962 by Soviet concessions to

> national sovereignty, has prompted the Rumanians to act more and more independently in various aspects of foreign policy.
>
> (CIA, 1964b, p. 4)

Another CIA report considered that 'the Dej regime is apparently convinced that the USSR cannot apply strong political pressure or economic sanctions and that it will not intervene militarily' (CIA, 1964a, p. 7).

This book's objectives

The aim of this book is to examine, within the broader context outlined above, the main organisational and social characteristics of the Romanian industrial enterprise under communist rule. The approach adopted is multi-disciplinary and trans-disciplinary. It draws on Industrial Management knowledge to understand the important role of communist enterprises and their management in the centralised management of the economy and its consequences. It draws on Economics in order to understand the significance of economic indicators, for example of production capacity, productivity, and plan indicators for the outcome of industrialisation policies, and to describe in a significant manner the failure of the centralised planning system. Organisation Studies provided the basic theoretical framework for the understanding of the complex relation between the communist ideology, the economic structure and the industrial organisations. Other social sciences bring an important contribution to the completion of the research objectives. Sociology supports the research, which employs complex concepts such as power, elites, social structure and demographic indicators in attempting to understand the social relations through which centralised planning was carried out and negotiated, and how the communist enterprise was managed through the interrelations between managers and planners on the one hand, and between managers and the workforce on the other hand. Political science provides the general framework for the analysis of the Romanian communist system. Finally, the research is trans-disciplinary because it aims to create an over-arching perspective on Romania's social and political evolution during the communist regime.

In focusing on the industrial enterprise under communism, it is important to note that, as discussed above, Romanian industrialisation was significantly different from the Soviet or other East European experiences, and therefore investigation of the role of the managerial elite in the evolution of the economic system in the specific conditions of Romania is important, and leads to relevant conclusions concerning the character of Romanian society. The book aims to investigate also the validity of the predominant top-down characterisation of Romania under communism and to explore evidence for key bottom-up processes, especially in the organisational environment, which would argue for a more complex and nuanced understanding. The empirical research had three main objectives which are outlined below.

The key features of Romanian industrial enterprises during the process of industrialisation under the communist regime

The specific character of the typical industrial enterprise that emerged in communist Romania can only be understood in the context of the industrialisation strategy of the communist leadership in a predominantly rural society with an uneducated formerly peasant workforce. As many authors have argued (e.g. Shafir, 1985, Gallagher, 2005), the predominantly rural character of Romania represented a serious challenge for the Party's leadership. According to official statistical data, the percentage of the urban population in Romania was 23.4 per cent in 1948 (Direcţia Centrală de Statistică, 1990, p. 51), and the percentage of the labour force in industry was 12 per cent in 1950 (Direcţia Centrală de Statistică, 1990, pp. 102–105). The urban population grew to 53.2 per cent in 1989 (Direcţia Centrală de Statistică, 1990, p. 51) while the industrial labour force reached 38.1 per cent in the same year (Direcţia Centrală de Statistică, 1990, pp. 102–105). These percentages had increased at the expense of the rural population and the agricultural labour force. On the one hand, the drive for industrialisation generated widespread social changes that further influenced the structure of organisations. On the other hand, the significant increase of the working class suggests that industrialisation had been based on extensive use of labour with a lower concern for labour efficiency and intensive use of human resources.

Through analysis of Romanian national census data, documents of Romanian industrial enterprises from 1945 to 1963, and other archival documents, the consequences of Romania's 'autarkic industrialisation' (Shafir, 1985, p. 93) for the social structure of Romanian working class and the closely connected issue of the changing structure of the communist party are described. These changes created the premises for what Katherine Verdery called 'the encounters between the national idea and a monolithic socialism' (Verdery, 1993, p. 202). This widely accepted perspective suggests that the emergence of national-Stalinism in Romania was mainly a survival strategy of the communist leaders under the threat of de-Stalinisation.

The PCR had tried to control what is usually supposed to be the 'covariance of development as a socioeconomic phenomenon and political participation' (Nelson, 1988, p. 19) through imposing new organisational structures such as the workers' councils (COM – Consiliul Oamenilor Muncii), or mechanisms such as self-management (*autoconducerea*). While COM was meant to be a key element of the new self-management by the industrial labour, *autoconducerea* was emphasised as a major step towards democratisation. Based on significant empirical data, Nelson (1988) argued, however, that workers' self-management was an illusion, and so was the democratisation at the organisational level: 'workers' councils are, in fact, not highly regarded, elected representatives in them are not well known, and council meetings are dominated by the party leadership in combination with party cadre who administer the enterprise's departments' (Nelson, 1988, p. 25). Empirical evidence collected from the archives of enterprises conducted for this research confirms Nelson's conclusions and gives useful insights into the decisional mechanisms governing the communist enterprises. Since the plan objectives were received from above and were the subject of complex and continuous negotiations, the enterprise's basic activities such as financial, supply or sales were also prescribed, and the COM and *autoconducerea* were essentially control mechanisms designed to improve productivity rather than mechanisms designed to involve the working class in decision-making processes. The lack of political involvement of the new working class created a problem for the communist leadership. The Party's power legitimacy was based on its links to the masses but those links were weak. The Romanian communist leadership's solution to this problem consisted in an extensive growth of its own membership so that by the 1980s it was the largest communist party in the world as a proportion of total population.

An in-depth description of the continuous process of negotiation of the plan objectives between enterprises and central state structures

This negotiation process represents an example of what Dahl and Lindblom (1953) named vertical bargaining. Authors such as Berliner (1957) and Kornai (1980, 1992) described extensively the bargaining process in the Soviet Union and Hungary. The conclusions presented in this book are based on first hand evidence of this process gathered from Romanian enterprises' archives. Special attention has been given to the causes and consequences of this negotiation process, as well to the arguments used by the parties involved in it. The extent to which central planning of the economy was in fact the outcome of systematic plan negotiation from the early beginning of communist rule in Romania was also subject of this study. The influence on the industrialisation process of factors like the blatant exploitation through Sovroms which had made the Soviet government 'the only large industrial capitalist owner' (Ionescu, 1964, p. 164) from 1945 until 1956, and the failures of the first economic plans, will be extensively analysed. The following quotations identified in the enterprise archives illustrate the character of the negotiating process: 'On these bases, we cannot agree with the increase of productivity indicated in your previous letter. We request a reduction of the productivity task from 127,5% to 124,5%'. These words were addressed to the Planning Department of the Romanian Ministry of Metallurgy and Machines Building by the director of an industrial enterprise in 1961 (in a document entitled 'Request regarding the workload plan'). Another person from the same enterprise wrote, 10 years earlier: 'for the 183587 hours of workload you allocated 571 workers, which seems completely discordant with the workload' ('Justification for salaries and workers') and '... each trimester we have been obliged to seek plan modification, especially regarding the average and the total salaries...' ('Report regarding the difficulties faced in the realisation of the workforce plan'). These messages are first-hand evidence of the bargaining process and they can be contrasted to the predominant understanding of communist Romania as a state in which 'deeply unequal relations were encouraged within a rigidly hierarchical system of political control' (Gallagher, 2005).

The findings support a more balanced perspective of power in the Romanian industrial system, revealing a complex network of dependencies and factors within a hyper-centralised and over-regulated economy.

The documents from enterprises' archives show an ongoing process of negotiations between the enterprises and the state structures that definitely required not only technical knowledge but also political skills. This process was ongoing only two years after the launching of the first five-year plan and four years after nationalisation. This suggests that the precondition of economic and technological progress was not the main reason for the greater influence of the technocrats over the apparatchiks. The dysfunctionalities of the Romanian economy were acknowledged as early as 1953. In the verbatim record of a bi-lateral meeting held in Moscow on 8–14 July 1953, the Soviet delegation rebuked the Romanian communist leaders, calling the Romanian economic policy 'erroneous, illiterate and even dangerous' (Berindei, Dobrincu, Goşu, 2009, p. 428). The Soviet analysis of the Romanian economy will be discussed in detail in Chapter 3. Another important reason for this continuous negotiation could be the financial mechanism set in the economy: the enterprise was able to access salary funds only if they produced evidence of fulfilling the monthly plan. In this way, the bank gained a controlling role in the economy, and the enterprise's management became keen to fulfil the plan or to adapt the indicators to reality on a monthly basis. Designed probably as a pressure mechanism to assure plan fulfilment, it turned out as well to be an efficient tool for negotiation in the hands of managers: any failure in plan fulfilment would generate insufficient funds for salaries and could generate workers' protests. The research's findings suggest that the main causes of failure were the systematic miscalculations of the indicators either in terms of outputs or in terms of inputs, the insufficient number of employees, and the impossibility of receiving specific resources. All these arguments were used by managers in the process of negotiation of the plan targets, and all of them were to blame the planning authorities. At the highest political level the shortcomings of planning were also acknowledged: 'there are still cases when various tasks of the national economic plan are insufficiently correlated or substantiated' (Ceauşescu, 1967, p. 55).

The analysis of the human side of the communist enterprise

As noted above, in developing a strategy for rapid industrialisation, the Romanian communist leadership was confronted with a series of contradictory pressures. They had to justify their strategy in terms of a Marxist-Leninist orthodoxy laid down by the Soviet Union, they had to legitimise their rule and the profound social changes they were imposing on the population, and they had to educate and train new generations of managers, specialists and technicians to build and operate the new industrial enterprises. Unlike other more developed communist countries, after World War II, Romania experienced 'a woeful lack of experts, technicians, and managers; it also lacked the skilled manpower necessary to begin large-scale industrialisation' (Ionescu, 1964, p. 164). On the other hand, before World War II, the PCR was 'a marginal organisation, completely dominated by the Comintern apparatus' (Tismăneanu, Dobrincu and Vasile, 2007, p. 52). Unlike the Bulgarian, Hungarian, Polish or Yugoslavian communist parties, the PCR was a small organisation with fewer than 1,000 members on 23 August 1944 (CIA, 1944, p. 4; Tismăneanu, Dobrincu and Vasile, 2007, p. 56). In this context both the Party apparatchiks and the technocrats had to be significantly developed as social categories in communist Romania. The only source for this extensive development was the working class and the peasants. While the former was reduced as a proportion of the total population, the latter were more important because of the country's predominantly rural character. This created the premises for a specific context of industrialisation in terms of socio-demographic evolution. Therefore, a deeper insight on the enterprises' evolution from the personnel perspective should contribute to a better understanding of the complex relations between workers, managers, planning authorities and other organisational structures.

In exploring these issues, the book both draws on and aims to contribute to the extensive existing literature on the tensions between political orthodoxy and technical expertise in communist development. Some authors (e.g. Lowenthal, 1974, 1976; Huntington, 1970) have argued that the tensions inherent in such economic development in communist countries was characterised by a conflict between 'red' and 'expert', between Party apparatchik and economic technocrat, and that communist systems lost ground because by their nature they systematically promoted 'reliable' people with the appropriate political qualifications in preference to the better qualified. But other authors (Jowitt, 1975; King, 1980) have argued that more important was the emergence of the political manager characterised by technical knowledge and 'manipulative skills in socio-political settings' (Jowitt, 1975, p. 77).

The book analyses the wider implications of the dilemma of 'red' versus 'expert' in the context of the Romanian command economy and extensive industrialisation. The classic dilemma, 'red versus expert', was described and at the same time supposedly solved by Chairman Mao on 31 January 1958: 'Red and expert, politics and business are the unification of two pairs of opposites.... There is no doubt that politics and economy, and politics and technology should be united' (Mao Zedong, 1958). Romania, as well as other communist countries faced the same dilemma, but in a different context. The book addresses the context in which a conflict between 'red' and 'expert' was able to appear, the existence of this conflict at the organisational level and the emergence of the political manager in communist Romania. Evidence supporting the existence of this conflict is identified. This approach takes its roots in themes raised by Max Weber in classical sociology, and in some of the classics of Western sovietology such as works by Berliner, Azrael, Szelenyi, Kornai and Burawoy. Joseph Berliner's *Factory and Manager in the USSR* (1957), Jeremy Azrael's *Managerial Power in Soviet Politics* (1966), George Konrad and Iván Szelényi's *The Intellectuals on the Road to Class Power* (1979) and János Kornai's *Economics of Shortage* (1980) are probably among the best-known publications on this topic.

Contributions of insiders such as Leon Trotsky and Milovan Djilas are also important sources for a better understanding of the emergence and evolution of the new managerial group.

Berliner's book (1957) presents the results of a significant number of interviews with former Soviet managerial officials. The interviews were conducted in the Harvard Project on the Soviet Social System between 1950 and 1956. The *safety factor*, plan fulfilling simulation and *blat* were the three categories of managerial practices identified and described by Berliner. These practices were in conflict with the laws, regulation and official discourse, but they were tolerated by the authorities and, Berliner argued, they made an important contribution to the system. In 1988, Berliner published a book entitled *Soviet Industry from Stalin to Gorbachev*, in which the concluding chapter was based on the findings of another research project based on interviewing Soviet emigrants. This project's results allowed Berliner to draw a few important conclusions regarding the most persistent managerial practices in Soviet industry.

Azrael (1966) extensively described the Soviet managerial elite, from the bourgeois specialists to red directors and post-Stalin new managers. Azrael placed his investigation in the wider context of the discussions regarding the 'docility and political impotence that have characterised the role of the technical intelligentsia and managerial elite' in the development of the Soviet system (Azrael, 1966, p. 173). While in political development theories the engineers and the managers were considered the 'gravediggers of communism', events had failed to confirm the theories, at least until Azrael wrote his book.

George Konrad and Iván Szelényi's book, *The Intellectuals on the Road to Class Power* (1979), was focused on the social structure of communist Hungary and mainly on the rise of intellectuals as a class and their relation to the ruling political elite. The authors argued that, contrary to common understanding, it was not the working class who ruled East European countries but the intelligentsia, which was on the way to become the new ruling class. This publication brought a lot of problems for the authors and resulted in Szelényi leaving the country. A manuscript was smuggled abroad and the book was published in the West in 1979. According to the review published by John C. Campbell, the book 'is centred on the rise and the social role of the intellectuals as a class, their relation to the ruling political elite, and the keys they may hold to the future' (Campbell, 1979–80). The authors argued that the East European intelligentsia was on the way to becoming the ruling class, while the working class was the most underprivileged class (Konrad and Szelényi, 1979). This assertion needs more evidences, considering at least the status of collectivised peasantry in Romania which, in terms of access of public services, was undoubtedly less privileged than the working class. Moreover, in the authors' understanding, the intellectual class also included experts, technocrats and bureaucrats. The authors were also criticised for their 'propensity to lump together all East European societies – along with the Soviet Union – in sweeping generalizations' (Hollander, 1980).

János Kornai investigated Hungary's command economy for more than three decades. He made his first impact on the reform debate in 1957 when his dissertation was published. Entitled *Overcentralisation in Economic Administration* (published in Hungarian), the book made an in-depth critical analysis of the system of mandatory plan indicators and of its system of incentives and penalties. Kornai continued to dedicate his efforts to investigating the problems of planning in the Hungarian economy. A series of publications in Western and Hungarian academic journals addressed the problems of planning, programming, control, shortage and other issues faced by communist economies. The publication of *Economics of Shortage* (Kornai, 1980) finally concluded his researches and provided his complete perspective on command economies dysfunctionalities.

Iván T. Berend dedicated an important effort to describe and analyse the reforms experienced by the Hungarian economy during the communist regime. According to Berend's analysis, most of the reforms of the Hungarian economic system were either partial corrections affecting only parts of the economy or experimental measures (Berend, 1990). However, an intense debate regarding the possible paths of reform can be observed in Berend's account.

The British sociologist Michael Burawoy realised a long-term field research in two Hungarian enterprises – Bánki and Lenin Steel Works. His findings and conclusions were published with János Lukács as a collection of essays entitled *The Radiant Past: Ideology and Reality in Hungary's Road to Capitalism* (Burawoy and Lukacs, 1992). This book appeared as a sequel to his previous work, *Manufacturing Consent* (Burawoy, 1979). Though Burawoy had a distinctive Marxist approach, his work is particularly important because it reflects not only his field research in Hungary, but also because it allows comparison between socialist and capitalist industrial relations.

The book's structure

The discussion proceeds as follows: the next chapter is focused on the theoretical framework in which the research was done. The theoretical framework has been built up on the significant knowledge regarding the Soviet industrial organisation developed by Azrael and Berliner, regarding the Hungarian communist economy and society studied by Kornai, Berend and Szelényi. The main features of the communist industrial enterprise are framed into the model proposed by Burrell and Morgan (1979), which frames the fundamental assumptions of the main theories regarding organisational analysis. The political sociology of state socialism developed by David Lane (1976, 1978) and Burawoy's perspective on socialist industrial relations are used to help to position the communist industrialisation policies and practices within Burrell and Morgan model. Burrell and Morgan's (1979) meta-theoretical frame helps to outline the communist system's internal contradictions between the ideological core values and the bureaucracy's rationalisation of the planned economy.

The third chapter is focused on the main characteristics of Romanian industrial development during the communist period. The industrialisation process is described on the basis of information collected from official documents, statistical data, and from recollections, memoirs of people who had witnessed or had been involved in the events. The main aspects analysed in this chapter are the description of the centralised planning system, the labour legislation, the impact of extensive industrialisation and the cadre selection and training processes. Special attention is paid to social unrest, events such as strikes, protest or attempts to establish independent unions, experienced during the communist regime. The findings suggest that social unrest was probably generated by systemic failures, when no negotiation or dissimulation could fix the problems. The impact of Soviet exploitation of the Romanian economy through *sovroms* is also brought into the discussion. These aspects are analysed from the early years of the communist regime until the last decade of communism.

The fourth chapter outlines the methodological framework, and the sources of information and evidence used in this study. The chapter begins with the author's self-positioning within the Burrell and Morgan (1979) framework. The research methods and the information sources used in the empirical study are presented in the second part of the chapter. The chapter also includes a brief description of the investigated enterprises' history.

The fifth chapter describes the main organisational practices of Romanian communist enterprises. The empirical research was framed by the conclusions of Berliner's studies regarding the Soviet factories. The chapter is focused on the relations between the enterprises and the planning structures – mostly industry branch ministries. This part of the book is based mostly on documents identified in Romanian National Archives and on interviews with former communist enterprises' employees.

The sixth chapter is focused on the personnel aspects, on the evolution of the working-class structure, on the processes of selection and promotion of managers and specialists, and on the relations between these processes and the Party's strategies, directives and plans. A number of cases of specific human resources management problems are extensively described within the political context.

Finally, the seventh chapter summarises the findings and the main conclusions.

References

Azrael, J. 1966. *Managerial Power in Soviet Politics*. Cambridge, MA: Harvard University Press.

Axenciuc, V. 1992–2000a. *Evoluţia economică a Romaniei. Cercetări statistico-istorice 1959–1947. Vol. I. Industrie şi transporturi*. Bucureşti: Editura Academiei Române.

Axenciuc, V. 1992–2000b. *Evoluţia economică a Romaniei. Cercetări statistico-istorice 1959–1947. Vol. II. Agricultura*. Bucureşti: Editura Academiei Române.

Axenciuc, V. 1992–2000c. *Evoluţia economică a României. Cercetări statistico-istorice 1959–1947. Vol. III. Monedă, credit, comerţ, finanţe publice*. Bucureşti: Editura Academiei Române.

Axenciuc, V. 1997. *Introducere în istoria economică a României. Epoca modernă*. Bucureşti: Editura Fundaţiei România de mâine.

Banu, F. 2004. *Asalt asupra economiei României – De la Solagra la Sovrom (1936–1956)*. Bucureşti: Editura Nemira.

Berend, I.T. 1990. *The Hungarian Economic Reforms 1953–1988*. Cambridge: Cambridge University Press.

Berindei, M., Dobrincu, D. and Goşu, A. 2009. *Istoria comunismului din România: documente. Perioada Gheorghe Gheorghiu-Dej (1945–1965)*. Bucureşti: Humanitas.

Berindei, M., Dobrincu, D. and Goşu, A. 2012. *Istoria comunismului din România: documente. Nicolae Ceauşescu (1965–1971)*. Iaşi: Polirom.

Berliner, J. 1957. *Factory and Manager in USSR*. Cambridge, MA: Harvard University Press.

Berliner, J. 1988. *Soviet Industry from Stalin to Gorbachev*. Aldershot: Edward Elgar.

Brown, V.F. 1979. The Movement for Reform in Rumania after World War I: The Parliamentary Bloc Government of 1919–1920. *Slavic Review*, 38(3).

Brucan, S. 1996. *Stâlpii noii puteri în România*. Bucureşti: Nemira.

Brucan, S. 2012. *Generaţia irosită*. Bucureşti: Editura Teşu.

Burawoy, M. 1979. *Manufacturing Consent*. Chicago: University of Chicago Press.

Burawoy, M. and Lukacs, J. 1992. *The Radiant Past*. Chicago: University of Chicago Press.

Burrell, G. and Morgan, G. 1979. *Sociological Paradigms and Organisational Analysis*. Aldershot: Ashgate.

Campbell, J.C. 1979–80. Review: The Intellectuals on the Road to Class Power. *Foreign Affairs*, Winter 1979–80.

Ceauşescu, N 1967. Report Concerning Measures for Perfecting the Management and Planning of the National Economy and for Improving the Administrative-Territorial Organization of Romania, National Conference of the Romanian Communist Party. Bucharest: Agerpres.

Central Intelligence Agency. 1944. *Rumania: The How of Enslavement*. [Online]. [Accessed 18 June 2017]. Available from: www.cia.gov/library/readingroom/docs/DOC_0000483695.pdf.

Central Intelligence Agency. 1958. *Outlook for Stability in the Eastern Europe Satellites*. National Intelligence Estimates. 12–58. [Online]. [Accessed 19 June 2017]. Available from: www.cia.gov/library/readingroom/docs/DOC_0000269478.pdf.

Central Intelligence Agency. 1964a. *Rumania's Position in the Soviet Bloc*. [Online]. [Accessed 19 June 2017]. Available from: www.cia.gov/library/readingroom/docs/DOC_0000567349.pdf.

Central Intelligence Agency. 1964b. *Changing Patterns in Eastern Europe*. National Intelligence Estimates. 12–64. [Online]. [Accessed 19 June 2017]. Available from: www.cia.gov/library/readingroom/docs/DOC_0000012082.pdf.

Constantinescu, N.N. ed. 1997. *Istoria economică a României. De la începuturi până la cel de-al doilea război mondial*. Bucureşti: Editura Economică.

Constantinescu, N.N. ed. 2000. *Istoria economică a României. Vol. 2. 1939–1989*. Bucureşti: Editura Economică.

Dahl, R.A. and Lindblom, C.E. 1953. *Politics, Economics and Welfare: Planning and Politico-Economic Systems Resolved into Basic Social Processes*. Piscataway, NJ: Transaction.

Deletant, D. 1999a. *Romania under Communist Rule*. Iaşi: Center for Romanian Studies.

Deletant, D. 1999b. *Communist Terror in Romania*. London: Hurst.

Direcţia Centrală de Statistică. 1972. *Anuarul statistic al Republicii Socialiste Romania*. Bucureşti.

Direcţia Centrală de Statistică. 1979. *Anuarul statistic al Republicii Socialiste Romania*. Bucureşti.

Direcţia Centrală de Statistică. 1980. *Anuarul statistic al Republicii Socialiste Romania*. Bucureşti.

Direcţia Centrală de Statistică. 1990. *Anuarul Statistic al României*. Bucureşti.

Direcţiunea Recensământului General al Populaţiunei. 1931a. *Populaţiunea actuală a României. Cifrele preliminare ale recensământului general dela 29 decembre 1930*. Bucureşti: Ministerul Muncii, *Sănătăţii* şi Ocrotirilor Sociale.

Direcţiunea Recensământului General al Populaţiunei. 1931b. *Recensământul general al populaţiei României din 29 decemvrie 1930, Vol. II: Neam, limba materna, religie*. Bucureşti: Monitorul Oficial.

Djilas, M. 1957. *The New Class. An Analysis of the Communist System*. London: Thames and Hudson.

Fischer, M.E. 1980. Political Leadership and Personnel Policy in Romania: Continuity and Change 1965–1976. In Rosefielde, S. ed. *World Communism at the Crossroads*. Boston, MA: Nijhoff.

Fischer, M.E. ed. 1996. *Establishing Democracies*. Boulder, CO: Westview Press.

Frunză, V. 1999. *Istoria comunismului în România*. Bucureşti: EVF.

Gallagher, T. 1998. The Balkans: Bulgaria, Romania, Albania and the Former Yugoslavia. In White, S., Batt, J. and Lewis, P.G. eds. *Developments in Central and East European Politics 2*. Basingstoke: Macmillan.

Gallagher, T. 2005. *Theft of a Nation. Romania since Communism*. London: Hurst.

Gavrilovici, O. and Iacob, G. 2006. Romania and the Western World from the 1800s. *Journal of Organizational Change Management*, 19(6).

Georgescu, V. 1988. Romania in the 1980's: The Legacy of Dynastic Socialism. *Eastern European Politics and Societies*, 2(1).

Gerschenkron, A. 1962. *Economic Backwardness in Historical Perspective*. Cambridge, MA: Belknap, Harvard University Press.

Holmes, L. 1997. *Post-Communism. An Introduction*. Oxford: Polity.

Hollander, P. 1980. Review: The Intellectuals on the Road to Class Power. *Commentary*. June.

Huntington, S. and Moore, C.H. eds. 1970. *Authoritarian Politics in Modern Society*. New York: Basic Books.

Ionescu, G. 1964. *Communism in Rumania 1944–1962*. London: Oxford University Press.

Ionete, C. 1993. *Criza de sistem a economiei de comandă şi etapa sa explozivă*. Bucureşti: Editura Expert.

Janos, A.C. 1982. *The Politics of Backwardness in Hungary 1825–1945*. Princeton, NJ: Princeton University Press.

Jowitt, K. 1970. The Romanian Communist Party and the World Socialist System: A Redefinition of Unity. *World Politics*, 23(1).

Jowitt, K. 1971. *Revolutionary Breakthroughs and National Development: The Case of Romania*. Berkeley, CA: University of California Press.

Jowitt, K. 1974. An Organizational Approach to the Study of Political Culture in Marxist-Leninist Systems. *The American Political Science Review*, 68(3).

Jowitt, K. 1975. Inclusion and Mobilization in European Leninist Regimes. *World Politics*, 28(1).

Jowitt, K. ed. 1978. Social Change in Romania, 1860–1940: A Debate on Development in a European Nation. *Institute of International Studies, Research Series*, 36.

Kideckel, D.A. 2008. *Getting by in Postsocialist Romania: Labor, the Body, and Working-Class Culture*. Bloomington and Indianapolis, IN: Indiana University Press.

King, R.R. 1980. *History of the Romanian Communist Party*. Stanford, CA: Hoover Institution Press.

King, C. 2007. Remembering Romanian Communism. *Slavic Review*, 66(4).

Kirițescu, C.C. 1997. *Sistemul bãnesc al leului si precursorii lui*. București: Editura Enciclopedicã.

Konrad, G. and Szelényi, I. 1979. *The Intellectuals on the Road to Class Power*. New York: Harcourt Brace Jovanovich.

Korkut, U. 2006. Nationalism Versus Internationalism: The Roles of Political and Cultural Elites in Interwar and Communist Romania. *Nationalities Papers: The Journal of Nationalism and Ethnicity*, 34(2).

Kornai, J. 1980. *Economics of Shortage*. Amsterdam: North Holland.

Kornai, J. 1992. *The Socialist System. The Political Economy of Communism*. Oxford: Clarendon.

Lane, D. 1976. *The Socialist Industrial State. Towards a Political Sociology of State Socialism*. London: George Allen & Unwin.

Lane, D. 1978. *Politics and Society in the USSR*. New York: New York University Press.

Lee, C. 2009. Towards a Professional Civil Service in Post-Transition Romania. *Public Administration and Development*, 29(4).

Lowenthal, R. 1974. On 'Established' Communist Party Regimes. *Studies in Comparative Communism*, 7(4).

Lowenthal, R. 1976. The Ruling Party in a Mature Society. In Field, M.G. ed. *Social Consequences of Modernization in Communist Societies*. Baltimore, MD and London: Johns Hopkins University Press.

Maddison, A. 1998. Measuring the Performance of a Communist Command Economy: An Assessment of the CIA Estimates for the USSR. *Review of Income and Wealth*, 44(3).

Maddison, A. 2003. *The World Economy: Historical Statistics*. Paris: Development Centre of the OECD.

Maiorescu, T. 1868. În contra direcţiei de astãzi în cultura românã. *Convorbiri literare*.

Mao Zedong. 1958. Red and Expert. *Selected Works of Mao Tse-tung*. [Online]. [Accessed 19 June 2017]. Available from: www.marxists.org/reference/archive/mao/selected-works/volume-8/mswv8_04.htm.

Marin, G.Gh. 2000. *În serviciul României lui Gheorghiu-Dej. Însemnãri din viaţã*. Bucureşti: Editura Evenimentul Românesc.

Murgescu, B. 2010. *România şi Europa. Acumularea decalajelor economice (1500–2010)*. Iaşi: Polirom.

Nelson, D.N. ed. 1981. *Romanian in the 1980s*. Boulder, CO: Westview Press.

Nelson, D.N. 1988. *Romanian Politics in the Ceauşescu Era*. New York: Gordon and Breach Science Publishers.

Roberts, H.L. 1951. *Romania. Political Problems of an Agrarian State*. New Haven, CT: Yale University Press.

Shafir, M. 1985. *Romania: Politics, Economics and Society*. London: Frances Pinter.

Siani-Davies, P. 2005. *The Romanian Revolution of December 1989*. Ithaca, NY: Cornell University Press.

Snyder, R. 1992. Explaining Transitions from Neopatrimonial Dictatorships. *Comparative Politics*, 24(4).

Tãnase, S. 1998. *Elite şi societate. Guvernarea Gheorghiu-Dej 1948–1965*. Bucureşti: Editura Humanitas.

The Maddison-Project. 2013. *Maddison Project Database 2013 version.* [Online]. [Accessed 19 June 2017]. Available from: www.ggdc.net/maddison/maddison-project/home.htm.

Tismăneanu, V., Dobrincu, D. and Vasile C. 2007. *Raport Final al Comisiei Prezidenţiale pentru Analiza Dictaturii Comuniste din România.* Bucureşti: Humanitas.

Verdery, K. 1991. *National Ideology under Socialism.* Berkeley, CA: University of California Press.

Verdery, K. 1996. *What Was Socialism, and What Comes Next?* Princeton, NJ: Princeton University Press.

White, S. 2001 *Communism and its Collapse.* London and New York: Routledge.

Wolfe, B.D. 1967. Backwardness and Industrialization in Russian History and Thought. *Slavic Review*, 26(2).

2 Organisation, power and politics in the communist regime

The main purpose of this chapter is to propose a theoretical framework for the analysis of the extensive industrialisation in communist Romania and the position of the communist managerial class in the power structure generally and the complex relations they engaged in with the state and its economic planners. The chapter is an attempt to bring together in the same framework the industrial organisation, the communist ideology, the ruling elites and the industrial managers, and to understand the way each offered different ways of seeing their world. The main assumption is that the evolution of communist industrial organisation was significantly influenced by the latent conflict between the perspective on the society of the communist leadership and the bureaucracy's perspective on the industrial organisation required by a planned economy. The shortcomings of industrialisation and, finally, the economic failure resulted on the one hand from the limits of the communist ideology regarding the organisation's management and on the other hand from the strategies pursued by the communist leadership.

The chapter begins with an examination of different views on the character of the society that emerged under the communist regimes in Eastern Europe, the nature of its ruling group and the character of power and production relations in communist regimes, and the sources of the problems faced by the planned economies as they became more mature. This is followed by sections examining the problems faced by the state-managed economies of communist-ruled societies and the problems this created for its managers, and the detailed research on the new managerial class in the communist economy developed by authors such as Jeremy Azrael, Joseph Berliner and others on managers in the Soviet economy, and then a discussion of the work of Janos Kornai, Ivan Berend, Michael Burawoy and János Lukács on managers in the Hungarian planned economy.

The social character of societies under communist rule

There is a wide variety of views on the nature of the society created by communist economic and social policies but the main division is between those who argued that the communists coming to power created a workers' state which went on to build a socialist society, operating in the interests of the population as a whole, and those who argued the revolution was usurped by a new ruling elite, or even a new ruling class.[1]

The building of socialism

The standard view offered by communist writers was that the system of political management of the economy employed by the ruling communist parties had created a new socialist form of society which operated in the broad interests of the people as a whole. The profit motive and market criteria had been replaced by a process of decision making based on rational assessment of the long-term general interests of the population. State ownership and planning of the economy meant that the production process could be organised in a scientific and orderly way. With the political revolution against capitalism achieved, further changes were held to have taken place as part of the 'scientific and technical revolution' in which the party, armed with its 'scientific' theory of society, would supervise the application of science in production and devise the most appropriate policies for overall social development. The stress here was on the controlled introduction of scientific discoveries and technological innovations into the economy, with the aim of improving productivity, the quality of production and general standards of living. In such a society, although inequalities remained, it was claimed that they were not associated with fundamental differences of material interests or ideologies. Since all people worked with different forms of socially owned property, in conditions where their activity was guided by the general policies of the party, they all shared common general interests and aspirations which would be met by a gradual improvement of the publicly owned, centrally managed system.

As a result of these policies nearly all means of production were held in the form of some kind of socialised property. Working people worked either with state-owned property, in which case they were working class, or with collective property, making them collective farmers. These were the two main classes of socialist society, and because they both worked with socialised forms of property in the means of production, they were both regarded as socialist classes whose relations were non-antagonistic. Unlike classes in capitalist society, they are not thought to conflict in terms of any basic interests, but rather to share common interests in the further development of the socialist organisation of society.

As a consequence of the harmony of interests between classes, it was argued, social change in Soviet-type societies would follow a peaceful, evolutionary path, under the general direction of ruling Communist parties. Managed technological change was seen as the main determinant of social change. Since there were no basic divisions of interest to be overcome, remaining inequalities were the result of differences in culture and education between different social groups, or differences in the availability of various goods and services.[2]

Critical theories

In the Western political and social science literature, most writers have rejected the claims of the communist theorists regarding their societies. Many writers have argued that the ruling group in communist regimes can best be described as an elite, albeit one that exercises power more exclusively and in a more authoritarian way than elites in Western societies. The most commonly held theory of this kind argued that the communist regimes were examples of totalitarian control, based on the exclusive and 'total' power of communist party states.[3]

Meanwhile, in contrast both to official Marxism-Leninism and to totalitarian theory, a number of critical Marxist theories argued that class distinctions were important and new class divisions were developing. It was argued that the ruling elite had been able to use their political power to appropriate a surplus, not by market exchange, but by a mixture of political control and bargaining. There are many variations on this theme in Marxist critical writing on the communist regimes, including for example, writers such as Tony Cliff, who argued that the Communist Party and its state apparatus had established a capitalist economy, in the form of state capitalism (Cliff 1974, pp. 153–154), and those such as the dissident Hungarian writers Georg Konrad and Ivan Szelenyi, who argued that the basic division in Soviet-type societies was between the direct producers and the intelligentsia, who were in the process of using their specialist knowledge to become a class of redistributors of the surplus.

Although there was a wide and often heated debate between these different views, the main point to note for our discussion here is that there has been very broad agreement in the literature on societies under communism that the ruling group took control and ruled in their own interests rather than those of the population as a whole, and employed a version of Marxism, official Marxism-Leninism, to legitimate their rule and to provide the language through which policies were to be discussed. This will be explored further below through a focus on three of the most influential critical theories, those of Leon Trotsky, Milovan Djilas and Herbert Marcuse.

Was there a new ruling class?

The title above represents a combination between Milovan Djilas's book *The New Class. An Analysis of the Communist System* (1957) and Alec Nove's paper *Is there a Ruling Class in USSR? (1975)*. As noted above, the problem of a new class, a new ruling stratum, or new elite had been observed and discussed from the very beginning of the Soviet regime in Russia. While Nove's paper was published in 1975 and Djilas's book in 1957, the problem of a new ruling class in the Soviet Union had been raised much earlier. Nove (1975, p. 620) cited an observation of Bukharin in 1922:

> Even proletarian origin, even the most calloused hands … are no guarantee against turning into a new class. For if we imagine that a section of those

> who have risen out of the working class becomes detached from the mass of the workers and congeals into a monopoly position in its capacity of ex-workers, they too could become a species of caste, which could also become a 'new class'.

According to Bukharin (cited by Nove, 1975), the divorce between worker bureaucrats and the working class was more dangerous in Russia because of the conditions of general misery and cultural backwardness of the working masses, when the administrative apparatus enjoyed far better life conditions. Another communist leader who observed the transformation of the Soviet bureaucracy was Rakovsky in 1929. According to Rakovsky (cited by Nove, 1975) the Soviet administrative and Party bureaucracy had ceased to be members of the working class 'not only objectively, but subjectively and not only physically but morally'.

Probably the first book that extensively analysed and critiqued this issue was Trotsky's *The Revolution Betrayed*, published in 1937. Leon Trotsky was initially a member of the Menshevik faction of the Russian Social Democratic Labour Party. He joined the Bolsheviks immediately prior to the 1917 October Revolution and he had become a leader of the Party. During the early days of the Soviet Union, he was the People's Commissar for Foreign Affairs and later the founder and first commander of the Red Army as People's Commissar of Military and Naval Affairs. He was a major figure in the Bolshevik victory in the Russian Civil War (1918–23). He was also among the first members of the Politburo. Lenin's retirement from active political life in 1923 was followed by an interregnum during which several leading candidates struggled for supremacy. Lenin's long-time associate and Communist International chief Grigory Zinoviev, Moscow Party leader Lev Kamenev, nationalities expert and party organisation secretary Joseph Stalin, and military leader Leon Trotsky represented the most important contenders for primacy. Trotsky was considered by the other contenders as the most important political threat and an alliance was formed against him. Over the next several years Trotsky and his supporters were marginalised and isolated by this alliance in the Soviet leadership group. This process was accentuated by successive exiles of Trotsky, first in 1928 to Central Asia, followed the next year by Trotsky's expulsion to Turkey.

The Revolution Betrayed was completed and sent to the publisher in 1936, immediately prior to the public announcement of the first great public Moscow trial, the beginning of the Great Purge. The trials would ultimately end in the execution of Grigory Zinoviev, Lev Kamenev and other prominent Soviet political figures. The book is an in-depth critique of the USSR and its leadership, and advocates a new political revolution to overthrow the Stalinist dictatorship. The book begins with the chapter entitled 'What has been achieved' – a positive description of the economic advances of the USSR since the death of Lenin, citing growth in electrical power, industrial production and agricultural output. Trotsky argued that the task of democratisation in Russia 'as liquidation of the monarchy and the semi-feudal slavery of the peasants, could be achieved only through a dictatorship of the proletariat'. According to Trotsky, the concentration of the means of production in the Soviet state's hands was the only solution in order to efficiently industrialise and develop the country, and socialism was proved as being correct 'not in the language of dialectics, but in the language of steel, cement and electricity'. Once the first five-year plan had been started (1923–28), the state and Party bureaucracy had the opportunity to escape not only the masses' political control 'upon whom this forced industrialisation was laying an unbearable burden' but also the monetary control. Official propaganda announced that the first five-year plan was completed in four years and three months but Trotsky argued 'that means only that the cynicism of the bureaucracy in its manipulations of statistics and public opinion is without limit' and this put the fate of the Soviet state at stake. Trotsky also cited Christian Rakovsky's words regarding the bureaucracy as a new class: 'in a proletarian state, where capitalist accumulation is forbidden to the members of the ruling party, the differentiation is at first functional, but afterward becomes social. I do not say it becomes a class differentiation, but a social one'. Trotsky dedicated an important part of his work to the analysis of *the social physiognomy of the ruling stratum*. The analysis started with the observation that it was impossible to describe the Soviet bureaucracy in accurate figures, for two main reasons: on the one hand the Soviet state was almost the sole employer; therefore, it was hard to say where the administrative apparatus ends; and on the other hand, Soviet statisticians, economists and publicists kept silence on this topic. However, after analysing the Soviet state structure, and taking into consideration aspects such as consumption and income, Trotsky concluded that '15 per cent, or, say, 20 per cent, of the population enjoys not much less of the wealth than is enjoyed by the remaining 80 to 85 per cent'. But it is Chapter 9, entitled 'Social Relations in the Soviet Union', where Trotsky sharply attacked the bureaucracy:

> The cadres are in their very essence the organs of domination and command. A cult of 'cadres' means above all a cult of bureaucracy, of officialdom, an aristocracy of technique. In the matter of playing up and developing cadres, as in other matters, the Soviet regime still finds itself compelled to solve problems which the advanced bourgeoisie solved long ago in its own countries. But since the Soviet cadres come forward under a socialist banner, they demand an almost divine veneration and a continually rising salary. The development of 'socialist' cadres is thus accompanied by a rebirth of bourgeois inequality.

According to Trotsky, the bureaucracy escaped from the control of the political leadership using its monopoly over economic planning. This monopoly represents the most important assets the bureaucracy holds and the mechanism of control over the whole of Soviet society. While in capitalism the bureaucracy is accountable to the bourgeoisie because the latter owns and controls the means of production, in the Soviet state the means of production were nationalised and the state's leadership had only political control over the apparatus. The real control in the Soviet state was the bureaucracy's control over the means of production, which had led to a new social differentiation in the society. Trotsky argued that

> the real divisions of Soviet society, which should and might easily be revealed with the help of an honest census, are as follows: heads of the bureaucracy, specialists, etc., living in bourgeois conditions; medium and lower strata, on the level of the petty bourgeoisie; workers and collective farm aristocracy – approximately on the same level; medium working mass; medium, stratum of collective farmers; individual peasants and craftsmen; lower worker and peasant strata passing over into the *lumpen proletariat*; homeless children, prostitutes, etc.

This new social differentiation was visible not only in differences in living standards, but in 'the revival of the exploitation of man in its most barbarous form – that of buying him into slavery for personal service'. It can be noted that Trotsky divided Soviet society using living conditions as the main criterion, largely ignoring salaries and even education.

The second section of Chapter 9 has a very descriptive title: *Is the Bureaucracy a Ruling Class?* Following Marxism, Trotsky argued that classes are characterised by their relation with the means of production, and in civilised countries these relations are validated by laws. But in the Soviet Union, the state owned almost everything. The Soviet bureaucracy was seen by Trotsky as any other bureaucracy from a capitalist country, especially as one from a fascist regime. But it had its specific characteristics, the most important being the higher degree of independence from the dominating class. In capitalist countries, the bureaucracy represents the interests of the bourgeoisie, which has many means of control over its administration of affairs. In a fascist country, the bureaucracy is related with the bourgeoisie through a wide range of relations – common interest, friendship, marriage – and therefore a certain degree of mutual control still exists. The Soviet bureaucracy was completely out of the control of the working class, 'which is hardly emerging from destitution and darkness, and has no tradition of dominion or command'. Therefore, argued Trotsky, the bureaucracy represented 'the sole privileged and commanding stratum in Soviet society'. More than that, the Soviet bureaucracy had appropriated the political power, creating a new social relationship with the means of production. The only legitimate owner of the political power found itself expropriated, and the state – the formal owner of almost everything, became captured by the bureaucracy. According to Trotsky, in the long run these developments would lead to a complete liquidation of the proletarian revolution's social conquests. Trotsky predicted that the bureaucracy would have to create new forms of property in order to establish its dominance as a class. While this would conflict with the state property principle, the bureaucracy had to defend and extract benefits from the current status quo. Trotsky argued that proletariat dictatorship was the last weapon that would restore working class leadership.

But Trotsky was aware that representing the Soviet bureaucracy as a class of state capitalists would not withstand criticism. The bureaucracy did not formally own anything and its social position was not the subject of inheritance. The privileges, the undeserved and important share of the nation's income appropriated by the bureaucracy, were the results of power abuse and represented a form of social parasitism. The bureaucracy's social position was 'in the highest degree contradictory, equivocal and undignified, notwithstanding the completeness of its power and the smoke screen of flattery that conceals it'. Trotsky concluded that the bureaucracy had betrayed the revolution, but it didn't succeed in overthrowing the revolution. The proletarian revolution resisted because of the established property relations and because of 'the living force of the proletariat, the consciousness of its best elements, the impasse of world capitalism, and the inevitability of world revolution'. One important and disputable aspect of Trotsky's argument is the conscious character of the bureaucracy as political force. Trotsky suggested that it was more than common interest behind the behaviour of the commanding stratum of Soviet society. But since neither property nor education were among the distinctive features of this social group, Trotsky failed to explain the sources and characteristics of this conscious character. According to his detailed descriptions, the Soviet bureaucracy represented a mass of individuals in command positions seeking better life conditions in the frame of Soviet society. Better life conditions were associated with command positions based not only on control over organisational structures, but also on a certain expertise in commanding those structures. Moreover, as other researchers would argue later on, in the conditions of chronic shortages and demanding targets, the ability to survive in command positions depended on negotiation with other individuals in command positions. In this social structure, the enterprises' managers were the bureaucrats that acted as an interface between the bureaucratic system and the working class.

Djilas joined the Communist Party of Yugoslavia as a student in 1932. In 1938, he was elected to the Central Committee of the Communist Party and became a member of its Politburo in 1940. He was one of the closest associates of Tito in the partisan resistance. After the establishment of the Federal People's Republic of Yugoslavia, Djilas had been appointed as vice-president in Tito's government. He became one of the leading critics of Stalin's attempts to bring Yugoslavia under Soviet control. Later, Yugoslavia broke with the Soviet Union and left the Cominform. Djilas was involved in pursuing the policy of independent socialism by the Yugoslav Communist Party. Self-management of workers in state-owned enterprises was an important part of these experiments. Djilas also encouraged freethinking based on his involvement in the propaganda apparatus. After a series of newspaper articles criticising the benefits of high rank officials, he was expelled from the Party's Central Committee and lost all political position. After other public criticisms, he was sentenced to prison. In 1957, Djilas published abroad *The New Class: An Analysis of the Communist System*, which was followed by another prison sentence.

According to Djilas, in communist societies a new class had appeared that exercised the same dominating, exploitative and repressive functions as the bourgeoisie in capitalism. Unlike other authors such as Herbert Marcuse who analysed Soviet Marxism from a Left philosophical position, Djilas built his arguments from the position of a former communist politician who had 'travelled the entire road open to a Communist' (Djilas, 1957, p. vi). The book aimed 'to establish the nature of relationships which arise in the course of the Communist revolution and ultimately become established in the process of industrialisation and collectivisation' (Djilas, 1957, p. 35). The author argued that the state apparatus didn't really determine social and property relations, it just protected these relations. A new form of ownership and exploitation and a new class had emerged in the communist states. The communists were unable to act differently than any other ruling class before them. Djilas also observed that unlike other classes who reached power after new economic patterns had taken shape in old societies, in the communist case, the new class took power to complete a new economic order. Therefore, a new form of discipline was required in order to overcome its weaknesses. The continuous class struggle, the external enemies and the centralised and extensive industrialisation provided the frame in which the strong morale discipline was enforced. According to Djilas, the members of the new class were those 'who have special privileges and economic preference because of the administrative monopoly they hold' (Djilas, 1957, p. 39). The Party was the source of this new class, but the stronger the class grew, the weaker the Party became. The new class was born in the working class and acted in the name of the working class but practised its monopoly primarily over the working class and this was the biggest deception the new class had to accomplish. This is the reason why the new class needed industry and industrialisation – to maintain and enhance its monopoly over the working class. This explains why industrialisation was a crucial goal for both the Party leadership and the new class.

Following his release from the second imprisonment, Djilas completed *The Unperfect Society: Beyond the New Class*, which was published in the USA in 1969. Conceived as a sequel to *The New Class*, *The Unperfect Society* reasserts the main arguments in a more cohesive way. Djilas observed and tried to explain the conflict between sciences and the Marxist-Leninist doctrine.

Herbert Marcuse published in 1958 the book entitled *Soviet Marxism: A Critical Analysis*. Associated with the Frankfurt School of critical theory, Marcuse's main theme regarded the dehumanising effects of capitalism and modern technology. During World War II he worked for the Research and Analysis Branch of the Office of Strategic Services (OSS), a fact that helped him write *Soviet Marxism*. According to Kellner (1984, p. 197), the book represents 'an interpretation of both the political phenomenon of Communism in the Soviet Union and its ideological doctrine and departures from classical Marxism'. In a synthesis of Marxist ethical tenets, Marcuse argued that the main appeal of the Soviet state was the claim 'to unite, on a scientific basis, values and facts, ideal and reality, the particular interest of the individual and the general interest of society, even of mankind, as a whole'. In contrast with Western ethics' tensions between ideal justice and unjust practices, between affirmed equality and reality's discriminations, between growing resources and their limited availability, the socialist society promised to offer effective solutions for all these tensions. In the economic realm, while capitalist society offers unequal opportunities and chances, the planned economy would eliminate all insecurities based on scientific management of all economic and social aspects. Marcuse argued the absurdity of the Soviet society in which the 'realisation of the Marxian promises appeared – only to be delayed again – and in which the new productive forces are again used as instruments for productive repression' (Marcuse, 1958, p. 89). According to Marcuse (1958, p. 106), the role of the first five-year plan was 'to revolutionise the economic order of the country not only over, above and against the "immediate interests" of workers and peasants, but also by subjecting them to the bureaucratic-authoritarian organisation of production'. The five-year plans represented the institutionalisation of the revolution-from-above state, in which total industrialisation with a strong focus on means of production represented a distinctive feature. Another feature identified by Marcuse (1958, pp. 78–79) was the 'universal work morale, competitive efficiency, elimination of all transcendent psychological and ideological elements'. The state, military, managerial and party apparatus represented the vehicles for the implementation of all these processes.

Marcuse's *Soviet Marxism* was critiqued by Kellner for its lack of 'serious and sustained critique of Stalinism, the Soviet bureaucracy and Soviet political repression' (Kellner, 1984, pp. 211–212). As well, according to Kellner, Marcuse ignored the question raised by Trotsky – as to whether the Soviet Union is truly a socialist society and to what extent it shared features with the capitalist society. However, Marcuse sharply criticised Soviet work ethics and observed the fundamental conflict between technological progress and the ideological pressure for conformity and submission to the Party's directives. While production automation and rationalisation free individual time and energy, the same processes produce standardised conformity and routinised reactions. According to Marcuse (1958, pp. 84–85) nationalisation and centralisation of the economy counteracted the first of these tendencies, therefore 'progress in industrialisation is tantamount to progress in domination: attendance to the machine, the scientific work process, becomes totalitarian, affecting all spheres of life'. The uninterrupted growing of the economic system became the only rationality of the whole society, and the union between ideal and reality 'remains a mere promise'. Nationalisation and centralised control didn't constitute a distinctive feature of the socialist society, they represented just 'a change in the mode of domination, streamlining of domination' (Marcuse, 1958, p. 82), a device for increasing productivity and accelerating the development. Therefore, control from below was required in order to demonstrate the qualitative superiority of the Soviet system. Marcuse argued that in the Soviet state where all means of production were nationalised, the decisive factor was control and not ownership. But while in capitalist society ownership could be usually identified, in the Soviet state the locus of control was vague and unclear. Marcuse also made a further distinction between technical-administrative and social control. Marcuse argued that in practice, the centralised command economy had exercised the function of domination against the working class by a group which had decided the society's needs independently of collective control. The Soviet state bureaucracy had developed a *caste character* and maintaining and enhancing its privileged position had become its main interest. Moreover, Marcuse defined the concept of class as a 'group which exercises governmental (including managerial) functions as a "separate" function in the social division of labour – with or without special privileges' (1958, p. 105). From this perspective, Marcuse's analysis can be compared with Djilas's (1957) new class theory.

The problem of the state-managed economy

After rapid growth rates in its early years, economic performance in the centrally managed economies experienced a dramatic decline. The rate of technological innovation gradually slowed down and the quality of production was often poor. As a result, policy makers continued to be preoccupied with questions of production to the detriment of consumption, and these concerns created pressure on the industrial managers and what was expected of them by their superiors. In the years of rapid forced industrialisation, it had been possible to achieve high rates of growth by extensive development of new sources of raw materials and peasant labour. However, as state socialist industrial society became more complex after the 1960s, and untapped sources of materials and labour became less accessible, the need became more urgent for a radical restructuring of production relations to promote more intensive development.

A range of different explanations for the problems were offered by economists. For example, Alec Nove argued that the basic problem was the growing complexity of the economy and the impossibility of economic managers having adequate information to plan and administer the system centrally (Nove, 1965, pp. 89, 201). Nove also indicated the communication and common understanding between industrial managers and central planners as the core issue of a non-market economy: 'The trouble lies in the near-impossibility of drafting micro-economic instructions in such way that even the most well-meaning manager will not be misled' (Nove, 1980, p. 89). An implication of this argument was that solutions might be found in decentralisation of some decision making and the introduction of market criteria in the management of the economy. The question of how to decentralise decision making and to introduce some elements of a market mechanism were explored in several countries in Eastern Europe, including in the Soviet Union, but practical attempts to implement changes, while staying within the parameters of central management and public ownership, went furthest in Hungary, although even there the reforms were constrained by powerful barriers to change inbuilt in the state managed system. A review of the debate in Hungary therefore provides insights into the problems faced more broadly across communist Eastern Europe.

Iván T. Berend dedicated an important effort to the study of the reforms experienced by the Hungarian economy during the communist regime. In 1990

Berend published a book entitled *The Hungarian Economic Reforms 1953–1988* in which he analysed the evolution of the centralised economy in a detailed manner, including not only the relevant economic indicators but the debates regarding possible development paths. The author argued that except for the 1966–68 reform, the other changes of the Hungarian economic system were rather 'partial corrections made within a previously adapted Soviet economic model, affecting only one or another sector of the economy, or, say, measures introduced only as experiment' (Berend, 1990, p. x). The author described in a detailed manner the Hungarian centralised system. Like most other communist countries, the Soviet system of centralised planning was adopted in Hungary. The first five-year plan started in 1950 under the new system of planning. Detailed annual plans were produced for each enterprise, containing an important number of indicators. The authorities were responsible for the successful implementation of plans, for enterprises' management and performed operative, supervisory and controlling functions. The negotiation of the plan indicators between the authorities and enterprises became one of the usual practices. According to Berend, an important characteristic of the Hungarian planned economy was the price system. The prices of industrial products were seen 'simply as a technical accounting instrument' (Berend, 1990, p. 5). State subsidies were largely used to bridge differences between prices and costs. All incentives, including the managers' bonuses, were related to the fulfilment of plan indicators. Therefore, the enterprises were encouraged to overfulfil the quantitative targets at all costs.

Another important factor considered by Berend was Hungary's industrial backwardness. Because the Soviet model was attractive to countries struggling against backwardness, the Hungarian communist government decided 'to adapt the Soviet model rather than seek new paths' (Berend, 1990, p. 7). Rapid industrialisation of backward countries was also seen as preparation for the inevitable war with capitalist countries. In spite of a few short-term advantages, the negative consequences of the command system appeared from the very beginning. As a consequence of eliminating the real relation between price and value, investment and production were wasted to a large extent. Vast quantities of unsaleable goods were produced because of the obsession with plan fulfilment. The monopolistic position enjoyed by most enterprises reduced the interest in innovations or new technologies. By 1950, the decline in quality and range of products was admitted by the communist leadership. The command system reacted by issuing more directives, more indicators and finally 'an increasingly incomprehensible mass of detailed instructions' (Berend, 1990, p. 11). Obviously, the bureaucratic apparatus required to control the whole economy in such a manner had expanded significantly. In order to control and to increase the political commitment, various forms of disciplinary procedures were issued and used in enterprises. Even prison sentences were prescribed for significant infringement of plan targets. A sentence of a maximum of five years in prison was prescribed for crimes involving 'grave danger to or infringement of the national economic plan or any of its detailed plans' (Berend, 1990, p. 12). In spite of a growing number of regulations and procedures, and of an expanding bureaucracy, the Hungarian economy had experienced an increasing number of shortcomings that finally led to corrective efforts. Moreover, a serious crisis broke out in the winter of 1952–53 and it appeared that the first five-year plan would be unsuccessful.

All these economic aspects together with the political changes generated by Stalin's death had led to the first attempt to reform the Hungarian economic system. According to Berend, this reform aimed to make a modest adjustment, basically to reduce the bureaucracy and the excessive number of plan indicators. The National Planning Office also carried out a simplification of the planning process, and experimental reforms were introduced in a few enterprises aiming at greater freedom of action for enterprises in plan fulfilment. The period between 1953 and 1956 had been marked by an intense and public debate regarding the reform of the economic system. Many authors, among them Gyorgy Peter and János Kornai, argued for the introduction of other mechanisms in order to obtain a better resource allocation and to reduce waste. Most of these authors argued for a significant reduction in the role of centralised planning. However, the limits on the extent of economic reform that could be allowed by the communist leadership was expressed by Tamas Nagy: 'the economic mechanism connected with the law of value should function within the framework of central planning' (cited in Berend, 1990, p. 28).

After the 1956 revolution, discussions regarding economic reform resumed both among political leaders and in academic circles. Some proposals were drafted by the Ministry of Finance, the National Bank and the National Planning Office. The philosophy behind the proposals was to combine central planning with a market economy based on the introduction of a few market mechanisms in the frame of the central planning system. The central element of the new economic mechanism was to be played by the workers' councils. Workers' self-management was conceived as the replacement for the centralised bureaucratic system and became the fundamental institution of the new system of economic management, in the official discourse. But soon this new structure generated an intense debate regarding the double subordination of enterprise managers. As a solution for this contradiction, workers' councils had to be involved in enterprise management. However, the debate around the fundamental principles of the command economy continued long after the establishment of workers' councils. The mandatory plan indicators, enterprises autonomy, price reform and shortages of goods were among the most important topics discussed in the context of the new economic mechanism. Finally, few significant reforms were introduced in 1957 – the price system was changed, state subsidies were reduced, compulsory deliveries in agriculture were eliminated, and private initiative was encouraged. The number of plan indicators was drastically reduced, labour management centralisation was relaxed, and in a few areas, especially in light industry, production planning was based on direct negotiations between industry and commerce. Moreover, the enterprises were involved to a greater extent in plan preparation, an aspect which could 'be seen as a degree of institutionalisation of the plan bargaining' (Berend, 1990, p. 76). Prices were adjusted periodically in connection with real values.

All these reforms had an important impact on the industrial structure. Industrial enterprises were re-structured in order to ensure a higher degree of autonomy and industrial directorates lying between the ministry and enterprises were abolished. However, according to Berend, all these changes in the industrial structure of the Hungarian economy 'ultimately became a powerful and resilient obstacle to reform, whose extremely adverse effects were to be felt for a quarter of a century' (Berend, 1990, p. 92). The reason for this evolution was the emergence of new monopoly companies through voluntary mergers, which narrowed the market significantly, re-built the bureaucracy at enterprise level and reinforced directive planning. In conclusion, the economic reforms pursued until 1964 had been unsuccessful, bringing only small corrections in the system. But the possibility of drawing further recruits into the workforce had been exhausted by the rapid and extensive industrialisation process. Therefore, further industrialisation could not rely only on increasing the amount of labour; it had to be built on an increase of productivity.

This persistence of central control despite attempts at reform in Hungary's command economy was investigated in detail by János Kornai. In 1956, he published his candidate's thesis entitled *A Few Problems of Overcentralization and Material Incentive Relying on Experiences Gained in the Light Industry*, which offered a critical analysis of the system of mandatory plan indicators and of its system of incentives and penalties. Kornai's main conclusion was that all the system's dysfunctionalities were related, forming a coherent system, and any attempt to partially adjust the command economy would generate as many negative effects as it would eliminate. He suggested using economic compulsion instead of the compulsion of directives, therefore arguing for a fundamental change of the command system. Thereafter, Kornai continued to dedicate efforts to investigating the problems of planning in the Hungarian economy. A consistent series of publications in Western and Hungarian academic journals addressed the problems of planning, programming, control, shortage and other issues faced by communist economies. The publication of *Economics of Shortage* in 1980 had finally concluded his researches and it provided his complete perspective on command economy dysfunctionalities.

According to Kornai (1992, p. 161) the promise to eliminate backwardness was 'a major constituent on the official ideology' and it was based on a belief in the socialist system's superiority. Consequently, the leaders of the communist parties had to insist on fast growth 'because it will provide further evidence of that superiority' (Kornai, 1992, p. 161). The economic growth experienced by the communist states was forced, being generated not by the society's structure but by top-down bureaucratic decisions. This kind of growth was unsustainable and sooner or later it slowed down. In the same manner, after some initial steps to fulfil communism's basic promises, complete fulfilment 'never occurs and never can occur' (Kornai, 1992, p. 54). Kornai argued the accumulation of 'soft budget' constraints inevitably leads to the system failure in what he coined as 'economy of shortage'. The author identified as the main source of chronic shortage the leadership's commitment to maintain employees and production regardless of the enterprises' efficiency. This commitment permitted the accumulation of systematic losses that exhausted the economy's resources. According to Kornai, taut planning contributed to the accumulation of losses, managers being focused on plan fulfilment regardless of the required costs. The lack of strong financial constraints generated a systematic accumulation of losses, due to the existence of more important ideological and political constraints. Thus, the system was unable to encourage enterprises to maximise productivity and profitability. In a system based on 'vertical bargaining' between different levels of political hierarchy instead of market relations, politically formulated directives only offered 'soft budget constraints'. In other words, the constraints were of an administrative nature and could be relaxed by subsequent political decision if targets were not met and an enterprise failed to operate profitably.

A few decades later on, Michael Ellman investigated the characteristics of the socialist planning systems in a broader comparative manner. The first edition of his book *Socialist Planning* appeared in 1979, and it explored the problems faced by the planned economies of the Soviet Union and China during Brezhnev and Mao leaderships. The second edition appeared in 1989, and it reflected the economic reform attempted by some socialist countries. This second edition also served as an important source of information about the causes of the socialist system's collapse. The third edition appeared in 2014, when socialist planning 'has become a historical phenomenon' (Ellman, 2014, p. ix), and significantly more information is available. Very importantly for the understanding of the Soviet centralised plan, Ellman presents the historical context in which the centralised planning system appeared and was developed. Ellman describes the ideological debates, the bureaucratic struggles and successive developments of various types of plans used by the Soviet authorities. The author also summarises the main critique, reform attempts and international impact of Soviet planning. The ritualistic function of planning was also brought into the discussion. Ellman concluded that 'it is more nearly correct to call the economy "centrally managed" rather than "centrally planned"' (p. 48). The numerous reform attempts pursued by the Soviet Union, Yugoslavia, Poland, Hungary and, post-1990, by China are also discussed.

Ellman also argues that 'much of the waste usually ascribed to "the inefficiency of central planning" was actually a by-product of the system of mobilisation planning' (p. 133) – the rapid transition to military production in case of war. According to Ellman, investment planning in socialist economies was not a 'socially rational process for achieving the efficient allocation of scarce investment resources' but rather a 'part of the relationship between individuals and groups' (p. 178), in which different aspects, notably *gigantomania*, played important roles. Ellman argues that the main objective of labour planning was fulfilment and over-fulfilment of the national economic plan. But considering the mobilising and ritualistic roles of the plan, it can be argued that other rationalities were behind labour policies and planning. For example, the plan could be designed to integrate all available labour into state-controlled organisations. Ellman argues that the socialist system has not been successful in making any progress towards a more human labour process.

According to Ellman, the international trade of socialist countries experienced five different models. The wealth extraction exerted by the Soviet Union on its new Eastern European satellites immediately after World War II marked the beginning of international trade among the socialist countries. Few attempts to coordinate and increase the trade by creating a socialist world market ultimately failed despite some temporary and limited successes. In contrast, China's strategy of integration in the world economy after 1978 represents a success based probably on lessons learned from the Soviet system collapse.

Ellman concludes that in spite of some successes as an intensive method of modernisation, socialist planning ultimately failed. While physical and human capital were significantly developed in most socialist countries, the effect on social capital, at least in Eastern Europe and in the USSR was rather negative. Ellman concludes that especially in more developed countries 'state socialism led to a steadily increasing lag behind' (p. 364) the capitalist countries.

The role and position of industrial managers

In the context described above, of the consolidation of a ruling elite or class operating in its own interests in maintaining its position and power and justifying its decisions in the framework of a theory that claimed to be scientific and supported top-down decision making, and of an economy that displayed inbuilt resistance to decentralising reforms and persistently generated its own inefficiencies, the industrial managers were confronted with the task of increasing production and securing the cooperation of their workers.

The first scientist who focused his empirical research on the Soviet industrial system was Joseph Berliner. His book *Factory and Manager in the USSR* was published in 1957. The book presents the results of a significant number of interviews with former Soviet managerial officials, within the framework of the Harvard Project on the Soviet Social System. A brief description of the project of which Berliner's study of the Soviet industrial enterprise was only a part is summarised by Raymond Bauer, Alex Inkeles and Clyde Kluckhohn in their book, *How the Soviet System Works* (1956). According to the authors, in the spring of 1950, the Russian Research Center of Harvard University accepted support from the US Air Force for a systematic study of the emigrants from Soviet Union. At that time knowledge regarding the Soviet Union was 'handicapped by the absence of certain types of data, principally that bearing on the day-to-day life experiences of Soviet citizens, on the informal aspects of the functioning of Soviet institutions, and on the psychological characteristics of the Soviet population' (Bauer, Inkeles and Kluckhohn, 1956, p. 7). In the first stage of the research, 329 persons responded to a battery of interviews regarding the individual's work and educational history, their family background, the sources of information, social and political attitudes and the history of their relations to the regime. The second stage comprised a written questionnaire covering the same topics, administered to 2,718 respondents. A supplementary 435 interviews and 9,748 questionnaires regarding special topics were administered in the third stage. One of those special topics was the operation of the Soviet enterprise. Other psychological tests were given in order to describe the personality, and to identify possible bias in respondents. Furthermore, a few intensive case studies were developed in order to obtain further insights in specific problems. These details show one of the distinctive aspects of the Harvard project – the large body of collected data regarding multiple aspects of the Soviet system.

The fourth chapter of Bauer, Inkeles and Kluckhohn's book deals with the planning and controlling system. The authors identified the main vulnerability of the Soviet economic system as over-control and over-centralisation (p. 44). The centralised bureaucracy generated a rigid control apparatus and, in response, many illicit methods adopted by people in order to 'get things done'. On the whole, the authors suggested, Soviet managers showed acceptance of the Soviet system and this was one important element of the system's strength. The investigation showed 'the apparent competence and vigour of the Soviet industrial managers'; and the authors were impressed by 'the degree to which the managerial group accepts the main structure of Soviet society, particularly the organisation of such realms as industry, and regards it as worthy of respect and emulation' (pp. 227–228). However, within this context, the managers also showed a desire for mainly ameliorative measures of the managerial world, especially to deal with the lack of trust and confidence, and political interference in day-to-day activity. Finally, the authors suggested, this might lead to increasing pressure on the Soviet elite towards better morale in organisations. They suggested that modern technology would ask for a more educated work force with a higher degree of autonomy; therefore performance would depend on the workers' morale.

Subsequently Berliner (1957) made a more detailed report of the Harvard project findings regarding the Soviet enterprise viewed through the eyes of former managers. The main conclusion of this study suggested there were more pronounced tensions in the system than identified earlier. He concluded that 'managers follow an entirely different set of rules which have no officially recognised existence and which, moreover, sharply contradict the official rules' (Berliner, 1957, p. 318). These practices were constantly criticised in the official discourse, but their persistence showed their important role in the Soviet planned economy. According to Berliner, these managerial practices fell into three groups: 'the safety factor', the simulation of plan fulfilment and *blat*. The 'safety factor' could take different forms – from manipulating the planning process in order to obtain targets smaller than what could actually be produced to hoarding materials, spare parts and workforce. Reducing the quality of output or producing a different range of quantities than those supposed to be produced were simulation practices noted by Berliner. Finally, Berliner defined *blat* as 'the use of personal influence to manipulate ministry officials into giving the enterprise an easy production target or to persuade a bank official to overlook an unplanned use of enterprise funds' (Berliner, 1957, p. 319). The *blat* practice was connected with the invisible occupation of the *tolkach* – 'the specialist in obtaining all manner of scarce commodities through a combination of influence and gifts' (ibid).

Since all these practices conflicted with laws, regulations and the official Party discourse, the question Berliner tried to answer was why the Soviet manager engaged in such practices. The research findings showed the manager 'feels compelled to do so, that the pressures exerted by the economic environment leave him no other way in which to achieve his goals' (Berliner, 1957, p. 320). The unreasonably high level of the plan targets combined with constant shortages and delays in deliveries were the two dominant features of the Soviet economy that generated the managerial practices described before. As Berliner synthesised the phenomenon, 'the manager with good *blat* in the proper quarters and the services of a competent *tolkach* is a step ahead of his colleagues in the competition for scarce resources' (ibid.). The control system also contributed to the survival of these practices. The control agencies focused on special problems such as repeated plan under-fulfilment. Therefore, the best strategy to avoid control was to report plan fulfilment regularly. On the other hand, a strict control would show the large scale of these irregular practices. Consequently, a 'looking the other way' attitude of control officials was often mentioned by the interviewed managers. Moreover, a 'family relationship' between Party secretary, chief accountant and manager often appeared, all of them sharing the rewards and prestige that came with regular plan fulfilment. This was generally supported by the later study of *blat* by Alena Ledeneva (1998). She analysed extensively the phenomenon of *blat*, and its pervasiveness in Soviet society. According to Ledeneva, 'blat is a matter of belonging to a circle' (1998, p. 40). Rather than being just an influencing method, *blat* (and its Romanian counterpart – *pile*) expressed a kind of favour accessible just to *people of the circle, to one of us*.

Finally, Berliner analysed the reasons for which the Soviet state tolerated these practices. The author considered that the high rate of industrial growth required that people be pushed beyond the limits to which they would voluntarily go. Therefore, these managerial practices were 'the price the state has been willing to pay for the achievement of its objective' (Berliner, 1957, p. 329). On the other hand, Berliner argued that these practices had some advantages, serving as counterweights to forces which, if uncontrolled, would result in greater dysfunctionalities in the economy. For example, the plan negotiation compensated for the 'constant bias in the planning system toward unrealistically high targets' (Berliner, 1957, p. 326).

Jeremy Azrael has also extensively examined the Soviet managerial elite, from bourgeois specialists to red directors and to the new post-Stalin generation of managers in the book *Managerial Power in Soviet Politics* (1966). Azrael placed his investigation in the wider context of the discussions regarding the 'docility and political impotence that have characterised the role of the technical intelligentsia and managerial elite' in the development of the Soviet system (Azrael, 1966, p. 173). In the first two decades after the revolution the *red directors* were assigned to the top positions in the industrial establishment. They had a diverse social origin, but they had in common the skill of organisation-building and an immense energy that often compensated for their lack of technical expertise. In the political realm, they supported Stalin's rise to power and 'took no steps to prevent the definitive consolidation of that power' (Azrael, 1966, p. 102). In contrast to some extent with the red directors was the group that had emerged after Stalin's death. This group had been educated in first-class schools and institutes, so they were highly skilled engineers with significant technical expertise. Furthermore, they were 'strong-minded realists, well aware of the "imperatives" of economic and technical rationality and anxious to see that these imperatives are taken into account in the policy process' (Azrael, 1966, p. 162). Confirming Bauer, Inkeles and Kluckhohn's (1956) observation regarding the high degree of acceptance of the Soviet system, Azrael concluded that 'what political influence they have had has been primarily a function of their unquestioning acceptance of an instrumental and dependent role' (Azrael, 1966, p. 173). According to the author, the primacy of politics and ideology over economic rationality was the rule in the Soviet system and this principle would be maintained in the future as well – 'the politics will continue to dominate economics and will remain largely in the hands of committed technicians of power' (Azrael, 1966, p. 177).

A further contribution to this literature was Berliner's book entitled *The Innovation Decision in Soviet Industry* (1976). Focused on innovation processes in industry, the book provided a detailed account of Soviet economy structure, economic planning, research and development organisations, prices and profits, and incentives and decision rules. According to Berliner, there was a significant degree of bias against innovation generated by the structural uncertainty over the supply of materials and equipment (Berliner, 1976, p. 92). The author considered as a sufficient explanation of this problem the state of disequilibrium that characterised inter-enterprise transactions. The policy of excessively taut planning, the imperfections of pricing methods and centralised planning were the reasons for this disequilibrium (Berliner, 1976, p. 62).

Berliner also analysed the changes taking place more widely in the Soviet economic system in 'Planning and Management', the fifth chapter of his book *Soviet Industry from Stalin to Gorbachev* (1988). Analysing five cases of changes in the economic mechanism between 1957 and 1979, Berliner argued that the process of changing the system of planning and management had become routinised and, for the most part, the changes were technical rather than fundamental (Berliner, 1988, p. 97). The author also identified a conflict between planning and management in the view of the Party leaders. System failures were usually blamed on inadequate management while the efficacy of the central planning system was beyond any doubt (Berliner, 1976, p. 109). Moreover, the importance and efficiency of the planning system was systematically reinforced in the official discourse.

In the final chapter of this book, Berliner drew on a new research project based on interviews with a significant number of Soviet citizens who had been allowed to leave the country in the 1970s. This 'Soviet Interview Project' (SIP) had one portion devoted to interviews with individuals who held management positions in Soviet enterprises or in the higher economic bureaucracy. Berliner also cited a few SIP project reports authored by Susan Linz – 'Managerial Autonomy in the Soviet

Firm' (1985) (a preliminary draft), 'The Role of Tautness in Soviet Planning' (1986) and 'The Treadmill of Soviet Economy Reforms: Management's Perspective' (1987). The chapter describes the continuities and changes in industrial management over almost five decades of development. While the economic structure had faced significant changes, and national planning was more sophisticated and based on computers and mathematical modelling, 'many of the practices of the past have survived virtually unchanged' (Berliner, 1988, p. 277). The most important change identified by the author was in technology, which exhibited 'the fruits of the arduous industrialisation drive' (Berliner, 1988, p. 271). In the same period the labour force had changed dramatically. Most of the workers were urban-born, with a consistent technical education, and living in far better conditions than their predecessors. The new managers were also better educated, more self-confident, with a higher social status and with a far better living standard. But while so many aspects of the industrial realm had improved in three decades of industrialisation, many others had remained constant according to the discourse of interviewed managers: 'portions of the SIP interviews read as if they came right out of the Harvard interviews' (Berliner, 1988, p. 277).

Berliner described 10 practices that had survived virtually unchanged during that period. Almost all of them were identified in interviews with managers of Romanian communist enterprises, and will be discussed in following chapters. First, the 'ratchet' principle consisted in raising the target for the next period to the level realised in the current period if this level over-fulfilled the plan. This practice was one of the main sources of plan tautness. The second persistent practice identified in the SIP project was production reserves – the systematic interest in obtaining plan targets lower than the production capability. Materials hoarding was also a common practice due to the chronic supply problems. Related to materials hoarding was another practice – barter and resale. The SIP informants reported that barter and resale were more often practiced than in the past. Hoarding of labour was a practice less present in the responses of SIP informants than in the Harvard study. The reason for this evolution was a stronger control by the authorities. Enterprise autarky was also a persistent practice used for minimising the risk of dependence on uncertain deliveries. The lower level of enthusiasm about innovation and new technologies had also been a persistent practice. The managers' preference for producing established products using existing technology was another form of the safety factor. A side effect of the planning system had been a lower concern for the quality of products. In spite of strong official propaganda and even of criminal penalties imposed on persons guilty of producing sub-quality products, this practice had persisted through Soviet industry. The uneven pace of production, with a lower rate during the first part of the plan period followed by storming in the last part was another practice almost impossible to eradicate in Soviet industry. Finally, the constant focus on relating wages to performance was identified among the persistent practices. Almost all Soviet leaders from Stalin to Gorbachev expressed the need to connect salaries with workers' contribution.

According to Berliner, the *shortage syndrome* was the main reason for most of these practices. The *shortage syndrome* included 'quality deterioration, hoarding, barter, supply expediters, gifts and bribery, organisational autarky and so forth' (Berliner, 1988, p. 286). Berliner argued that a *shortage syndrome* occurred whenever an economy functions under conditions of persistent shortage, regardless of the political system in which it exists. But in the case of Soviet industry, the practices described above derived from the Soviet economic system's characteristics: 'mandatory quantitative output targets and centralised distribution of intermediate products' (Berliner, 1988, p. 291). Therefore, the persistence of centralised economic planning had generated the persistence of these managerial practices, in spite of successive attempts to reform the planning system.

Further interesting insights into the problems facing industrial managers in the centrally managed economies can be seen in the case of Hungary. In particular, the well-established tradition of Hungarian sociography offers useful insights regarding the relation between working class and industrial enterprise. Miklós Haraszti is one of the well-known examples with his book *A Worker in a Workers' State* (1977). After a personal experience as a worker in the Red Star Tractor Factory, Haraszti wrote a detailed sociographic account of his experiences. His first attempt to publish his book was declined in 1973 with the publishing house's comment 'hostile'. Iván Szelényi agreed to publish sections of Haraszti's manuscript in *Szociológia*, one of Hungary's main social sciences journals. As soon as the authorities were alerted, Haraszti was arrested and Szelényi dismissed from his editorship. The original manuscript entitled *Darabbér* (*Piece-rate*) was published in 1975 by Rotbuch Verlag under the title *Stücklohn*. His book offered a first-hand account of the way the plan was perceived by the workers, of the various mechanisms used to increase the salaries and avoid or dissimulate targets' un-fulfilment.

While being focused mostly on a specific work system – the piece-rate – Haraszti's book offers a very consistent perspective on the workers' perception on two key aspects discussed here: the salaries and the managers. When the author had been working for Red Star Tractor Factory, Hungary was already using payment by results system. Called by a Hungarian expert 'the ideal form for socialist wages' (Haraszti, 1977, p. 21), payment by results had generated a high level of insecurity for the working class. According to Haraszti (1977, p. 56) this insecurity was 'the main driving force in all payment by results' systems, and this is why it was considered as the best incentive system of all. Haraszti's account expresses workers' dissatisfaction with this salaries system, over which they had almost no control. It also describes how this apparent fair and measurable reward system was affected by subjectivism in norm setting and work allocation. Haraszti dedicated an entire chapter to the systems of norms, arguing that even in a communist state, the norms system was a coercion mechanism designed to continuously increase the industrial output. But the efficiency of the system is doubtful, norms being 'far more effective at shackling the imagination than at stimulating production' (Haraszti, 1977, p. 132). Moreover, norms were more successful in producing workers' adverse reaction: 'each new increase in output extracted by the norms excites pain and anger in us' (ibid.). The Romanian version of payment by results and its effect is detailed in the next chapter, confirming Haraszti's sociographic account.

Another interesting aspect of Haraszti's story is the radical dissociation between the workers and *them* – 'the management, those who give orders and take the decisions, employ labour and pay wages, the men and their agents who are in charge – who remain inaccessible even when they cross our fields of vision' (Haraszti, 1977, p. 71). In contrast with the official '*we*', the working class was defining itself by exclusion. Moreover, according to Haraszti, 'workers never use, either by chance, or in jest, or by slip of the tongue, or in error, and probably not even in their dreams, the '*us*' which forms the counter-balance' to *them* (Haraszti, 1977, p. 72). This suggests not only a disconnection between the working class – officially branded as the leading force of a communist society, and the managers, but also a rather antagonistic relation between these two social groups. This relation is also supported by Romanian miners' demand to discuss directly with the Party's leader during the 1977 Valea Jiului strike.

Haraszti's book influenced significantly Michael Burawoy's interest in the socialist industrial relations. Initially Burawoy planned to study the Polish workers' movement, but the 1982 events and Martial law put an end to his plan. Burawoy finally decided to focus on Hungary. The results of his sociological study were published together with János Lukács in 1992 as a collection of essays entitled *The Radiant Past*. The authors' conclusions contribute to a more accurate understanding of the main principles, assumptions and perceptions of the communist industrial management from the shopfloor perspective. Some of the observations made earlier by Haraszti are confirmed by Burawoy and Lukács. According to the authors, the workers' main concern was the norm: 'Norms are the true dictator. They drive one to fury and panic' (Burawoy and Lukács, 1992, p. 43). The reason for this perception is definitely the correlation between norms and salaries. The authors also describe how the relation between the enterprise's management and the workers was centred on the relation between norms and salaries. These crucial elements were the results of complex bargaining strategies aiming to maximise the benefits of all actors involved in the process. Therefore, one may conclude that, at least in the Hungarian case, negotiation was a method of adjustment between the working class and the managerial class, having the norms at the core of this process.

An important theme that has emerged from the discussion in the three sections above has been the underlying conflict between two different sets of assumptions about the fundamental nature of organisations in communist regimes. One crucial assumption of the ruling elite or class was that the society at large, but especially the planned economy, had to be managed according to scientific methods and principles. Besides the legitimisation sought in this way, this principle also reveals the belief that a set of scientific principles and methods for managing the economy exists – in the writings of Marx, Lenin and Stalin. While for the Party's leadership this claim of using scientific methods was a way to legitimise their decisions and policies, no matter how absurd or ideologically driven they were, for the state apparatus involved in the process of planning the economy, both at central and at organisational levels, the question of the rationality of decision making was crucial. In a market economy, Adam Smith's invisible hand of unobservable market forces acts to reach an equilibrium between demand and supply. Regardless of how disputed this concept is, it is widely accepted that market forces, more or less combined with state regulation, generate a dynamic equilibrium between supply and demand. In the case of communist societies, the elimination of the free market represented an ideological imperative. Therefore, the whole economy had to be regulated and carefully planned by the state. This conclusion was based on the assumption that such planning is possible, it has to follow scientific principles and rules, and it will produce an optimal state for all actors.

This book argues that the communist ideology, and social engineering strategies and policies based on its assumptions, were in conflict with those required by a rational bureaucracy responsible for the country's over-ambitious and tightly planned development. From the Party's top level to enterprise managers, rational decisions were over-ridden by political imperatives and by pragmatic negotiations, all at the expense of economic performance.

Meta-theories of communist society and organisation

A useful way of understanding this basic contradiction at the basis of the communist development strategy is the theoretical framework proposed by Burrell and Morgan (1979) based on two dimensions which generate four main sociological paradigms regarding organisational analysis. The two main dimensions synthesise two sets of mutually exclusive assumptions about the nature of social science and the nature of society. Burrell and Morgan's analytical scheme has had an important impact on organisational theory, creating the opportunity to 'become more aware of the nature of the broad intellectual traditions at work' (Burrell and Morgan, 1979, p. 396). The authors argue that it is important to know possible alternative avenues for development in order to analyse more consciously the social philosophy upon which these avenues are based. According to Gioia and Pitre (1990, pp. 591–592), the dividing lines between these main sociological paradigms are permeable to a certain extent rather than well defined, and 'the boundaries between paradigms are therefore more usefully conceived as *transition zones*'. Moreover, new theoretical currents within critical management studies (CMS) have complicated the scheme considerably. But both despite and because of these caveats, Burrell and Morgan's meta-theoretical map can be heuristically useful as a way to locate management and organisational practices and their theoretical roots. According to Burrell and Morgan (1979, pp. viii–xii) 'social theory can be conceived in terms of four key paradigms based upon different sets of meta-theoretical assumptions about the nature of social science and the nature of society'. These paradigms are based on mutually exclusive views of the social world. According to the authors, each paradigm generates specific theories and perspectives on organisations which are 'in fundamental opposition to those generated by other paradigms' (ibid.).

Burrell and Morgan's discussion of the two dimensions begins with the different assumptions of each about the nature of social science. The authors' central idea is that 'all theories of organisation are based upon a philosophy of science and a theory of society' (Burrell and Morgan, 1979, p. 1). Any approach to social science is based on some philosophical assumptions. According to Burrell and Morgan (1979, pp. 1–3) within each dimension there are four sets of assumptions: of an ontological nature, if the investigated reality is external or it is created by the individual consciousness; of an epistemological nature, regarding the grounds of knowledge; concerning human nature and the relation with the environment; and assumptions involved in the debate between determinism and voluntarism. These sets of assumptions concern the methodological approach to be employed in the analysis of any given set of social arrangements.

The extreme positions on each set of assumptions are represented in the two intellectual traditions which have dominated the social sciences in the last two centuries: sociological positivism and German idealism. The first intellectual tradition is based on the principle of similarities between the natural sciences and social science, in which a realist approach to ontology is backed up by a positivist epistemology, a relatively determinist view of human nature and the use of nomothetic methodologies. The second intellectual tradition based on German idealism stands in complete opposition to the first – reality is constructed by humans rather than existing outside activity; it stresses the subjective nature of social reality, rejecting the relevance and utility of natural science methods in the study of human realm; it supports ideographic methods for investigating social reality, arguing for the voluntarism of human nature. Epistemologically it is essentially anti-positivist, and its approach to social reality is fundamentally nominalist. The authors refer to these different dimensions as the 'subjective' and the 'objective' dimension. They are represented in Figure 2.1.

The subjective dimension	Assumptions	The objective dimension
Nominalism	Ontology	Realism
Anti-positivism	Epistemology	Positivism
Voluntarism	Human nature	Determinism
Ideographic	Methodology	Nomothetic

Figure 2.1 Assumptions about the nature of social science.

Source: adapted from Burrell and Morgan, 1979, p. 3.

The forms of analysis in each dimension are differentiated according to whether they focus on order, regulation and consensus, or on change, transformation and conflict. The 'order' or 'integrationist' view of society emphasises stability, integration, functional co-ordination and consensus. The 'conflict' or 'coercion' view of society emphasises change, conflict, disintegration and coercion (Burrell and Morgan, 1979, p. 13). The authors use the term *sociology of regulation* to refer to 'theorists who are primarily concerned to provide explanations of society in terms which emphasise its underlying unity and cohesiveness', and the term *sociology of radical change* to refer to ideas concerned to find 'explanations for radical change, deep-seated structural conflict, modes of domination, and structural contradiction which its theorists see as characterising modern society' (Burrell and Morgan, 1979, p. 17). The two independent dimensions briefly presented above define four distinct sociological paradigms as shown in Figure 2.2.

According to Burrell and Morgan, these four paradigms are 'defined by very basic meta-theoretical assumptions which underwrite the frame of reference, mode of theorising and modus operandi of the social theorists who operate within them' (Burrell and Morgan, 1979, p. 23). The scheme also provides a map in which each theory's frame of reference can be located. The authors argue that very few theorists are able to switch the paradigm in which they frame social life (Burrell and Morgan, 1979, p. 24).[4] Ultimately moreover, the authors argue, these four paradigms are mutually exclusive, offering alternative views of social reality because they are based on opposing meta-theoretical assumptions.

It can be suggested that a deeper understanding of the contradictory situation of enterprises' managers under a communist regime can be gained by attempting to locate the different views of the ruling class or elite and the managers within the framework offered by Burrell and Morgan. In order to do this, it is necessary first to decide where best to place the official Marxism-Leninism and the centralised

'Radical humanist'	'Radical structuralism'
'Interpretive'	'Functionalist'

Figure 2.2 The four paradigms of social theory.

Source: adapted from Burrell and Morgan, 1979, p. 22

planning system of the ruling group among Burrell and Morgan's categories. Then it may be possible to understand the contradiction experienced between managers and ideologues in communist countries as they tried to achieve economic development and remain in conformity with Marxist-Leninist ideology, or whether the managers in finding solutions to the problems of management, were in fact moving implicitly to a different and contradictory paradigm to the one asserted by the ruling group.

In the coordinates of Burrell and Morgan, the communist ideology could be placed in the quadrant of radical change theory. After all, the official ideology stated the need for the radical change of society, for new social and work relations and for a continuous struggle with internal and external enemies. But once the Party's leadership won the absolute control over the society, their approach changed to a less conflictual and more 'scientific' one.

As David Lane (1976, p. 20) has noted, Marxist-Leninist doctrine was assumed by all state-socialist countries; therefore this doctrine was assumed as 'the only true science of society', and moreover, that only the Communist Party held the only true account of the doctrine. Lane argued that the official value system of Marxist-Leninist doctrine has three pillars: Lenin's acceptance of the unity of thought of Marx and Engels, the acceptance of Lenin's theory of imperialism, and the acceptance of Lenin's theory of the Party as the articulator of the working class's interest. This resulted in an emphasis on economic determinism and class antagonism. According to Lane, these three components formed an organic whole legitimating all the actions of the Party leaders. The Marxist-Leninist Party had a central place and its main task was to express what it claimed to be the interests of the working class. Strict discipline and the organisational centralism were fundamental conditions to achieve the main objective – victory over capitalism through an alternative socialist industrialisation strategy. With this aim, the Party also leads and organises the socialist economy as a single process. In socialist society, contradictions are resolved not through class struggle but through joint efforts of friendly classes. The communist narrative reads as follows: there are scientific laws of economics which permit society's development while avoiding exploitation and inequality, and the Communist Party is going to apply these laws. Ruling communist ideology thus came to position itself in the objective dimension, both in terms of axiological claims – communist society is the objective and deterministic final stage of human evolution – and in terms of immediate actions. It was pure science which was used to offer legitimacy for all decisions either in social or economic realms. Scientific materialism (*materialismul ştiinţific*) was claimed to be the fundamental base for all decisions, policies and strategies of Romanian communist leaders.

In an ideal communist society, where the strategies, policies and practices developed would have been 'scientific', they will be perfectly matched by the requirements of the bureaucratically managed economy, in which the managers' only task would be to implement the plans and directives coming from above structures. In real life, a continuous struggle to survive and control had been Party's leadership strategy in competition with internal challengers – both from inside the Party or from the society, and with external pressures for change. The communist leaders' behaviour manifested a stronger ideological orthodoxy, a tightening control and a focus on industrialisation, suggesting that despite its origins in revolutionary Marxism this had become a mode of thinking.

Moreover, as noted by Lane (and the Marxist 'new ruling class' critics discussed in the first section of this chapter), nationalisation of the means of production may create a new ruling stratum which derives its power from the control over means of production, in spite of the principle of collective ownership over all national wealth.

But while in the political and social realms objectivity was only the claim used to offer a scientific legitimacy for the arbitrary, dictatorial and terror-backed domination over society, in the economic realm scientific management imposed a strict necessity. Any malfunction of the economic sector had a cost which must be paid, and which eroded the support for the elite. In the case of the Romanian communist regime, the whole society paid the cost of economic errors while the support for the leading clique was enforced through nationalism, control and Ceauşescu's cult. Finally, it was economic failure which completely delegitimised the regime, in spite of complex policies used by Ceauşescu to create and control a disciplined and educated managerial stratum.

This evolution had created problems for the industrial managers who were faced in practice with problems of achieving efficiency and increasing production permanently while motivating their workforce, implementing effective recruitment and promotion strategies and levels of remuneration that would be acceptable or at least tolerated by the workforce. From the literature discussed in this chapter, it seems clear that the increasingly rigid, deterministic and functionalist character of official Marxism-Leninism doctrine restricted the possibilities for reforming the system of central planning and failed to offer the managers a framework within which to analyse their problems and devise practical solutions. Instead, managers had to innovate solutions which implicitly belonged more in the subjective dimension and were more voluntarist in nature, perhaps moving unconsciously towards Burrell and Morgan's 'Interpretative' quadrant. However, given the strict control exerted by the ruling groups, the heavy censorship they applied to all 'unorthodox' ideas, and the insistence on political loyalty as a criterion for appointments and promotions, it was impossible in the communist context to give voice to any expression of an alternative way of looking at problems of management, and still very restricted even in the more liberal context of Hungary after the 1968 reforms.

Conclusions

The emergence of a new managerial class in communist societies had been observed since the beginning of the Soviet regime. Insiders such as Leon Trotsky and Milovan Djilas, or external observes such as Herbert Marcuse critically analysed the development, role and influence of the new-born social category – the state and Party bureaucracy. The significant knowledge regarding the communist economy developed by authors such as Jeremy Azrael, Joseph Berliner, Janos Kornai and Ivan Berend also included a detailed description of the new managerial class. Azrael and Berliner dedicated their work to the study of Soviet industry and managers, while Kornai and Berend studied the Hungarian planned economy. Michael Haraszti and Michael Burawoy contributed with the detailed perspective on the relations between Hungarian workers and their managers.

Because of the similarities between the historical evolutions of Romania and Hungary, the conclusions regarding the Hungarian communist regime argued by Kornai, Szelényi, Janos and Berend must be considered in the analysis of Romanian economic and social developments during communism. Some of the underlying causes of these developments are similar as well – economic backwardness, low urbanisation and obsession with reducing the development gap. In addition, Romania was facing a larger skills gap between the education level of the emergent working class and the requirement of industrialisation.

In both cases, in the day-by-day practice of building the communist economy a new social group had emerged from the very beginning. The new class, or command stratum, had tried to rationalise the economy in order to fulfil the Party's directives and probably to conserve its power over the system. From this perspective the extensive industrialisation, centralised planning and targets tautness were used by the Party's leadership as control strategies over the working class, rather than imperatives of the communist ideology. In this context, the permanent conflict required by the ideology was useless and counter-productive. The industrial enterprise was one of the arenas of this conflict, the place where the central planning targets met the real economy performances.

The model of Burrell and Morgan represents a useful frame to analyse these contradictions and conflicts that emerged in communist Romania between the ideology and interests of the ruling group, and the rational requirements of the planned economy. Scientific materialism was the banner under which the society in general and the economy in particular were managed by the communists. From this perspective, the Communist Party perspective on leading society had changed from the radical change approach to a regulated, bureaucracy-based strategy. It may be better therefore to locate official Marxism-Leninism in Burrell and Morgan's functionalist quadrant. However, the problems created by the power struggle and by the prevalence of few fixed ideas had generated an environment in which a much more subjective approach based on *blat, pile şi relaţii* was the receipt of success for industrial managers.

Notes

1 For more detailed discussion of this wide range of approaches, see Lane 1978, pp. 171–201.
2 For a more detailed discussion see Cox, 1979, pp. 21–34.
3 One of the most detailed accounts of the main features of totalitarian society was put forward by Carl Friedrich and Zbigniew Brzezinski in their book *Totalitarian Dictatorship and Autocracy* (1965).

4 It can be argued that Karl Marx was one of the few theorists who shifted paradigms in moving from the radical humanist paradigm to the radical structuralist paradigm – the 'epistemological break' between the work of the young Marx and the mature Marx.

References

Azrael, J. 1966. *Managerial Power in Soviet Politics*. Cambridge, MA: Harvard University Press.

Bauer, R.A., Inkeles, A. and Kluckhohn, C. 1956. *How the Soviet System Works*. Cambridge, MA: Harvard University Press.

Berend, I.T. 1990. *The Hungarian Economic Reforms 1953–1988*. Cambridge: Cambridge University Press.

Berliner, J. 1957. *Factory and Manager in USSR*. Cambridge, MA: Harvard University Press.

Berliner, J. 1976. *The Innovation Decision in Soviet Industry*. Cambridge, MA and London: MIT Press.

Berliner, J. 1988. *Soviet Industry from Stalin to Gorbachev*. Aldershot: Edward Elgar.

Burawoy, M. 1979. *Manufacturing Consent*. Chicago: University of Chicago Press.

Burawoy, M. and Lukacs, J. 1992. *The Radiant Past*. Chicago: University of Chicago Press.

Burrell, G. and Morgan, G. 1979. *Sociological Paradigms and Organisational Analysis*. Aldershot: Ashgate.

Cliff, T. 1974. *State Capitalism in Russia*. London: Pluto Press.

Cox, T.M. 1979. *Rural Sociology in the Soviet Union*. London: C. Hurst.

Djilas, M. 1957. The New Class. An Analysis of the Communist System. London: Thames and Hudson.

Djilas, M. 1969. *The Unperfect Society: Beyond the New Class*. London: Methuen.

Ellman, M. 2014. *Socialist Planning*. 3rd edition. Cambridge: Cambridge University Press.

Friedrich, C.J. and Brzezinski, Z. 1965. *Totalitarian Dictatorship and Autocracy*. Cambridge, MA: Harvard University Press.

Gioia, D. and Pitre, W. 1990. Multiparadigm Perspectives on Theory Building. *Academy of Management. The Academy of Management Review*, 15(4).

Haraszti, M. 1977. *A Worker in a Worker's State*. London: Penguin.

Janos, A.C. 1982. *The Politics of Backwardness in Hungary 1825–1945*. Princeton, MJ: Princeton University Press.

Kellner, D. 1984. *Herbert Marcuse and the Crisis of Marxism*. Berkeley, CA: University of California Press.

Konrad, G. and Szelényi, I. 1979. *The Intellectuals on the Road to Class Power*. New York: Harcourt Brace Jovanovich.

Kornai, J. 1980. *Economics of Shortage*. Amsterdam: North Holland.

Kornai, J. 1992. *The Socialist System. The Political Economy of Communism*. Oxford: Clarendon.

Lane, D. 1976. *The Socialist Industrial State. Towards a Political Sociology of State Socialism*. London: Allen & Unwin.

Lane, D. 1978. *Politics and Society in the USSR*. New York: New York University Press.

Ledeneva, A.V. 1998. *Russia's Economy of Favours: Blat, Networking and Informal Exchange*. Cambridge: Cambridge University Press.

Marcuse, H. 1958. *Soviet Marxism: A Critical Analysis*. New York: Columbia University Press.

Nove, A. 1965. *The Soviet Economy: An Introduction*. London: Allen & Unwin.

Nove, A. 1975. Is There a Ruling Class in USSR? *Soviet Studies*, XXVIII(4).
Nove, A. 1980. *The Soviet Economic System*. London: Allen & Unwin.
Trotsky, L. 1937. *The Revolution Betrayed: What Is the Soviet Union and Where Is It Going?* [Online]. [Accessed 12 July 2017]. Available from: www.marxists.org/archive/trotsky/1936/revbet/.

3 Romanian industrialisation

Legal frame, characteristics and social consequences

This chapter describes the context of the relations and processes analysed in the empirical chapters of this book. It is focused on the main characteristics of economic development in the Romanian communist period from the early years until the last decade of communism. It draws on official documents, statistical data and the recollections and memoirs of people who witnessed or were involved in the events. The chapter provides a description of the centralised planning system, labour legislation, the impact of extensive industrialisation and the cadre selection and training processes. Special attention has been paid to social unrest – strikes, protests or attempts to establish independent unions – that were experienced during the communist regime. Some of those events were explicitly related to failures of the central planning system. Therefore, the directors were held responsible not only for plan fulfilment but also for social harmony at the local level. Their bargaining power to negotiate plan targets had substantially increased in view of the dramatic consequences that protests could have had for the communist regime. The 1977 Valea Jiului miners' strike had shown that the local authorities and the centralised industrial structures were the scapegoats who were officially blamed for the unrest and consequently, all these structures had become more interested in avoiding the risks of plan failures. This was an important incentive for them to use all possible mechanisms to fix problems before their consequences became visible, including effectively negotiating plan targets. The fact that such negotiations had been the usual procedure from the very beginning of the communist regime suggests that social unrest had probably been generated by systemic failures, when no negotiation or dissimulation could fix the problems. Discussion in this chapter will also include the impact of the Soviet exploitation of the Romanian economy through *sovroms* which seriously aggravated the post-war economic and social environment, already affected by war devastations, post-war inflation, severe drought and famine.

The Soviet Union and the Romanian economy

According to Murgescu (2010, p. 332), Romania had sustained larger losses than other European countries after World War II, mainly resulting from the Soviet occupation. It then experienced three decades of economic growth above the European average, before a catastrophic last decade of communism. Mureşan and Mureşan (1998, p. 323) estimated Romania's total loss generated by World War II at US$3.7 billion (at the 1938 exchange rate). Roughly US$1 billion of loss was generated before 23 August 1944, US$1.2 billion between 23 August 1944 and May 1945 and US$1.5 billion was generated by the armistice convention and consisted of the war reparations owed to the Soviet Union.

According to Wolff (1967) the Soviet occupation brought economic misery to Romania. The armistice convention of 1944 (Convenţie de armistiţiu, 1944) and the Paris Peace Treaty (Tratat de pace, 1947) set the war reparations at US$300 million, but the Soviet Union arbitrarily valued the goods at the level of 1938 world prices. This permitted the Soviet Union to extract 'between twice and three times as much as it would have obtained using 1944 prices' (Wolff, 1967, p. 344). In addition, Romania had to return everything that had been taken after 1941 in Bessarabia and Bukovina by the Romanian authorities. But it was the Soviet authorities who identified such properties, 'and they took full advantage of the opportunity to help themselves to Romanian trucks, cars, barges, and the like' (ibid.). The Soviet authorities also claimed all German assets but without assuming the German liabilities. According to Wolff (1967, p. 345), especially in the early months of Soviet occupation, the Russians took everything they wanted from individuals or from companies, calling it 'war booty'. Wolff estimated the loot at approximately 2 billion US dollars.

The Romanian oil industry represented the first and the most important objective for the Soviet Union. After the Soviet troops occupied Romania, about 50,000 tons of pipe and drilling equipment were seized and the entire current production was also taken as war reparations (Wolff, 1967, p. 345). According to Wolff, the Soviet Union took over 11 French and Belgian companies that previously had been seized by the Germans. A pipe line was built from Ploieşti to Odessa using material from a former German pipe line. Wolff estimated the total value of the seized companies at one quarter of the entire industry. These companies formed the Soviet share in a new joint Soviet-Romanian company called *Sovrompetrol*. An agreement between the two countries regarding the establishment of common enterprises was signed in Moscow on 8 May 1945. According to this agreement, in the industry sector 'Romanian-Soviet enterprises will be created with the purpose of exploiting metal ore deposits in Romania' (Békés *et al.*, 2015, p. 71). *Sovrompetrol* was the first *Sovrom*, created on 17 July 1945, and had as its objective the oil exploitation of areas of Prahova County and the oil refineries in Ploieşti. By 1947, it was responsible for 37 per cent of oil drilling, roughly 30 per cent of the total production of crude oil, and over 36 per cent of refined oil, controlling 37 per cent of internal oil supplies and 38 per cent of external ones. At the same time, the Romanian government put significant pressure on the American, British and Dutch companies operating in the same industry, and finally nationalised them in December 1947. In this way, 'without investing any of its own resources [the Soviet Union] managed to obtain control of the richest single industry in southeast Europe' (Wolff, 1967, p. 346).

Sovrompetrol was followed by *Sovromtransport* and *Tars* (transportation), and later by *Sovrombanc* (banking and commercial monopoly), *Sovromlemn* (wood processing), *Sovromgaz* (natural gas), *Sovromasigurare* (insurance), *Sovromcărbune* (coal exploitation in the Jiu Valley and other areas), *Sovromchim* (in the chemical industry), *Sovromconstrucţii* (construction materials), *Sovrommetal* (iron extraction – around Reşiţa), *Sovromtractor* (future *Tractorul*, in Braşov), *Sovromfilm* (importing Soviet cinema productions), *Sovrom Utilaj Petrolier* (producing oil refining equipment) and *Sovromnaval* (shipbuilding in Constanţa, Giurgiu and Brăila). *Sovromtransport* controlled all Romanian harbours, port equipment and shipyards. The *Sovroms* enjoyed substantial advantages like 'extra-territorial privileges, exemption from stamp duties and taxes, and all had Soviet managers and controllers' (Ionescu, 1964, p. 164).

Ostensibly the *Sovroms* were joint Romanian-Soviet ventures aimed at generating revenue for reconstruction and were created on a half-share basis in respect to the two states. However, they were mainly designed as a means to ensure resources for the Soviet side, and generally contributed to draining Romania's resources in addition to the war reparations. The Soviet contribution in creating the *Sovroms* consisted mostly in reselling leftover German equipment to Romania, which had been systematically overvalued.

But the *Sovroms* were not the only form of Soviet economic influence in Romania. By 1952, 85 per cent of Romanian exports were directed at the Soviet Union. The total value of goods sent by Romania to the Soviet Union surpassed by far the demanded war reparations, being estimated at around 2 billion dollars. The *Sovroms* were liquidated between 1956 and 1959, amid 'numerous animosities between the governments of both countries' (Tismăneanu, Dobrincu and Vasile, 2007, p. 217).

Sovromcuarţit was a Romanian-Soviet mining company which dealt with the extraction of uranium and exploration for uranium deposits in Romania. The name chosen for this *sovrom* was meant to hide the true purpose of the activity, which was the extraction not of quartz but of uranium. The convention establishing *Sovromcuarţit* was signed on 31 December 1951. It was one of the last three *sovroms* set up, and also one of the last terminated, with a short but intense activity. Because of the secrecy of this activity, there is very limited information regarding *Sovromcuarţit*. During that period, uranium had gained strategic importance in the struggle for nuclear supremacy which had engaged the great powers and especially the Soviet Union. In this context, the Soviet Union expressed its great interest in uranium exploitation in Romania. According to a former director of Băiţa-Bihor (North-West region) uranium exploitation, the Soviet exploration activities searching for uranium deposits had started as early as in 1946. In April 1949, an important deposit was located at Băiţa-Bihor, and the whole area was declared of strategic importance by the Soviet occupation authorities. *Sovromcuarţit* started its production activity in April 1952. Each country owned half of enterprise's capital, and the costs and benefits were to be, at least theoretically, equally divided. *Sovromcuarţit* focused on best quality and most accessible uranium ore, ignoring the rational exploitation of uranium and the special protection measures needed to handle radioactive material. Later on, the negative impact caused by the irrational exploitation of the mines was supported by Romania. Despite the availability of educated personnel in Romania, the Soviet Union imposed its own specialists in every key position, preventing the training of Romanian employees. Although Romania had tried to negotiate the development of the refining and processing activities in Romania to increase value added remaining in the country, the Soviet side had declined. In secrecy, Romania delivered 17,288 tons of uranium ore to the Soviet Union between 1952 and 1960, which was used, at least partly, in the Soviet atomic bomb project. All ore was shipped out of Romania for processing, initially to Sillamäe in Estonia; the uranium concentrate was then used exclusively by the Soviet Union. On 22 October 1956, Romania and the USSR signed a Takeover Convention, which led to the abolition of *Sovromcuarţit* and *Sovrompetrol*, the last two remaining *sovroms*. The Convention stipulated that Romania would redeem the USSR stake, valued at 413 million roubles in a period of 10 years in equal instalments starting with 1961. The Romanian government also established the company *Cuarţit* which took over the *Sovromcuarţit* activity. Romania had to commit the entire production of the new enterprise *Cuarţit* to be sold to the USSR. However, Romania stopped shipping uranium ore to the Soviet Union in 1965, and later on facilities for industrial preparation of uranium ore were developed.

Finally, it must be observed that there are no estimations of the losses of national wealth through *sovrom* companies. However, Tismăneanu, Dobrincu and Vasile (2007, p. 412) estimate that 40 per cent of the national income was extracted through *sovrom* companies by the Soviet Union for more than a decade.

Another account of the Soviet influence over the Romanian communist economy can be found in the transcript of the meetings held on 8–14 July 1953 in Moscow published by Berindei, Dobrincu and Goşu (2009, pp. 428–438). Romania was represented by Gheorghiu-Dej, Miron Constantinescu and Chivu Stoica. The Soviet Union was represented by Khrushchev, Malenkov, Molotov, Mikoyan, Pervukhin and Lavrentiev. The meeting held on 8 July had as its main discussion topic the Romanian economic development plan. The Soviet representatives were highly critical of Romanian plans, especially regarding the Danube-Black Sea channel, the excessive development of heavy industry, and the underinvestment in agriculture and consumer goods industries. The Soviet approach can be easily synthesised by Molotov's statement: 'you feel safe under the protection of the Soviet Union. Without our support you would be overthrown in less than two weeks. If you won't connect with the people, even we won't be able to help you' (p. 430). The Soviet leaders expressed detailed concerns regarding the imbalances of the Romanian economy and its development plans. The criticism is very sharp, Malenkov calling the Romanian economic policy 'erroneous, illiterate and even dangerous' (Berindei, Dobrincu and Goşu, 2009, p. 428). The main aspects criticised by the Soviet leaders were:

- the exaggerated focus on heavy industry;
- the Danube-Black Sea channel, which was not needed and which required significant investment and a huge mass of workers;

- excessive import of technology and equipment without integrated use of it;
- reduced imports of food and consumer goods;
- reduced investment in agriculture, and the food and clothing industries;
- important work force fluctuation, including over 40,000 soldiers working in *sovrom* enterprises;
- excessive military expenses.

On the other hand, the Soviet leaders assumed the responsibility for some of Romanian decisions and policies. The transcript of this meeting recorded at least five statements acknowledging the Soviet Union as the cause of some wrong decisions. However, the Romanian leaders were accused of complacency in the current state of affairs, not admitting their errors and ignoring the possible effects in the long run. According to the Soviet leaders' arguments, such mistakes had been made not only in Romania but in Hungary, Bulgaria and East Germany. All these mistakes had to be corrected as soon as possible because otherwise 'in case of war we'll be all criticised by weapons' as Molotov put it. This first meeting concluded with the agreement that Romania would produce a draft of a preliminary document containing ideas to correct the situation. This document was produced and presented at the second meeting held on 13 July 1953. In spite of some shallow criticism, the document had been accepted by the Soviet leaders. It contained six main categories of measures, including an overall reduction in investment, an increase in agricultural investment, a reduction in military spending, improvement in the balance of trade, taxation and the supply of consumer goods. The first part of document's preamble, which was classified as top secret, is translated below:

> Our Party and government have made serious mistakes in economic policy, which have generated the danger of a separation from the masses. The pace of industrial development has been forced at the expense of agriculture and consumer goods production. The slogan 'Five years plan fulfilled in four years' had been launched erroneously and each year's plan targets were increased without taking into account the real economic possibilities. A lot of erroneous measures were taken in the area of economic relations with the peasants, weakening the alliance between the working class and the working peasantry and reducing the peasants' interest in increasing production. Sufficient quantities of food have not been ensured for the urban population. In order to make a significant turn in economic policy and to correct the mistakes, we propose the following measures.
>
> (p. 435)

The discussions with the Soviet Union regarding the Romanian economic crisis were resumed in October 1953 when the Romanian government asked for a substantial loan. On 3 October 1953, Gheorghiu-Dej asked the Soviet ambassador personally for a three years loan of 350–400 million roubles (Buga, 2004, p. 108). Their discussions were held in the first months of 1954 with the new

Soviet leaders and they were concluded with recommendations for the Romanian government.

After Stalin's death and Khrushchev's assumption of power, Romania's relations with the Soviet Union shifted from complete obedience to 'the three phases of the Romanian-Soviet cold war' as described by Frunză (1999). According to Frunză (1999, p. 385), the first phase had been generated by the ideological conflict between China and the Soviet Union. The PMR's position had been balanced between the two contenders, Romanian representatives even travelling between Moscow and Beijing in an attempt to mediate the conflict (Frunză, 1999, p. 388).

The second phase of the conflict had been induced by the Comecon plan to assign specific tasks in the development of the communist bloc. In this plan, officially announced in 1959, Romania and Bulgaria were designated to be agricultural countries, while the other communist Eastern European countries were designated to further develop their industry (Tănase, 1998, p. 185). The determined opposition of the PMR leaders in the name of national independence, mutual advantages in economic development and voluntary participation in common programmes finally led to the failure of the Comecon plan. The CIA report, *A Crack in the CMEA Facade – Rumania* (CIA, 1963, p. 1), noted that

> significant conflicts of interests over economic policy appear to have arisen between Rumania and other members of the Soviet Bloc's Council for Mutual Economic Assistance (CMEA). The precise nature of these conflicts is not known, but clearly they are related to the direction of future Rumanian industrialisation.

The failure was officially admitted at the XVII Comecon session in June 1963. To demonstrate PMR fidelity to the industrialisation dogma, Romania amplified its efforts towards developing big machine-building, chemical and metallurgical enterprises. Arguing for the value of bilateral agreements, in June 1963 an agreement with Yugoslavia was signed for the building of the first hydro-power plant on the Danube at Iron Gates (Frunză, 1999, p. 390).

The peak of the second phase was reached in April 1964, with the issuing of The Declaration of the PMR's position Regarding the Problems of the International Communists and Workers Movement, later known as the April Declaration. In this document, the Romanian communist leadership clearly identified national independence and sovereignty as principles of official Party policy. For the first time in its history, the PMR's leadership had considered the application of the principles of 'national independence and sovereignty, mutual advantage, comradely assistance, non-interference in internal problems, respect for the territorial integrity and socialist internationalism'. The April Declaration was followed by an intense campaign of closed meetings in the Party regarding Romanian-Soviet relations (Frunză, 1999, p. 394). A series of replies followed from both parties, culminating in the so-called Valev plan. At the Fourth Congress of the USSR Geographical Society, E.B. Valev – a geography professor, presented a system of integration of the communist countries in a single economic complex. Valev had argued for the creation of an economic complex by merging a part of Romania with the southern part of Bessarabia and another part of Ukraine. The Romanian reply was sharp and violent, the Valev incident representing 'the culmination of the Romanian-Soviet cold war' (Frunză, 1999, p. 402).

After 1964, the Romanian leaders decided to reduce Russian influence in Romanian society. A CIA report considered that the 'intransigence was the product, primarily, of Gheorghiu-Dej's early opposition to de-Stalinisation, of longstanding economic grievances against the USSR and of increased confidence as a result of economic success' (CIA, 1964, p. 4). After Gheorghiu-Dej's death, Ceauşescu pursued a visibly independent policy especially in the foreign relations area. However, the level of independence is still disputed among researchers because Romanian positions, declarations or actions overtly opposed to the Soviet Union, such as public opposition to the invasion of Czechoslovakia, were mixed with constant cooperation such as that between the *Securitate* and KGB in espionage.

The Romanian command system

There are three main sources for an understanding of the Romanian command system: the laws, regulations and directives issued by the state or by the Communist Party regarding the centralised socio-economic system; statistical data regarding economic and demographic evolution; and interviews, recollections and memoirs of people involved in the system.

The inconsistency and unreliability of official statistical sources regarding Romanian communist society is widely known. According to Tismăneanu, Dobrincu and Vasile (2007, p. 163) the official communist statistical data regarding the economic development of Romania between 1938 and 1989 rather disorient the researcher. The statistics had a largely propagandistic character, used unsteady and unclear definitions, and often displayed contradictions between different indicators. Furthermore, the variable methodologies used in the calculation of prices and other macro-economic indicators, and changes in monetary system affected comparability over time. The first statistical yearbook after World War II was published in 1957 and it included data mainly from 1955. To partially overcome the lack of precise statistical data, the Romanian Statistical Yearbook for 1990 has been used. It includes recalculated data for the period mentioned above, as well as new indicators. Other statistical data and results of economic analysis are taken from academic works of reliable scientific reputation published before and after 1989 in Romania or abroad.

An important effort has been made by Ionete (1993) to estimate the real impact of the crises experienced in the last decade of the communist regime on the Romanian economy. His book *Criza de sistem a economiei de comandă si etapa sa explozivă* (*The System Crisis of the Command Economy and its Explosive Phase*) offers a revealing perspective of this period, especially regarding basic economic indicators.

The memoirs of Gheorghe Gaston Marin offer a different perspective on the industrialisation process, especially on its first three decades. His book *În serviciul României lui Gheorghiu-Dej* (2000) (*In the service of Gheorghiu-Dej's Romania*) contains the memories of a person deeply engaged in the process of creating the centralised planning system, and who managed this system in whole or in part for more than two decades. While the author's opinions regarding the communist period are consonant with his involvement in the system, a part of his arguments behind the decisions and other information can be used for a better understanding of the system. Details of Gheorghe Gaston Marin's biography can be found in his memoirs (Marin, 2000) and in data presented in Berindei, Dobrincu and Goşu (2009, p. 126). He was born in 1918 in Transylvania in a Jewish family as Gheorghe Grossman. He graduated from Sorbonne University in mathematics and physics and from the Polytechnic Institute of Grenoble in engineering. At the beginning of the World War II, he was studying for a PhD in engineering. After the Nazi occupation of France, he enrolled in the *Jeunesse Comuniste* and the *resistance* in 1942. In 1945, he returned to Romania as veteran of the *resistance* and of the French army. At the end of 1945, he became the political secretary of Gheorghe Gheorghiu-Dej, the general secretary of the PCR and at that time the minister of Communication and Public Works. Because of his education and in spite of his bourgeois origin, he was appointed to various positions in the Romanian government: counsellor at the Presidency of the Ministers Council (1945–48), General Secretary and Deputy Minister at the National Economy Ministry (1948–49), Minister of the Energy and Electrotechnical Industry Ministry (1949–54), President of the State Planning Committee (1954–65), President of the State Council for Nuclear Energy (1955–66), Vice-President of the Ministries Council (1962–69), President of the State Committee for Prices (1969–82) and member of the Great National Assembly (1952–85). In all these positions, he was involved in the main decisions regarding the economic development of the country and the trade agreements with other countries – especially with Western countries – as well as in political decisions. Gaston Marin signed the agreement between the Soviet Union and Romania regarding the transfer into Romanian possession of the Soviet share in *Sovromcuarţit*. At that time, 22 October 1956, Gaston Marin was the Chairman of the Romanian Atomic Commission.

Another book of memoirs used in this research is Silviu Brucan's *Generaţia irosită* (*Wasted Generation*) and *Stâlpii noii puteri în România* (*The Pillars of New Power in Romania*). Silviu Brucan, born as Saul Bruckner in 1916, was one of the most important journalists and diplomats in the first three decades of the Romanian communist regime. The 1929 financial crisis made his father, a small bourgeois, go bankrupt (Brucan, 2012, pp. 21–24) and the young and educated Silviu Brucan had to work hard for the survival of his family, giving private lessons in Latin to the children of rich families. This was the period of his revolt against the huge social discrepancies experienced by Romania. Soon after this period Brucan became a journalist for illegal communist newspapers. After World War II, he worked for *Scînteia*, the Party's official newspaper (Berindei, Dobrincu and Goşu, 2009, p. 421). Between 1956 and 1959 he was appointed as

Ambassador to the United States and between 1959 and 1961 he was the Romanian representative at the UN. In 1962, he was appointed Vice-President of Radio-TV. Once Ceaușescu became the Party Secretary, Brucan resigned and spent the rest of his active life as a professor. In the next 15 years the Party leadership permitted Brucan to travel extensively abroad, both in the West and in communist countries, for academic conferences or for teaching. The relations between Brucan and Ceaușescu deteriorated in the 1980s, culminating in letters and articles published in the Western mass-media after the 1987 Brașov workers protests. He had been influential in the first decade of the Romanian transition. He died in 2006 in Bucharest. His books offer personal insights into several important events in the Romanian communist history. The author admitted his Stalinist perspective until 1956, but after reading the Khrushchev secret report delivered at the XX Congress he realised that 'if such a man was able to rise and to maintain for so long at the top of the communist party and of the Soviet state, something is fundamentally wrong in the system' (Brucan, 2012, p. 101). His social sciences education had been constantly updated through contacts with Western and communist countries' academic environments. This allowed him to observe and to draw useful conclusions regarding the communist system.

Preparations for the command economy

There were three main developments in the period between 1944 and 1948 that had an important impact on the economy and on the population: the efforts towards economic recovery after the World War II; the preparations for the takeover of the whole Romanian state and economy by the communists; and the beginning of the Soviet exploitation of the Romanian economy. From an economic point of view, the evolution of Romania was dramatically affected by factors such as nationalisation, the systematic draining of resources and assets by the Soviet Union, and the severe drought and famine of 1946. All these factors generated a severe devaluation of the Romanian leu that culminated in forced stabilisation through monetary reform in 1947. The monetary stabilisation was carried out with the support of Soviet advisers.

In the post-war circumstances, aggravated by the severe drought of 1946, many measures were taken in order to improve living standards as well as to limit and eventually eliminate private initiatives. Prices, salaries, commodity-trading, speculators and citizens' control were subjects of different laws issued in 1945–46. The National Institute of Cooperatives became the state representative responsible for cereals acquisition. The same organisation became responsible for sales of basic products in rural areas. These sales were related to the peasants' deliveries of cereals. In February 1946, the County Economic Offices were reorganised and became responsible for the control of production, acquisition, distribution and prices. In April 1947, the Ministry of Industry and Trade was established through the re-organisation and merging of the Ministry of National Economy with Commission of Prices, Office of Supplies, Commission of Foreign Trade and Office for State Industry.

The conquest of political power by the Communist Party with the support of the Soviet Army and Soviet advisers enabled the preparations for nationalisation. The PCR's victory in the 1946 elections allowed it to use the democratic appearance of parliamentary mechanisms to impose the desired socio-economic transformation, but behind this appearance operated an extensive mechanism of repression. At the end of 1947 the Party concentrated all state structures – the public administration, the legal system, army and media – under its own control. All *hostile elements* were purged from these structures. At the end of May 1947, the Romanian government empowered the Minister of National Economy with control over all details of industrial production.

On 13 April 1948, the Grand National Assembly adopted the first Constitution of communist Romania. The document contained specific provisions regarding nationalisation. The Constitution stated that all underground riches, mining deposits, water, forests, natural energy sources, ways of communication by rail, road, water and sea, post, telegraph, telephone and radio belonged to the state. It also expressly stipulated that 'when public interest requires it, means of production, banks and insurance companies, which are the private property of individuals or legal entities, may become state property, or property of the people, as provided by law' (*Constituția Republicii Populare Romîne, Art. 11*).

According to Mureșan (2012, p. 249) there were four other legislative documents that had an important economic and social impact. The preparation for the centralised economy consisted in a set of political measures culminating with the nationalisation law (*Legea nr. 119 pentru naționalizarea intreprinderilor industriale, bancare, de asigurări, miniere și de transporturi*) voted by the Great National Assembly on 11 June 1948; 8,894 industrial organisations precisely nominated in the law's appendices were nationalised. Before the nationalisation law, the agrarian reform, the National Bank nationalisation and the monetary reform were the most important decisions. On 23 March 1945 began the first 'assault on the Rumanian social system' (CIA, 1944, p. 10) – the agrarian reform (*Decret-lege nr. 187 pentru înfăptuirea reformei agrare*). It aimed to gain the support of the masses by the expropriation of land exceeding 50 hectares per person, and distributing it to the peasants who owned less than 5 hectares. On 28 December 1946, the National Bank of Romania was nationalised (*Legea nr. 1056 pentru etatizarea și organizarea Băncii Naționale a României*) in order to obtain control of the credit system. State control of the banking system permitted the monetary reform of 15 August 1947 (*Legea nr. 287 pentru reformă monetară*).

Nationalisation was labelled in official documents as 'a fundamental act' with 'a decisive role' in the revolutionary transformation of Romanian society. The implementation of the nationalisation law was carried out according to a very detailed and systematic plan of action (Tismăneanu, Dobrincu and Vasile, 2007, p. 413).

A census of economic enterprises was carried out on 15 October 1947 following an Industry and Trade Ministry decision published in Monitorul Oficial no. 228, on 3 October 1947. The census provided an accurate picture of the Romanian economy and allowed the government to prepare detailed lists of the enterprises and assets subject to nationalisation. At the moment of the census, the state owned roughly 15 per cent of the extractive industry companies and 21 per cent of processing industry in terms of employee numbers. Overall, the state owned 1,186 industrial enterprises out of a total of 36,729 enterprises. In addition, the state owned more than 94 per cent of the total assets of the transport sector and had a monopoly in industries such as tobacco, salt and alcohol (Tismãneanu, Dobrincu and Vasile, 2007, pp. 413–414).

The Communist Party organised commissions for each county and committees for each enterprise that was to be nationalised. The committees, made up of individuals carefully selected by party cadres, had as their main objective the supervision of the owners of the enterprises. All the operations were kept secret until the law had been officially approved to prevent any acts of resistance. Take-over operations were actually completed in just two days, on 10 and 11 June 1948. All these operations required the combined action of the Communist Party with other state structures (Tismãneanu, Dobrincu and Vasile, 2007). Also, all private medical organisations were nationalised on 3 November 1948.

For reasons of political opportunism, in order to enjoy greater public support for the new policies, nationalisation did not include land, small businesses, companies with fewer than 10 employees and less than 20 horse-power machinery, and small trade. However, all businesses in these categories were subject to a systematic policy of containment and were wound-up between 1950 and 1960.

On 1 July 1948, the State Planning Commission (*Comisia de Stat a Planificării*) was created, and later re-labelled the State Planning Committee (*Comitetul de Stat al Planificarii – CSP*) in 1959. From that moment on, all state enterprises began to operate in a centralised and controlled manner. The first chairman of CSP was Gheorghiu-Dej, the National Economy Minister and General Secretary of the PRM. At the end of 1950, the CSP announced the first five-year plan for the industrial development of the country.

According to Marin (2000, pp. 130–133) nationalisation was an essential decision for the Romanian economy and was required in order to stop the decline in production and for a better concentration of the country's resources. The nationalisation required a detailed but also difficult preparation. Hundreds of cadres had to be recruited and trained, including directors, chief accountants and engineers to take over the companies' management on the day before the nationalisation law was approved by the National Assembly. Their tasks were to keep all the assets intact during the process, to replace unreliable members of the management and to keep and eventually increase production levels. Marin (2000, p. 131) noted that all new cadres were recruited from former capitalist companies, and almost all of them confirmed the trust placed in them. The production of the new nationalised companies grew with an average 4 per cent compared to the period before nationalisation.

Over the following decades, the success of the central plan remained an unchanged dogma in communist Romania. Market mechanisms had been destroyed, small businesses had disappeared, and the plan had become an object of worship. From Gheorghiu-Dej to Ceaușescu, state property over all economic resources was considered the essential principle in the building of an ideal Marxist society without classes (Tismăneanu, Dobrincu and Vasile, 2007, p. 49). But as evidence identified in the archives shows, at enterprise level the plan was the object of continuous negotiation with planning structures mainly because of the many shortcomings of the industrialisation strategies pursued by the Party. In the last decades of the communist regime, Ceauşescu's obsession with heavy industry, with rigid and centralised planning, and his hostility towards reforms led to generalised failure (Tismăneanu, Dobrincu and Vasile, 2007, p. 97).

Extensive industrialisation

The main official aims of the extensive industrialisation policies were the transformation of Romania into an industrial state with an efficient economy, the reduction of the discrepancies between Romania and developed countries and between the country's regions, the intensive use of local resources and the creation of a modern economy. While all these aims were reasonable and justifiable, the means chosen by the communist elite and mostly the irrational focus on heavy industry and the shortcomings of the central planning system generated serious problems for Romanian economy.

The fact that Romania was a predominantly agricultural society, with peasants constituting 80 per cent of the workforce immediately after World War II, implied that the Communist Party had to create an industrial workforce. And apparently, it succeeded in this objective: by 1979 the urban population increased to almost 50 per cent, and industrial employment grew from 12 per cent to 34.7 per cent (Nelson, 1988, p. 9). In less than four decades Romania had been transformed into an urban and industrial-agrarian country. But, as many authors have argued, the development gap between Romania and other Western economies or even Eastern economies increased.

The 'industrial worker with peasant origin became the ideal social basis of the Communist Party' (Brucan, 2012, p. 166) and supported the modernisation process as long as it provided better living conditions. However, as Brucan (2012) observed, even the rudimentary urban conditions offered were much better than those existent in rural areas. Moreover, this new industrial worker was neither educated nor willing to exercise the political power granted by the communist ideology, therefore the Communist Party had played this role on behalf of the working class. For the new industrial worker 'political freedom seemed redundant, and the freedom of the press had never been the dream of the illiterate' (Brucan, 2012, p. 167). Brucan argued that the new working class was perfect for revolution from above. But this new working class was less suitable for the industrialisation process. Gerschenkron observed that the 'creation of an industrial labour force that really deserves its name is a most difficult and protracted process' (1962, p. 9). Stability, reliability and discipline are the main characteristics of a real labour force. Such a group that 'has cut the umbilical cord connecting it with the land' (ibid.) is extremely scarce in a backward country.

The growth of the Romanian economy was impressive: through the 1960s and 1970s it was 'among the highest in communist Europe as well as in the world' (Nelson, 1988, p. 7). Many 'key achievements of socialism' (Fotaki, 2009, p. 151) were granted by the state – a relatively accessible education system and a health system apparently free, workplaces for all according to their qualifications. Most of the workers' unrest was caused by the system's failures to maintain salaries and benefits at previous levels. Protests and strikes appeared when salaries were reduced because the plan had not been fulfilled, when other benefits (such as work conditions and meals) were reduced, or when general living conditions became significantly worsened.

According to Brucan (2012) the main disruptive event was technological development, especially the computer revolution. In Western societies, this event diminished the role, the status and prestige of blue collar workers and raised the importance of innovation. Because this was unacceptable, Ceauşescu (and Brezhnev as well) had stubbornly resisted the introduction of computer technologies in civilian industries. The main plan indicators had become not only more extravagant but also more costly in terms of resources and energy required. For example, in 1975, when market mechanisms had imposed structural change towards services and higher added value industrial sectors in Western economies, the Party's programme still announced the following new targets for 1990: at least 1,000 kg of steel per capita, 1,000 kg of cement per capita or 5,000–6,000 kWh power per capita (Partidul Comunist Român, 1975, pp. 75–77).

This resistance to change led to lower productivity and efficiency, and finally to economic collapse. The price Romanian society had to pay for these socialist achievements was heavy: mounting hard-currency debt, trade imbalances and growing dysfunction of the economy. The 1980s were a period of sharp economic downturn with a significant decline of living standards. Marvin Jackson calculated a fall of overall domestic consumption of 17 per cent between 1980 and 1983 (cited in Siani-Davies, 2005, p. 14). In the same period, Ceauşescu turned Romania in a neo-Stalinist state in terms of 'personality cult and form of rule' (Siani-Davies, 2005, p. 16), only the historical context limiting the full replication of the characteristics of Stalin's cult.[1]

Tismăneanu, Dobrincu and Vasile (2007) also argue that the industrialisation conducted by the communist regime was one of the main components of Romania's national economic disaster. Although it was necessary to bring about the industrialisation of a predominantly rural Romania, and they argue that not everything that has been done in the line of industrialisation was wrong, the

> superhuman effort imposed on the Romanian people in the 45 years of communism was dissipated mostly in aberrant, unproductive and non-functional investments, in creating parasitic industries, and hence in products usually of poor quality un-marketable or marketable on the international market at a loss, all these amplified by huge losses caused by stupid planning and management of the hyper-centralised economy.
>
> (Tismăneanu, Dobrincu and Vasile, 2007, p. 164)

According to the Nationalisation Law, after 11 June 1948 all nationalised assets were administered by the state and each branch ministry appointed directors who took over the management of the nationalised enterprises based on a summary statement from the owners or representatives of the owners. New directors had the capacity to exercise all managerial duties. In 1949 and 1950, the Romanian economy was developed on the basis of annual economic plans. According to Tismăneanu, Dobrincu and Vasile (2007, p. 415) the official documents announced that the first two annual plans targets were exceeded respectively by 8 per cent and 3.4 per cent, and that post-war recovery was achieved in 1950 once industrial production and national income exceeded the figures for 1938. In 1950 the communist leadership decided that starting with 1951–55 the economy should be developed based on five-year plans. Five-year plan objectives were further broken down by year and ministries, and other central economic organisations broke down the objectives and tasks of the Five-Year Plan into detailed components. Based on these data, the enterprises obtained their own plans with corresponding objectives. Each enterprise plan resulted after a consultation process with the authorities and finally it was sent to the State Planning Commission for centralisation. The same procedure was followed for each year of the plan.

All sectors of the economy were the subjects of planning, but heavy industry received most of the focus and less attention was paid to agriculture, consumer goods and public services (King, 1980, p. 53). This trend was one of the constant features of the communist regime.

According to Marin (2000, pp. 167–184) the metallurgical industry was at the centre of the Party's effort from the very beginning. An important effort was concentrated on improvement of existing capacities and the development of other plants. Technology was imported from the Soviet Union, as well as from West Germany, France, Austria and the United States. Some of these imports of technology were to replace equipment taken by the Soviet Union as war reparations. The main reason for these investments was the need for pipes for the oil extracting industry and metal sheets for other industrial sectors. An important decision taken by the Party, against Soviet opposition, was to develop the country's biggest metallurgical enterprise – Combinatul Siderurgic Galați (CSG) – at Galați. According to Gaston Marin, CSG was designed in accordance with world-class technology. In the same period, other non-ferrous industrial capacity was developed. In spite of the development of the extracting industry, the gap between ore production and the processing capacities had increased. 'The extraction of iron ore had increased four times between 1955 and 1965 … while coal extraction had increased more than five times, but both had fallen behind the requirements of the metallurgical and chemical industries' (Marin, 2000, p. 171).

The chemical industry had been developed simultaneously with the oil refining industry. According to Gaston Marin most of the technologies were imported from the United States or France. And since the refining capacity had soon exceeded the oil reserves, significant efforts had been invested in exploring new oilfields onshore but also offshore in the Black Sea. In the 1980s, Romania had an oil refining capacity of more than 16 million tonnes, while the most successful year in the history of oil extraction was 1976 with 14.7 million tonnes. Other authors (e.g. Brucan, 2012, p. 158) indicated a total refining capacity of 34 million tonnes in 1988–89. The latter figure is indirectly confirmed by Ceauşescu in his last meeting with Gorbachev on 4 December 1989: 'From the Soviet Union we have imported 5 million tons of petrol, beginning in 1984, and from other countries we have imported 15 million tons.… [We extract] only about 10 million tons since we no longer have reserves' (*Minutes of Conversation between Gorbachev and Romanian Leader Ceausescu*, p. 11). Consequently, a significant quantity of crude oil was imported for petrochemical and refining industries. The conditions of a rigid and disconnected system of prices, of a poorly developed infrastructure, and of the system's incapacity to concentrate R&D investment in industries with profitable export potential had led to an uncontrollable accumulation of losses.

The significant disproportion between the available resources and the production capacities seems to be a constant during the Romanian industrialisation. And the more sophisticated the economy was, the bigger was the loss generated by this disproportion. Ionete (1993, p. 76) calculated the use of the existing capacities between 1985 and 1989 and the main reasons for this disproportion as shown in Table 3.1.

In spite of under-used industrial capacities, investment in other capacities had stubbornly continued. Consequently in 1989 more than 21,400 industrial investment projects were in different development phases (Tismăneanu, Dobrincu and Vasile, 2007, p. 422), which exerted a heavy pressure on the country's budget. Important supplementary funds were necessary to complete investments and most of them were delayed. Another negative aspect was the extension of the operation period for equipment and machines. This extension induced increasing maintenance costs and lower levels of productivity. Consequently, although the whole economy had been concentrated towards increasing exports at any cost in order to reduce external debt, most exports were generating losses supported by internal consumption. The external debt had been generated by two main factors: imports of resources (oil, iron ore and other raw materials); and technology for heavy industry.

Table 3.1 The use rate of industrial capacity between 1985 and 1989

	1985	*1986*	*1987*	*1988*	*1989*
Indicators:					
Production capacity (billions lei)	1,731.2	1,810.0	1,863.0	1,929.5	1,829.8
Use rate (%)	79.3	80.7	78.8	79.5	78.1
Reasons for under-use:					
Shortage of materials and energy (%)	44.0	42.6	44.3	44.8	52.0
Shortage of workforce (%)	2.3	2.4	2.5	2.5	2.9
Lack of demand (%)	11.3	14.4	13.7	13.2	14.4

Source: Ionete, 1993, p. 76.

Another aspect was the supervision role assigned to banks. According to Gaston Marin, banks strictly controlled the financial flows, being able to intervene on a wide range of problems such as 'outdated technology, de-correlation of supply prices with sales prices, low productivity or the management incapacity to perform' (Marin, 2000, p. 189). So, in the Romanian centralised planning system the banks played the role of a regulatory institution. Bank inspectors had to be competent, not only in accounting and financing aspects, but in technology, productivity and even management performance.

Evidence presented in the following chapters will indicate the immediate effect of plan under-fulfilment. Usually this took the shape of a reduction in the salaries fund. This mechanism can be related to the causes of strikes that had begun in 1977. This mechanism also put a strong incentive on managers to develop alternative methods to ensure plan fulfilment, such as continuous target negotiation or dissimulation.

Gaston Marin (2000, pp. 195–198) also discusses the process of recalculation of prices (*reaşezarea preţurilor*) which began in 1971 based on a special law. In that period Gaston Marin was the president of the State Committee for Prices. According to Gaston Marin the main objective of recalculation was 'the knowledge of the costs of the real economy'. After a long and carefully considered process, the new prices system was announced in 1974. The numerous phases of price recalculation were discussed and approved by the Executive Committee, but when the results showed an increase of production prices by 14.1 per cent, a decline in national income, significant losses in the mining industry and inefficiencies of some exported products, Ceauşescu appointed a trusted man to 'improve' the price recalculation. According to Gaston Marin, Ceauşescu was troubled by the decline in national income and by the weight of some industrial branches which were considered pivotal. In order to obtain an improvement in prices, the prices of oil, cement and electrical energy were reduced below their 1973 level (the level before the first oil price shock). Since the original recalculated prices had led to a positive foreign trade balance through stimulating the export of profitable products, the new prices concealed the real image of the economy and amplified the losses generated by Ceauşescu's decision to increase exports at any cost.

It is surprising to some extent how at the end of his rule Ceauşescu blamed the enterprises for the irrational investments. In his last meeting with Gorbachev Ceauşescu argued against economic de-centralisation:

> About 20 years back, we gave them [factories] a lot of rights and, the first thing they did was to take loans and make all kinds of poor economic investments. Then we realized that we needed to control certain things so we took some of their liberties away. For Romania, $11 billion debt in 1980 was a grave problem.... My mistake was that I gave too much discretion to the factories and all of them decided that if they have discretion then they can take credits from outside.
>
> (Minutes of Conversation between Gorbachev and Romanian Leader Ceausescu, pp. 8–9)

Considering the very tight control and the over-centralisation present in the Romanian economy under communist rule, Ceauşescu's argument suggests a bitter relation between the communist leadership and the managerial class at the end of 1980s.

Labour and cadre policies

The impact of the plan and of other mechanisms of centralised control of the economy on labour legislation and cadre policy was significant and caused problems for the Party's leadership in its attempts to gain and maintain the commitment of the working class to extensive development.

Since the communists came to power not by a revolution but through Soviet occupation, which meant there was a lack of connection between the Party and the population, the effort to industrialise Romania was 'one with enormous political risk' (Nelson, 1988, pp. 38–39). This was because the working class originated in a peasant class which had no commitment to communist values, and which had undergone the very recent experience of the collectivisation process. Between 1949 and 1962 more than 114,000 peasants were arrested according to official communist documents (Deletant, 1999, pp. 139–141). Obviously, the risk was that the impetuous developmental policies would erode the Party's political control. Aware of this risk, the Party's leadership used terror in the first two decades of communism to change the society and eliminate all potential challengers, and reign through rigid political immobilism during the Ceauşescu's era. Or in the words of Nelson (1988, p. 217), the regime's survival was contingent on its immobilism while the same rigidity escalated the cost of conflict between more modern social structures and the Party's institutions. As part of the same process, the Party grew impressively to become in 1987 the largest communist party in Eastern Europe except for the Soviet Union, 'including within its ranks approximately a quarter of the total adult and a third of the working population' (Gafton, 1988 cited in Siani-Davies, 2005, p. 21). This represented a part of Ceauşescu's utopia in which every 'expert' should be 'red'.

The first law which established the frame of labour legislation in the new communist regime was *Codul Muncii* (Labour Code) approved by the Great National Assembly on 30 May 1950. This law contained general provisions regarding the collective labour contract between the employer and the enterprise's union as representative of all employees. The collective labour contract had as main objectives the fulfilment of the State Plan and the improvement of the workers' living and work conditions. The law clearly stated that 'for equal work the employees will receive equal salaries' (Art. 33), and only if the employee did not fulfil the production norms, would the salary be reduced according to the law's provisions detailed for each possible case. The enterprise's plans or the state plan were not mentioned in other parts of the law. Since the industrialisation process was at its beginning, no issues related to ideological commitment of cadres were raised at this stage. According to Marin (2000, p. 131), before the nationalisation process began hundreds of cadres were recruited and trained: directors, chief-engineers and accountants. They were trained to take over the management of the organisations subject of nationalisation a day before the law was adopted. A new organisational structure was developed in order to coordinate the enterprises – the industrial branch central. Gaston Marin also noted that almost all the selected cadres were employees of the former capitalist companies.

However, nationalisation and extensive industrialisation required more personnel with specialised knowledge, as is evident from continuous complaints about the insufficient number of technicians or engineers. In an attempt to address this problem, the Great National Assembly issued '*Decretul nr. 381 din 23 septembrie 1949 pentru înfiinţarea de cursuri speciale necesare formării de cadre tehnice inginereşti de exploatare*' (*Decree for establishment of special courses necessary for the training of technical engineering cadre for exploitation*). The courses had a duration of two years and were organised by higher education institutions. They were designed for experienced workers with a minimum of five years in the same field, the graduates receiving the title of exploitation engineer (*inginer de exploatare*) (Decret nr. 391, 1949).

As noted above, from the 1960s onward, the Romanian educational system was geared to the production of engineers and sub-engineers, while the number of humanities and social sciences graduates was significantly reduced (Siani-Davies, 2005, p. 199). The 'Raport privind măsurile de perfecţionare a conducerii şi planificării economiei naţionale şi de îmbunătăţire a organizării administrativ-teritoriale a României' (*Report Concerning Measures for Perfecting the Management and Planning of the National Economy and for Improving the Administrative-Territorial Organisation of Romania*, National Conference of the PCR) published in 1967, stated the need for not only expert but also red cadres: 'our society demands highly skilled managing cadres, with deep political knowledge, unswervingly devoted to the cause of socialism and communism' (Ceauşescu, 1967, p. 77). According to official documents, the Party leadership remained constantly dedicated to this solution. However, the late 1960s was a period of slight liberalisation characterised among other aspects by a switch from symbolic-ideological legitimisation to a remuneratively based legitimisation. In this period, the technical-scientific elite started to emerge and to play a key role. Hale observes how the new technocrats began to challenge the Party's power, because 'on them depends the success of the economy, and this is their hold over the Party' (Hale, 1971, p. 114). According to Hale this new middle class consisted of 'engineers, industrial managers, bureaucrats, scientists, and professional men and women' (ibid.). Gilberg (1975) has also noted the emergence of indispensable technical-scientific elites in Romania. They were members of the Communist Party, because party membership represented the only means of upward mobility. This social category 'shared a common, rather conventionally bourgeois culture, and developed personal ties both through general social contacts and, in particular, through Party membership' (Swain, 2011, p. 1677).

In 1968, a new document was issued by the PCR regarding the selection, training and promotion of cadres from the party's sections and regarding the management of the cadres' records (Partidul Comunist Român, 1968). According to these instructions, 'the National Conference of the Romanian Communist Party has decided that cadre policy will be conducted under the direct guidance of the party's Central Committee' (Partidul Comunist Român, 1968, p. 3). The document acknowledged the increased need of cadres in all domains of social life. The criteria imposed for a person to be promoted to responsibility positions were:

- solid professional and cultural knowledge, organisational skills and initiative;
- satisfactory political and ideological knowledge, loyalty and sacrifice to the cause of socialism and communism;
- a determination to work for Party and state discipline, for the preservation and development of the common wealth.

A minimum experience of four years of PCR membership was required before a promotion to a position in the *nomenclatura*. Additionally, local PCR authorities had the right to control all other organisations with regard to the application of cadre policies and decisions. The process of promotion to positions included in the PCR's *nomenclatura* was based on a document entitled *Referatul de cadre*. This document had to include biographical information and evaluations regarding political and ideological knowledge, organisational skills, moral virtues, personal contributions to task fulfilment and a final conclusion regarding the appropriateness of the candidate for the respective position in the *nomenclatura* (Partidul Comunist Român, 1968, pp. 12–13). *Referatul de cadre* had to be elaborated based on the individual party file (*Dosarul de partid*), an evaluation from the job (*aprecierea activității*) and other references from people who knew the candidate for a *nomenclatura* position.

The evaluation of a cadre's activity had to be elaborated every time a person was suggested for a *nomenclatura* position, or had to be confirmed in a *nomenclatura* position. This evaluation had to include information about their professional and social activity, their level of political and ideological knowledge, their concern for the improving their knowledge, their managerial skills, their behaviour in their family and in society, and any shortcomings manifested in their activity and behaviour. *Referatul de cadre* had to be elaborated only when a person was promoted for the first time to a *nomenclatura* position. From that moment on, decisions would be made based on the initial *referat de cadre*, eventually amended with a note including the *apreciere* from the last job. Finally, the instructions required a probation period of six months for persons promoted for the first time to a *nomenclatura* position, or three months for persons with experience in a *nomenclatura* position. But if the party organisation considered the person appropriate for the respective position, the probation period could be reduced or even waived.

The first law with an impact on the labour relations was Legea Nr. 1 din 26 martie 1970 a organizării şi disciplinei muncii în unităţile socialiste de stat (Law of organising and work discipline in state socialist units). From the very beginning the law stipulated that

> the management structures of the state socialist units are accountable for efficient organisation of activities, for the integrity of common assets, for good management of material and financial resources, for taking all required decisions for completely and timely plan fulfilment, for the enforcement of socialist discipline principles and norms.
>
> (Art. 1)

Six specific tasks in relation to plan fulfilment were included in the long list of directors' responsibilities. The list below presents a selection of relevant responsibilities. The letter indicates the place of each responsibility in the list:

> a The thorough design of production and work plans;
> b The scientific organisation of production and rigorous control of the achievement of objectives;
> e The complete and timely supply of the enterprise's departments with all required materials, spare parts, fuels and energy and compliance with consumption norms;
> h The rigorous fulfilment of all delivery and services contracts,
> i The compliance with and fulfilment of all assumed commitments included in the collective labour contract
>
> (Art. 1)

The next article stated the duty of the unit's manager (*conducătorul unității*) was 'to take all required measures, within the limits of law, to fulfil the plan, to organise production, to assure proper work conditions, to improve the activity of the unit' (Art. 2). In the list of employees' rights, the law included the right 'to elect and to be elected to the unit's collective management structure (*organul colectiv de conducere al unității*), to express an opinion regarding any issue of the unit's activity' (Art. 4, h). One duty included in the list of employees' duties had a direct connection with the plan: 'the continuous improvement of professional levels for fulfilment of the plan's tasks, the continuous increase in the quality of products and services, and increase in productivity' (Art. 5, c).

The remaining part of the law contained provisions regarding the work contract, the transfer of employees to another unit, rewards and penalties. There was only one article (Art. 12) regarding rewards, and seven articles (Art. 13 – Art. 19) regarding penalties, sanctions and the procedures by which such cases had to be solved. This suggests increasing difficulties in controlling a more sophisticated economy, in which planning dysfunctions had an important impact on overall performance. According to this law, the main way of achieving a tighter control consisted in increasing pressure on the directors and in establishing a more comprehensive punitive mechanism. The working class were faced with more authoritarian directors and the threat of sanctions against disobedience.

This may have been related to the increasing number of workers recruited from rural areas, people with no industrial organisation culture, who probably experienced more difficulties in the integration process. This interpretation is intuitive however, since there are no statistics available regarding labour discipline problems in communist Romania. Significant labour conflicts started seven years later.

The evolution described above seems quite similar with the accounts of Haraszti (1977), Burawoy (1985), and Burawoy and Lukács (1992) regarding Hungary's industry. But after the visits Ceauşescu made in 1971 to China and North Korea, Romania experienced a significant turn. According to Siani-Davies, after these visits 'there was an unmistakable shift back from "expert" to "red" and ... the result, nonetheless, was the eventual exclusion from power of a segment of the scientific-technical elite who had pioneered the previous industrial expansion' (Siani-Davies, 2005, p. 201). According to Brucan (2012 p. 152), Ceauşescu discovered in China and North Korea 'a communist model and especially a political and cultural system which fitted him as a glove'. The extensive quotations provided below from the report made to the Executive Committee of the Central Committee of PCR on 25 June 1971 (Stenogram, 1971) aim to offer a better perspective on Ceauşescu's perceptions and understandings at this time.

First, the Ceauşescu family had been impressed by the official welcome, by the large popular mobilisation organised and by the high level of discipline. Ceauşescu declared:

> the population also gave us a very fine reception at the airport; afterwards, in the city, we were met by hundreds and hundreds of thousands of people, however not in thick crowds – as is the custom in our country – but in an organised manner: with schools, brass bands, sport games, and dances. The reception we were given in Korea was similar. I think we have to learn something from this, since everything was in good order. It was a kind of holiday, a festive manifestation. In the squares there was written, with flags and human bodies both in Chinese and Romanian languages: '*Long live the Chinese-Romanian friendship!*'
>
> (Stenogram of the Executive Committee of the Central Committee of the Romanian Communist Party's meeting, 25 June 1971)

Ceauşescu was also impressed by the Chinese commitment to develop their own capacities and to reduce the imports of technology especially from Western countries. Consequently, he decided to no longer approve technology imports: 'I told comrade Ioan Avram: I will not approve imports any longer' (ibid.). This decision will have a consistent impact on Romanian industry performance, and will be considered as one of the main causes of the economic crisis in the late 1980s.

The ideological activity of the Chinese Communist Party also had an important impact on Ceauşescu. In his opinion, the Chinese approach had been revolutionary: 'they put aside – maybe too suddenly, but in my view they did the right thing – all these petty bourgeois mentalities and started again from the very beginning. All of their cultural activity (ballet, theatre) was set on revolutionary bases' (ibid.). All these aspects confirmed Ceaușescu's vision of communist society as the record of the meeting shows:

> Before leaving I had a Secretariat meeting and there we decided to prepare a document for the plenary session to the effect that our propaganda was not satisfactory, that it did not correspond to the tasks of educating the youth and the people in general. I said this before going to China. What I have seen in China and Korea, however, is living proof that the conclusion we have reached is correct. Consequently, from this point of view as well, educating the people in a revolutionary, communist spirit is a very important activity. Naturally, they criticise imperialism a lot, the Americans, the Japanese, who are 'across the sea' from them, but in everything they compare the old with the new, they emphasise the efforts made to keep the fighting spirit awake.
>
> (Ibid.)

The Chinese experience gave the missing legitimacy to Ceaușescu's rudimentary understanding of a modern society, an understanding that would finally lead to 'a dynastic socialism, based on a personality cult un-equalled in communist Europe and on an extreme nationalistic policy' (Tismăneanu, Dobrincu and Vasile, 2007, p. 375).

But it was not only China that made a strong impression. Communist Korea also impressed Ceaușescu with new organisational structures that would be later imposed in Romanian enterprises:

> We went to the Heavy Equipment Works. There they build 6,000 tonnes presses. They do not import them as we do in spite of the fact that they do not have our machine-building industry. They too, want – by their own forces – to make man understand that he must do, not wait. They said so: we gathered together experienced engineers and workers and asked them to solve the problems together. In Romania we do not have old, experienced workers working together with engineers and solving certain problems. Otherwise nothing can be achieved. Where we involved workers as well the problems were solved. The engineer has never laid his hand on a hammer, he does not know how a machine is to be built; he knows how to make drawings for the machine and then sends you abroad to buy it. The Koreans build heavy machinery and equipment which we import from the USA, from Germany, machines that can process 22–25 meters long parts.
>
> (Stenogram of the Executive Committee of the Central Committee of the Romanian Communist Party's meeting, 25 June 1971)

The impressions from this visit were soon transposed into official documents. On 6 July 1971, Ceaușescu delivered a speech at a meeting of the Executive Committee of the Central Committee of the PCR, which would be later known as *Tezele din iulie* (*The July Thesis*) (Ceauşescu, 1971). The 17-points document marked a sharp turn in the Party's fundamentalist ideology. The speech was entitled *Propuneri de măsuri pentru îmbunătăţirea activităţii politico-ideologice, de educare marxist-leninistă a membrilor de partid, a tuturor oamenilor muncii* (*Proposals for improvement of the political and ideological activity, Marxist-Leninist education of Party members and of all workers*). All 17 theses were focused on raising the combative level of all people through educational measures established in all organisations. Socialist patriotism had become the essential task of education. Party education (*învăţământul de partid*) had to be improved in order to raise the level of Party work (*munca de partid*). Mass participation in the creation and implementation of state and Party policies in economic, social, ideological and cultural life had to become an expression of the Party's deep democracy. The volunteer work (*munca patriotică*) of younger generations in industry, agriculture and construction had to be widely stimulated. Ideological education had to be extended in schools, universities, mass-media, cultural events, radio and TV broadcasts. A tighter ideological control of books, movies, pop songs, opera, theatre and ballet performances was required. 'Art should serve the people, the motherland and socialist society'; therefore 'revolutionary, patriotic and worker songs must be created and broadcasted to the masses' (*creaţia de cîntece revoluţionare, patriotice, muncitoreşti*). A special and careful selection of foreign shows and songs was required. The mass media had to promote more the advanced image of the worker (*figura înaintată a muncitorului*) as devoted body and soul to socialism and to the development of the motherland.

This speech had been approved by a Party Plenary in November 1971, and it officially ended the period of the slight liberalisation of the 1960s. However, this shift from 'expert' to 'red' did not change enterprise management essentially in the last two decades of communism. The system of continuous negotiation of the plan established at the beginning of communism survived until the demise of communism, eventually becoming more sophisticated and adapted to technological advances. The dependence of the state on organisational performance grew at the same pace as the development and the sophistication of the whole economy. In the words of Noutcheva and Bechev (2008, p. 128), the state was captured not only from above by the Communist Party, but also from below by societal networks developed by this technocracy. However, the centralised planning system had visibly begun to fail in the last two decades of the communist regime, giving raise to social unrest especially in industrial centres.

Gilberg has suggested the emphasis on ideological orthodoxy also represented an effort to limit the political ambitions of specialised elites. The 'fundamental contradiction between the tight political control exercised by a centralised regime … and the interests of the many social and economic elites that can be now identified in Romania' (Gilberg, 1975, p. 245) was solved through a tighter ideological pressure which not only constrained other social groups' aspirations, but also improved the legitimacy of the communist elite. The new ideological orthodoxy was aimed at the phenomenon identified in the Soviet Union in the early 1920s by Bukharin of how the working class was dominated by an elite of professional managers and bureaucrats (Gelb and Gelb, 1981, p. 55).

The Romanian economy had to face similar challenges to those of other communist countries, but in a specific historical, social and economic context. Therefore, an objective of this research is to identify how far Romania developed similar organisational mechanisms to approach these challenges. Berliner (1957, p. 320) argued that a good *blat* at the right time and a competent *tolkach* were crucial preconditions of success in managerial activity in the Soviet economy. In the Romanian economy, the adaptation of the plan to economic realities was also widely used. Even the Party's documents admitted this behaviour: 'when life demands it, some amendments may be made to the original plan provisions by the forums which have approved them, according to some specially established rules and competences' (Ceauşescu, 1967, p. 58). As Ledeneva has observed in relation to the Soviet experience, in many cases such practices were tolerated and even stimulated by governments in order to 'resolve potential social conflicts or to promote political patronage' (1998, p. 50).

A significant change in labour legislation had appeared in Legea Nr. 12 din 21 octombrie 1971 privind încadrarea şi promovarea în muncă a personalului din unităţile socialiste de stat (The law regarding employment and promotion in state socialist units). If in the previous law access to collective management structures was a right, now it became also a duty: 'the employees have the right and the duty to directly participate in the improvement of organising and management of the enterprise's activity, to contribute to the promotion of the best cadres to management positions' (Art. 3). The law contained mainly provisions describing the procedures and criteria used in the processes of hiring and promoting people both in economic organisations and in central administration. There are few important aspects relevant for this study. The first aspect is the attempt to regulate the process of hiring, stating that 'in state socialist units the employees' hiring and promoting is done based on examination or competition. Competition is organised when there are more candidates for an available job' (Art. 7). The following articles contained details regarding hiring and promotion procedures. The law also established an evaluation system for 'knowing the possibilities and perspectives of development and promotion of cadres' (Art. 17). The system had been focused on technical, economic, speciality and administrative personnel. Some unspecified categories of workers could also be evaluated. The evaluations had to be done on an annual basis, and the personnel department archived the documents. The criteria used for the evaluation were:

- The results obtained in fulfilling the work tasks;
- The level of professional and general knowledge, and the degree of enrichment of their specialist knowledge;
- Their personal qualities;
- Their initiative, work discipline, perseverance in fulfilling work tasks, professional prestige;

- Their concern regarding the unit's wellbeing, care for socialist property, law enforcement and defence of state secrets;
- Their behaviour regarding the work collective, family and society, participation to collective activity, attitude towards the country's general interests.

(Art. 18)

General behaviour was mentioned among the evaluation criteria, but the law clearly reflected the concern regarding the professional qualities required by the economy. The hiring and promoting procedures also indicated the real need of professional knowledge. From a different perspective, probably the Party's leadership had tried to establish a more professionally oriented system in order to push forward the country's development.

One of the most important provisions of the law regarded the promotion to management positions. These provisions reflected the new approach of the Party's leadership to the red versus expert dilemma. Therefore Art. 36 stipulated that the

> general director of *centrala industrială* and director of other economic units can be promoted specialists with management experience, with a rich experience in organising and managing work and production, who have proved a high professional level, who actively supports the State and Party policies, who mobilise the collectives towards exemplary task fulfilment, who behave irreproachably in society.

Other conditions were required in the same article were graduation from a higher education institution, specific experience in industry and graduation from a training programme for management cadres. Consequently, directors were selected and promoted using two divergent categories of requirement – not only a more complex professional training but also a full devotion to the Party.

Regarding the state central structures Art. 48 of the same law required cadres with a profound professional training and long experience, who were good organisers and managers, with authority over the masses, but with 'a high political and ideological level, an endless allegiance to the interests of the working class and of the whole people, who actively participate in the firm accomplishment of internal and external policies of the Party and State'. Because it seemed that industrialisation had raised significant management problems, the law required that all directors and cadres must complete a training course on 'the management and organisation of production and work' by 31 December 1976 (Art. 69).

On 21–22 November 1972 a Plenary of the Central Committee of the PCR decided to establish workers' control councils in all state enterprises, state agricultural organisations, research institutes and other economic units. These control councils had the role of enhancing and improving the participation of all employees in the management process. According to the Central Committee decision, the control councils were to be focused on fulfilling the plan indicators, on product quality and on technological specifications. Other committees were established in every organisation with specific tasks: work organisation, cost reduction, production automation, quality, import-export problems, development and investment. All these committees had to support the 'collective management structures' to fulfil the plan objectives and to improve production efficiency. The Party organisation had to approve the employees nominated by the workers' council (*COM – Consiliul Oamenilor Muncii*) as members of these committees.

In this way, the PCR had tried to control what Nelson (1988, p. 19) defined as the 'covariance of development as a socioeconomic phenomenon and political participation' by imposing new organisational structures, the workers' councils, or mechanisms, self-management (*autoconducerea*). Assuming that along the socioeconomic development the working class will tend to increase its involvement into the political life, the communist leaders decided to create organisational structures adequate for such participation. While *COM* was to be a key element of the new self-management by industrial labour, *autoconducerea* was emphasised as a major step towards democratisation. Based on significant empirical data, Nelson (1988) argued that workers' self-management was an illusion, as was the democratisation at organisational level: 'worker's councils are, in fact, not highly regarded, elected representatives in them are not well known, and council meetings are dominated by the party leadership in combination with party cadre who administer the enterprise's departments' (Nelson, 1988, p. 25). Since the plan objectives were received from above and they were the subject of complex and continuous negotiations, the enterprises' basic activities such as financial, supply or sales were also prescribed, the *COM* and *autoconducerea* were essentially control mechanisms designed to improve productivity.

The most comprehensive document regarding labour relations was Legea Nr. 10 also known as *Codul Muncii* (1972). For almost two decades this law was the legislation general frame of work relations in communist Romania. *Codul Muncii* institutionalised a few main principles of the relation between the working class and the state and the managerial social category. It comprised 191 articles covering all main aspects of work relations. For the purpose of this research the most relevant articles for our discussion here are analysed below.

The first principle institutionalised by *Codul Muncii* was the collective management of socialist units. This principle had been labelled 'an expression of deepening socialist democracy' (Art. 9). The general assemblies of workers were considered a superior form of collective management, through which workers participated in the activity of management, in discussions and decisions regarding plan fulfilment, and in control over management structures. This principle together with the workers' control councils established by the Party plenary in the same month was an expression of the attempt to balance the influence of the emerging managerial class. At the same time, it reflected a rudimentary approach towards the efficient management of a more sophisticated economy. On the one hand the directors were directly responsible for plan fulfilment and they had multiple methods to control the workers; on the other hand the workers were supposed to control the enterprise management through structures such as *COM*. And as *Codul Muncii* and other directives or laws made clear, both directors and workers were responsible for the overall performance of the enterprise which was dramatically affected very often by the flaws of the central planning system.

Another relevant aspect was the reward system. *Codul Muncii* (1950) stated that 'for equal work the employees will receive equal salaries' (Art. 33). In 1972, a more complex economy required a more balanced perspective. Therefore Art. 11 mentioned that the workers 'receive a part of the national income, following the socialist principle of distribution according to the quantity, quality and the social importance of the work, in the spirit of the socialist norms of ethics and fairness'. The law represented the first official document showing a continuous oscillation between the egalitarian principle and the attempt to introduce other criteria in the salaries system. Art. 27 stated that 'the workers from industrial units have the right to a financial reward according to the quantity and quality of the realised work, as well as according to the place and importance of the industrial branch in the country's development'. Art. 82.1 added a new criterion: 'the rational distribution of the national income', re-stating the previous contradiction 'for equal work, an equal salary' but according to the social importance of the workplace. At the same time the salary had to reflect the complexity, responsibility, professional level and experience, and a fair ratio between low and high salaries (Art. 82.2). Art. 84 clearly related income to the degree of fulfilment of work tasks, and stated the possibility of reducing the salary of a worker who failed to meet their objectives.

A new concept – *retribuția în acord* – was introduced in Art. 93, but without a proper definition. The concept would have an important impact on the reward system, first in industrial branches, and later in the entire economy. Apparently, Art. 93 regarded the work norms, which had to be applied to all personnel categories, regardless of the payment system used. This is the only mention of this method of payment in this law. The work norms were defined as units for the evaluation of the work in duration, production, personnel or responsibilities. A literal translation of *retribuția în acord* is difficult, but as the concept will be defined and implemented later on, it meant a salary system correlated with the plan fulfilment either at individual level or at a higher organisational level.

The improvement of professional, political and ideological, and cultural training became a right and a duty for everybody, and also a promotion criterion. The work collective (*colectivul de muncă*) was accountable for the efficient use of society's assets, for fulfilment of the plan targets, and had the duty to mobilise all material, financial and human resources to contribute to the increase of the national economic-social development fund (Art. 20). This provision was a precursor of salary *în acord global* which later on would correlate the salary with plan fulfilment. The management of socialist units was again considered fully responsible for 'a normal deployment of production, at maximum efficiency' (Art. 21). But at the same time, management must consistently apply the collective management principle (*principiul conducerii colective*). Finally, in each and every socialist unit, it was necessary to ensure the full use of the workforce and the integral use of work-time (Art. 26.2).

In October 1974, a new law was issued called Legea Nr. 57 – a retribuirii după cantitatea şi calitatea muncii (The law of retribution according to the quantity and quality of work). From the beginning the law tried to integrate both principles into the same statement:

> in all fields of activity, workers are rewarded according to the quantity, quality and social importance of their work, according to the principle of equal salary for equal work. Unlike the capitalist salary which represents the price of the work in capitalist society, in socialist Romania the salary represents that part of the national income intended for individual consumption.

Art. 2 offered a new formulation: 'work is rewarded on the basis of the socialist principle of repartition according to the quantity, quality and social importance of the work, in terms of the contribution to the material and spiritual development of the whole society'. Art. 6 described this contribution:

- The fulfilment and over-fulfilment of production tasks;
- The improvement of product quality;
- The integral use of production capacities;
- The facilitation of technical, scientific and cultural progress;
- The improvement of productivity;
- The decrease of production costs, especially through reducing the consumption of raw materials, spare parts, energy and fuel;
- The increase of investments efficiency, shortening deliveries, reducing investments in buildings within total investments;
- The increase of export and of foreign trade efficiency;
- The permanent increase of efficiency in economic activities, but also in all areas of social life.

This law presented extended definitions of salary methods and forms in Art. 12. The most important method, with a significant impact on the work relations, was *în acord*. In this case, the individual salary was the result of multiplication of a unitary tariff by the total number of pieces. In spite of being an apparently fair and simple formula for calculating salaries, one of the forms of this method described in the law, *în acord global*, would later permit a decrease in salaries correlated with plan fulfilment. This form had to be applied when a comprehensive contract had been agreed between the work collective and the enterprise. All personnel categories were allowed to be rewarded through this form. Art. 13 stated that in the case of *acordul colectiv* the individual salary could be increased or decreased up to 20 per cent, related to the individual contribution to collective plan fulfilment.

Art. 39 stated that every person's salary from enterprises to ministries was to be calculated according to the fulfilment of individual and collective tasks.

Exceeding the planned task was rewarded additionally only if the superior structure ascertained that the plan took into account the full production capacity. A decreased salary was the consequence of task un-fulfilment. Art. 40 stated that salaries of all kinds of employees working *în acord* were to be established depending on the fulfilment of work tasks. Only if non-fulfilment of plan tasks had been generated by independent causes was the superior structure allowed to authorise a reduction in the amount of salary decrease. Art. 48 presented a long list of such independent causes, including delays in supplies, energy failures and delays in the installation of production capacities. The same article stated that if the production process could not be normally assured, the enterprise management must retain the minimum required personnel and dispose of the rest to other units. Art. 77 indicated the main objectives of the salaries system in industry, which was roughly the same as those stated in Art. 6. The extensive and intensive use of all production capacities, mainly through the second and third shift, was added. Art. 78 recommended the use of salary *în acord* wherever this form was possible and economically reasonable. Art. 80 stated that production target and the planned cost must be among the indicators used for calculating salaries.

On 1 July 1983 was issued Legea Nr. 2 cu privire la principiile de bază ale perfecţionării sistemului de retribuire a muncii şi de repartiţie a veniturilor oamenilor muncii (Law concerning the basic principles of the improvement of work retribution system and of workers income repartition). From this moment on, the egalitarian principle almost disappeared from official discourse. In the law's preamble, it was stated a direct correlation between income and work results was necessary. Moreover, the text explicitly stated that incomes were not limited. Art. 2 introduced the COM responsibility regarding the proper management of socialist property, productivity increase, the complete use of production capacities and material resources, the salaries system, strict compliance with consumption norms, product quality and professional continuous improvement. Basically, COM became fully responsible for the enterprise's performance. The general assembly of the employees (adunarea generală a oamenilor muncii) was the supreme control authority over COM and the enterprise managers.

Art. 5 expressed a completely new approach to the salaries system. While the first paragraph restated the possibility of increasing unlimited salaries if the planned production was over-fulfilled, the second paragraph stated that if the planned production was not fulfilled, salary was proportionally reduced, without ensuring a minimum guaranteed income. Basically, this provision opened the possibility of unlimited salary reductions, an unprecedented measure in communist Romania and probably in the communist system.

Art. 10 extended *acordul global* to the whole economy from industry to agriculture and research, and from workers to directors and ministers. The object of the *acordul global* contract between the work collective and the enterprise was the planned production of products, quantities and works. The salaries of management personnel from central and local authorities was to be calculated according to indicators such as production, export plans and productivity.

The evolution of the legal framework described above suggests a few important conclusions regarding industrial relations in communist Romania. First, both the economic and social indicators demonstrate an important increase in the size of the working class during the communist period. The main source for this increase was the rural areas – with a population with a low level of education and technical skills. The fundamental communist promises – a better urban life, better work conditions and becoming a part of the leading class had a huge attractive power. As many authors argued, the first stage of communist industrialisation was based on extensive use of labour. In a predominantly rural country such as Romania after World War II, rapid industrialisation was an opportunity for upward mobility for many social groups. But after almost two decades of extensive industrialisation, a higher degree of technological sophistication had required not only more educated employees but more sophisticated work relations. Moreover, efficiency had become an important factor to be considered in a more complex economic system managed in an over-centralised manner. This is probably why the legal system governing work had to deal with the contradiction between ideological commitments and the requirement of a modern economy, between the egalitarian principle and economic efficiency.

The workers' protests and strikes in communist Romania

The contradictions and tensions in the central planning system had a significant impact on the attitudes of the working class and had consequences in the emergence of criticisms and in generating protests. Furthermore, the changes over time in the organisational mechanisms discussed above can be related to these protests and strikes. For example, Nelson (1981, p. 177) has suggested that the renewed interest of the Party in workers' self-management 'had some relationship to the 1977 miners' strike and protests in the Jiu Valley'.

The academic literature on the history of the working class in communist Romania is extremely scarce. However, there are a few reliable sources providing data regarding the most important events such as protests, strikes and the emergence of free unions. For example, Tismăneanu, Dobrincu and Vasile (2007, pp. 345–359) offer a synthesis of the workers' protests in the communist regime. According to the authors, the Romanian communist period can be divided into three periods: 1945–58, 1958–77 and 1977–89, based on the main characteristics of the protests and strikes in each period.

The first period, 1945–58, was characterised by spontaneous, non-violent protests which had little impact, usually generated by hard work conditions, delays in salary payments or increases in production targets. Protests took place in areas with a strong industrial tradition in the oil industry (Valea Prahovei), machine building industry (Bucharest), the metallurgical industry (Resita, Hunedoara) and the Danube harbours (Galați, Braila). Information regarding these protests was mainly collected from oral testimonies. The authors argued that the protesters had some trust in communist leaders and there was no perceived difference between *us* (the people) and *them* (*nomenclatura*). A document entitled

'*Atmosfera politică din ţară în cursul lunei Februarie 1949*' (*The country's political background on February 1949*) issued by Serviciul de Sinteză (Synthesis Service) of the Central Committee of PMR noted that workers' discontent in some enterprises was generated by the new collective work contracts (Berindei, Dobrincu and Goşu, 2009, pp. 144–156). The same report indicated 64 cases of industrial sabotage in February compared with 74 cases in January 1949. Another report described a strike in Brăila port, generated by lay-offs and a new system of work norms (Berindei, Dobrincu and Goşu, 2009, pp. 189–192). The main reasons for workers' dissatisfaction were low salaries, the high cost of living, insufficient basic food and oil, and unreasonable work norms. These reasons were noted in reports issued in 1950 (Berindei, Dobrincu and Goşu, 2009, pp. 261–266), 1952 (Berindei, Dobrincu and Goşu, 2009, pp. 379–395). The 1952 report noted for the first time that supply problems in industry generated lower salaries and workers' dissatisfaction.

In the second period, following the de-Stalinisation process started by Khrushchev in 1956, the Romanian leadership launched a strategy of nationalisation of the Stalinist model. An important reason for this strategy was the Romanian leaders' fear of becoming victims of the changes initiated by Khrushchev. 'The awakening nationalism, encouraged since 1962 by Soviet concessions to national sovereignty' (CIA, 1964, p. 4), but also 'the Romanian-Soviet cold war' (Frunză, 1999, p. 385), culminating with the Party's *The Declaration of the PMR's position Regarding the Problems of the International Communists and Workers Movement* (PMR, 1964), were among the expressions of this strategy. Nationalistic values and a stronger emphasis on extensive industrialisation were the main coordinates of the strategy. Because the pace of industrialisation was higher than urbanisation, a significant number of workers were commuting from rural areas to urban industrial centres. Between 1960 and 1975 the percentage of the workforce employed in industry had increased from 19.2 per cent to 30.6 per cent. Tismăneanu, Dobrincu and Vasile (2007) suggested that both core values of this strategy were desirable for the new working class who tacitly accepted the communist leadership. Therefore, workers' protests during this period were insignificant.

The most important workers' unrest experienced under communist rule took place at the beginning of the third period, with the Valea Jiului miners' strike in 1977. Roughly 35,000 miners out of a total of 90,000 participated in the strike, starting a new period of conflict between the working class and the communist regime. Based on existing literature and documents describing this event, Tismăneanu, Dobrincu and Vasile (2007) argued that the protest had an essentially defensive character. The miners refused to have discussions with anyone other than Ceauşescu. This lack of trust in managers and in their ability and interest to solve workers' problems was also observed by Haraszti (1977). When Ceauşescu finally arrived, a list of 17 demands was presented and immediately accepted by the Party leader. The protests were generated by some decisions which aimed to increase productivity at the expense of work conditions: an increase from six to eight working hours per day, salary reductions of up to 35 per cent for plan non-fulfilment, worsened retirement conditions and other aspects strictly related to work conditions. The list of demands included one that the strikers should not be punished. Since Ceaușescu accepted all the demands, the miners resumed work immediately. Following the events an investigation was then undertaken by the Party. The results of the investigation were presented in *Raport privind activitatea politică, economică și socială din municipiul Petroșani, (Report concerning the politic, economic and social activity in the town of Petroșani)* (cited by Tismăneanu, Dobrincu and Vasile, 2007, pp. 350–351). According to the report, shortcomings generated by the local authorities 'had determined some dissatisfactions and an inadequate work climate'. However, the report identified the main causes of the protests as 'the insufficient supply of industrial and food products, flawed health assistance, other social service failures, as well as a chronic shortage of workers, and delays in implementing work automation'. The report also mentioned as consequences of these aspects 'an increasing frequency of salary penalties due to plan non-fulfilment'. Commenting on the failure of the automation programme on which the annual and five-year plans were based, the report noted that

> the automation programme for 1976–1977 required the import and the installation of 9 complex machines and 12 mining combines for thick layers, but until now only 6 and 4 respectively are procured; no extraction machine had been brought out of the 6 required; only 37 transformer stations are installed out of 160 required, and no device for explosions had been brought out of 293 required.

The report blamed all the faults and shortcomings on the local Party organisations, the Ministry for Mines, Oil and Geology, and on the Workers Councils of the mining enterprises. The report also included the measures and decisions that had been taken for improvement of miners' lives following the miners' strike: the reduction of the work programme to six hours, the improvement of supplies, medical assistance, housing, and work conditions, and the improvement of the Party and union activity in the political education field. The first Central Committee Plenary (26–27 October 1977) only mentioned 'dissatisfactions generated by accumulated abuses and failure to implement the laws and the Party decisions'. The same plenary identified as a scapegoat the former minister for Mines, Oil and Geology Bujor Almăș, who had held the post from 21 March 1961 until 27 January 1977. His punishment consisted of a vote of censure.

It was in this context that the first independent trade union was established in 1979, but the regime reacted immediately by arresting the founders. In spite of the significant social unrest, the extensive industrialisation policy was not re-evaluated. The solution identified by the regime consisted in partial concessions agreed with protesters regarding mostly work conditions combined with tighter ideological and security control. For Ceaușescu the main problem revealed by the miners' strike was the insufficient ideological level of the workers, their failed transformation into the desired 'new man'. So, they had to be more involved in political, social and artistic activities.

According to various sources, including Radio Free Europe, further strikes took place in Bucharest in 1980 in reaction to an increase in planned targets, a reduction of salaries, shortage of food supplies and deteriorating work conditions (Tismăneanu, Dobrincu and Vasile, 2007). In 1981 protests took place in Bucharest, as well as in other industrial centres such as Ploieşti and Piteşti. A violent protest against bread rationing took place in Motru – another important mining centre, in October 1981. Because of its violent character the protest was halted by the security forces in a few hours. A new wave of protests was generated by the 1983 extension of *acordul global* to the whole of industry and the consolidation in law of the reduction in salaries as a penalty in cases of plan non-fulfilment. According to Tismăneanu, Dobrincu and Vasile (2007), available sources also confirmed workers' protests in many industrial centres in the 1980s.

The last important protest took place in Braşov on 15 November 1987. The protest's trigger was the announcement of a 30 per cent reduction of salaries because production costs had been exceeded. As a result, thousands of workers gathered to demand an explanation from the management and then they left the enterprise. Other protesters joined in and they violently occupied the county's Party Committee. The security forces intervened on the same day, ending one of the most important protests of the workers against the Party leadership.

Conclusions

Until 1956 the Romanian communists had followed strictly the Soviet leadership in all areas of activity. The 1953 strong Soviet criticism was followed by economic plan adjustment and even by ceasing work on the Black Sea-Danube channel. The turning moments were Khrushchev's condemnation of Stalinism and the Hungarian revolution when, according to Brucan (2012, p. 77), Gheorghiu-Dej said, 'if we do not turn 180 degrees in our relation with the Soviets, we are lost'. From that moment, a secret policy was established, mostly for internal use, in order to show a higher priority to national interests. Some important measures were taken in the following years: the Soviet Army left the country, *Sovroms* were liquidated, and nationalism had begun to replace internationalism. Almost all Russian names of streets, towns or schools were changed, the Russian language was systematically replaced by Western languages in school curricula, and even Karl Marx's book *Note despre Români* (*Notes about Romanians*) was published. In this book, Marx condemned interference by the tsarist empire in Romanian affairs and especially the Bessarabia annexation in 1812. As noted in the first chapter, in 1963 the Romanian leaders successfully handled the issue of a supranational Comecon body, followed by the April 1964 Declaration which affirmed the sovereignty of the Romanian party. Finally, the first crisis of succession was successfully managed in 1965. The new leader, Nicolae Ceauşescu, would bring the manipulation of nationalistic symbols to the level of state policy (Brucan, 2012, p. 83).

Thus, in important aspects of its politics, internal as well as foreign policies, Romania adopted its own distinctive national form of communism. At the same time however, it retained many aspects of the Soviet model of state ownership, a centrally managed economy, and one-party government by a communist party whose role was closely interwoven with the functions and institutions of the state. A central question therefore, for any analysis of Romanian economy and society under communist rule concerns how distinctive was the situation in Romania, or how similar were the characteristics, problems and attempted solutions by the Romanian communist leadership and by managers and others throughout society. And such questions are particularly relevant for the subject of this book, the factory and the role of the factory management in the Romanian economy under communist rule.

Authors such as Jowitt or Berliner have observed that communist regimes exemplified some basic cultural traits. Jowitt (1974, p. 1179) noted that the communist regime 'has done more than unintentionally reinforce and enhance pre-Leninist political cultural postures'. Berliner (1957, p. 230) analysed the character and consequences of the command system in the Soviet economy and identified a series of informal-adaptive responses that included searching for a safety factor, hoarding, and dissimulation in conditions of extremely ambitious targets, tight time constraints, scarce resources and authoritative sanctions ('the plan is law'). Jowitt argued that Berliner's findings can be generalised to other communist countries and to sectors of society. And indeed, the Romanian case presents most of these adaptive responses, mostly hoarding, dissimulation and scarce resources. Defending the enterprise's interests had become the most important ability needed by directors 'just as in traditional peasant societies families jealously guard their own interests rather than cooperate extensively' (Jowitt, 1974, p. 1179). Hoarding production capacities represents an example of an adaptive response but there is evidence suggesting that this behaviour was present not only at enterprise level but at the whole economy level. The memoires of Gaston Marin, Silviu Brucan and statistical evidence show excessive production capacities from the very beginning of the planning system. This suggests that hoarding excessive capacities was a cultural characteristic rather than an adaptive response to a dysfunctional system. Over-capacities had charged the investment budget but also had generated supplementary operational costs. In order to fulfil these capacities, the imports of raw materials also increased consistently. Because the Soviet Union did not agree to deliver more oil, iron ore and other raw resources, Romania had to import them from Brazil, and even Australia. This is one example of how Romania had to adapt to contingencies, in this case resulting from its relations with the Soviet Union. However, the question of how far Romania departed significantly from the Soviet model will be addressed in the following chapters.

The analysis of work relations shows a relevant dynamic after Ceaușescu had become the Party leader. Until 1970 the egalitarian perspective on work relations had been the main principle – for similar work a similar salary should be paid. Starting with 1970, three main changes can be identified in work legislation: a stronger accent on work discipline, a developing focus on collective management and an increasingly stronger connection between salary and plan fulfilment. All these trends had as the main objective the increase of responsibility and commitment of the working class in an irrational process of development, based on Ceaușescu's obsessions.

The first change can be related to the increasing proportion of workers with rural origin. A more complex economy definitely required a disciplined workforce, and therefore legal mechanisms to enforce work discipline had to be put in place. Without any statistics regarding work discipline issues, it can be only supposed that such problems had significantly increased over the period. And as Jowitt (1974, p. 1186) observed, the Romanian leadership 'lacked the historical experience, political confidence, and consequently the ideological sophistication ... to approach the basic social force in a traditional society – the peasantry – in a flexible rather than dogmatic, repressive fashion'. Ceaușescu himself recognised the problem: 'we have had an easy time building factories. But it is incumbent on us to transform man at the same rate, so that he will be capable of mastering new techniques ... and new ways of thinking' (cited by Kligman, 1984, p. 167). Enforcement of the legislation regarding work discipline was the choice of Romanian leadership.

The growing power of the managerial class and technocracy, observed by Hale and Gilberg, had to be balanced by the authority of a more educated working class. The communist leadership was

> aware that in twenty-five years the regime has created social groups whose aspirations for recognition require a political response, whose skills require a restructuring of power relations, and whose understanding of authority allows for and requires new institutional formats and a corresponding political-cultural ethos.
>
> (Jowitt, 1974, p. 1974)

They had begun to institutionalise various structures and mechanisms – *COM* and *autoconducerea*. But those mechanisms had not been successful, as Nelson (1988) observed, because of the lack of interest and participative experience of the working class, and because of the lack of real content. The mechanisms were designed as an expression of democratic participation in the decision-making process, but all the main coordinates of organisational life were decided by the planning structures. So these structures and mechanisms had ended up being either irrelevant or being captured by the managers.

It is likely that the change from an egalitarian approach towards an apparently performative one had an important impact on the increase in events of social unrest. As the description of the main social unrest events show, most of them were generated at least in part by reductions in salaries and other benefits generated by plan non-fulfilment. Unlike the other transformations, this one had happened over quite a long period of time. The salary method *în acord* had been first announced in 1972 but without any proper definition. This method was then generalised to the whole economy more than ten years later. Officially the main reason for this change was to increase the productivity through a remunerative strategy. Therefore, a trade-off between the egalitarian approach and the stimulation approach began to be implemented in the early 1970s, and at the beginning of the 1980s the stimulation strategy was generalised. But under the constraints of a controlled and planned economy, the system not only failed to attain its objectives, but also created social side effects – protests and strikes – that soon eroded working class support of the Party's leadership. While in 1977 the miners did not trust the Party apparatus but they still had a certain degree of trust in Ceaușescu, in the next decade the few but violent protests showed the complete disruption of trust relations between the working class and the leadership. Most of the workers' protests were generated by the state's incapacity to improve or at least to keep constant the level of work and living conditions, in many cases because of plan fulfilment failures that led to reductions in salaries. In addition to plan fulfilment pressures, the worsening of work conditions, failures in the supply of food, health services or other basic services, had amplified further the working class dissatisfaction and frustration. However, as the case of 1977 Valea Jiului strike shows, the miners had still trusted Ceaușescu as having the capacity and intention to solve the problems. Just a few years later this trust had disappeared.

Hence this is the context in which in-depth archival and qualitative research was undertaken in order to understand the work relations at enterprise's level, to understand the extent to which Romanian experience was similar to that of other communist countries.

Note

1 For other authors who made comparisons between Romania in the 1980s, both with Soviet Union in 1930s and with other communist countries in the 1950s, see e.g. Sampson (1984).

References

Békés, C., Borhi, L., Ruggenthaler, P. and Trașcă, O. eds. 2015. *Soviet Occupation of Romania, Hungary, and Austria 1944/45–1948/49*. Budapest: Central European University Press.

Berindei, M., Dobrincu, D. and Goșu, A. 2009. *Istoria comunismului din România: documente. Perioada Gheorghe Gheorghiu-Dej (1945–1965)*. București: Humanitas.

Berliner, J. 1957. *Factory and Manager in USSR*. Cambridge, MA: Harvard University Press.

Brucan, S. 1996. *Stâlpii noii puteri în România*. București: Nemira.

Brucan, S. 2012. *Generația irosită*. București: Editura Teșu.

Buga, V. 2004. Relațiile politice româno-sovietice, 1953–1958. *Arhivele Totalitarismului*, 42–43(1–2).

Ceaușescu, N. 1967. *Report Concerning Measures for Perfecting the Management and Planning of the National Economy and for Improving the Administrative-Territorial Organization of Romania, National Conference of the Romanian Communist Party*. Bucharest: Agerpres.

Ceaușescu, N. 1971. Propuneri de măsuri pentru îmbunătățirea activității politico-ideologice, de educare marxist-leninistă a membrilor de partid, a tuturor oamenilor muncii. [Online]. [Accessed 21 July 2017]. Available from: https://ro.wikisource.org/wiki/Tezele_din_iulie.

Central Intelligence Agency. 1944. *Rumania: The How of Enslavement*. [Online]. [Accessed 18 June 2017]. Available from: www.cia.gov/library/readingroom/docs/DOC_0000483695.pdf.

Central Intelligence Agency. 1963. *A Crack in the CMEA Facade – Rumania*. [Online]. [Accessed 19 June 2017]. Available from: www.cia.gov/library/readingroom/docs/CIA-RDP79T01003A001600180001-4.pdf.

Central Intelligence Agency. 1964. *Changing Patterns in Eastern Europe*. National Intelligence Estimates. 12–64. [Online]. [Accessed 19 June 2017]. Available from: www.cia.gov/library/readingroom/docs/DOC_0000012082.pdf.

Codul Muncii. Legea nr. 3. 30 May 1950. [Online]. [Accessed 19 July 2017]. Available from: http://legislatie.just.ro/Public/DetaliiDocument/21523.

Codul Muncii. Legea nr. 10. 23 November 1972. [Online]. [Accessed 21 July 2017]. Available from: www.legex.ro/Legea-10-1972-500.aspx.

Constituţia Republicii Populare Romîne. 13 Aprilie 1948. [Online]. [Accessed 19 July 2017]. Available from: http://legislatie.resurse-pentru-democratie.org/constitutie/constitutia-republicii-populare-romane-1948.php#.

Convenţie de armistiţiu între Guvernul Român, pe de o parte, şi Guvernele Uniunii Sovietice, Regatului Unit şi Statele Unite ale Americii, pe de altă parte. 12 September 1944. Monitorul Oficial 219/22 September 1944. Bucureşti.

Decret nr. 381 pentru înfiinţarea de cursuri speciale necesare formării de cadre tehnice inginereşti de exploatare. 28 September 1949. [Online]. [Accessed 21 July 2017]. Available from: http://legislatie.just.ro/Public/DetaliiDocument/22102.

Fotaki, M. 2009. Maintaining the Illusion of a Free Health Care in Post-Socialism: A Lacanian Analysis of Transition from Planned to Market Economy. *Journal of Organizational Change Management*, 22(2).

Frunză, V. 1999. *Istoria comunismului în România*. Bucureşti: EVF.

Gelb, M. and Gelb, M. 1981. Roots of Soviet Industrial Management 1917–1941. *Review of Radical Political Economics*, 13(1).

Gerschenkron, A. 1962. *Economic Backwardness in Historical Perspective*. Cambridge, MA: Belknap, Harvard University Press.

Gilberg, T. 1975. *Modernization in Romania since World War II*. New York: Praeger.

Haraszti, M. 1977. *A Worker in a Worker's State*. London: Penguin Books.

Ionescu, G. 1964. *Communism in Rumania 1944–1962*. London: Oxford University Press.

Ionete, C. 1993. *Criza de sistem a economiei de comandă şi etapa sa explozivă*. Bucureşti: Editura Expert.

Jowitt, K. 1974. An Organizational Approach to the Study of Political Culture in Marxist-Leninist Systems. *The American Political Science Review*, 68(3).

King, R.R. 1980. *History of the Romanian Communist Party*. Stanford, CA: Hoover Institution Press.

Kligman, G. 1984. The Rites of Women: Oral Poetry, Ideology, and the Socialization of Peasant Women in Contemporary Romania. *The Journal of American Folklore*, 97(384).

Ledeneva, A.V. 1998. *Russia's Economy of Favours: Blat, Networking and Informal Exchange*. Cambridge: Cambridge University Press.

Legea Nr. 1 a organizării şi disciplinei muncii în unităţile socialiste de stat. 26 March 1970. [Online]. [Accessed 21 July 2017]. Available from: www.legex.ro/Legea-1-1970-444.aspx.

Legea Nr. 12 privind încadrarea şi promovarea în muncă a personalului din unităţile socialiste de stat. 21 October 1971. [Online]. [Accessed 21 July 2017]. Available from: www.legex.ro/Legea-12-1971-469.aspx.

Legea Nr. 57 a retribuirii după cantitatea şi calitatea muncii. 29 October 1974. [Online]. [Accessed 21 July 2017]. Available from: www.legex.ro/Legea-57-1974-564.aspx.

Legea Nr. 2 cu privire la principiile de bază ale perfecţionării sistemului de retribuire a muncii şi de repartiţie a veniturilor oamenilor muncii. 1 July 1983. [Online]. [Accessed 21 July 2017]. Available from: www.legex.ro/Legea-2-1983-752.aspx.

Marin, G.Gh. 2000. *În serviciul României lui Gheorghiu-Dej. Însemnãri din viaţã*. Bucureşti: Editura Evenimentul Românesc.

Minutes of Conversation between Gorbachev and Romanian Leader Ceausescu. 4 December 1989. History and Public Policy Program Digital Archive. First published in Săndulescu, S. 1996. December '89. The Coup D'Etat Confiscated the Romanian Revolution. (Bucharest: Omega Press Investment), pp. 283–298. Translated in CWIHP Bulletin Nos. 12/13 by Mircea Munteanu, pp. 217–225. [Online]. [Accessed 17 July 2017]. Available from: http://digitalarchive.wilsoncenter.org/document/116247.

Mureşan, M. 2012. Economia României în anii socialismului. In Bosomiti, S. and Burcea, M. eds. *Spectrele lui Dej. Incursiuni în biografia şi regimul unui dictator*. Iaşi: Polirom.

Mureşan, M. and Mureşan, D. 1998. *Istoria economiei*. Bucureşti: Editura Economicã.

Murgescu, B. 2010. *România şi Europa. Acumularea decalajelor economice (1500–2010)*. Iaşi: Polirom.

Nelson, D.N. ed. 1981. *Romania in the 1980s*. Boulder, CO: Westview Press.

Nelson, D.N. 1988. *Romanian Politics in the Ceauşescu Era*. New York: Gordon and Breach Science Publishers.

Noutcheva, G. and Bechev, D. 2008. The Successful Laggards: Bulgaria and Romania's Accession to the EU. *East European Politics and Societies*, 22(1).

Partidul Comunist Român. 1968. *Instrucţiuni cu privire la selecţionarea, pregătirea şi promovarea cadrelor din nomenclatura organelor de partid şi la organizarea evidenţei acestor cadre*. Bucureşti.

Partidul Comunist Român. 1975. *Program of the Romanian Communist Party for the Building of the Multilaterally Developed Socialist Society and Romania's Advance toward Communism*. Bucharest: Agerpres.

Partidul Muncitoresc Romîn. 1964. *Declaraţie cu privire la poziţia P.R.M. în problemele mişcãrii comuniste şi muncitoreşti internaţionale adoptatã la plenara lãrgitã a C.C. al P.M.R.* Bucureşti: Editura Politicã.

Sampson, S.L. 1984. *National Integration through Socialist Planning: An Anthropological Study of a Romanian New Town*. Boulder, CO: East European Monographs, distributed by Columbia University Press.

Siani-Davies, P. 2005. *The Romanian Revolution of December 1989*. Ithaca, NY: Cornell University Press.

Stenogram of the Executive Committee of the Central Committee of the Romanian Communist Party's meeting. 25 June 1971. [Online]. [Accessed 21 July 2017]. Available from: http://digitalarchive.wilsoncenter.org/document/112058.

Tãnase, S. 1998. *Elite şi societate. Guvernarea Gheorghiu-Dej 1948–1965*. Bucureşti: Editura Humanitas.

Tismãneanu, V., Dobrincu, D. and Vasile C. 2007. *Raport Final al Comisiei Prezidenţiale pentru Analiza Dictaturii Comuniste din România*. Bucureşti: Humanitas.

Tratat de pace între România şi Puterile Aliate şi Asociate. 10 February 1947. Monitorul Oficial 199/30 August 1947. Bucureşti.

Wolff, R.L. 1967. *The Balkans in Our Time*. New York: Norton.

4 Methodology

This chapter outlines the methodological framework, the methods and the sources of information and evidence used in the empirical research. The chapter begins with the author's self-positioning within the Burrell and Morgan (1979) framework, described previously in the Chapter 2. The research methods and the information sources used in the empirical study are presented in the second part of the chapter. The chapter also includes a brief description of the history of the three enterprises investigated in the main part of the empirical research.

An interpretive perspective on the communist enterprise

As argued in Chapter 2, the main reason for using Burrell and Morgan's framework is its potential to outline the underlying conflict between two different sets of assumptions about the fundamental nature of organisations in communist regimes. But the same framework can be used to place the researcher's own set of assumptions, which is very important for two main reasons: on the one hand, it clarifies his perspective over society and social science, and on the other hand it brings more clarity over the aims and means used to investigate the study's subject.

The approach employed in this study is definitely placed in the quadrant named by Burrell and Morgan 'interpretivist'. The author's set of assumptions lies on the subjective side of the philosophy of science dimension and is characterised by an integrationist view of society. According to this paradigm, 'people socially and symbolically construct and sustain their own organizational realities' (Gioia and Pitre, 1990, p. 588). While the functionalist paradigm has dominated organisational theory and research for a long time, the interpretive paradigm may offer a better understanding of events and evolutions 'so the systems of interpretations and meaning, and the structuring and organizing processes, are revealed' (ibid.). The dominance of the functionalist paradigm is based on the natural science model. Within this paradigm, organisational science has been driven by the assumption of an objective organisation, existing 'out there', available for exploration, measurement and assessment. The deductive approach, based on constructing and testing hypotheses using statistical methods, seems to be the predominantly used research methodology.

All these aspects are significantly different in the case of the interpretivist paradigm. The organisation is structured by the patterned relationships developed by individuals, these relationships serving as heuristic and symbolic forms. The organisation is not only a rigid, pre-determined structure, based on a set of rules and procedures established elsewhere, but it consists also in a pattern of relationships, more or less formal, with a significant influence over its existence and evolution. The theory-building tends to be more inductive, starting with collection of data that are relevant to the informants, theory generation being iterative and nonlinear.

In the case of communist societies and especially in the understanding of the communist enterprises, the subjective, interpretive perspective is even more needed. It is widely accepted that the statistical analysis of hard economic data was not reliable enough to understand and to forecast the system's evolution and final collapse. As it will be argued in the following chapters, the official data mostly reflected the outcomes of negotiation between various actors rather than quantitative measurement of real economic performance. The plan targets were subject of a lengthy negotiation ritual, before being officially set by the authorities. Some targets were also very often negotiated during the planned period. Finally, the reported indicators were also subject of various manipulations, both by the enterprises – by dissimulation, and by the planning authorities – by planning excessive quantities of products for which the resources existed. The widespread existence of various types of informal relationships (e.g. *blat*, *pile*) also supports this perspective. Moreover, the social groups involved in the economic realm – the working class, Party apparatchiks, planners, government administrators, and last but not least, the managers, had to accommodate each other and focus on stability and functional co-ordination. The Party, the administrative structures, the workers and the managers were all involved in the organisational life and directly interested in the organisation's performance according to the ideological imperatives and within the prescribed frame of reference. Any failure to meet the targets had direct consequences for all these groups. Of course, some actors had more power than others and, according to the evidence collected and analysed in this study, the managers had emerged as the key actor. Overall, the enterprises' activity was structured by the informal patterns of relationships among these actors, rather than the top-down directives and bottom-up reporting as the functionalist perspective would suggest.

Another argument supporting the use of the interpretive paradigm in this research is based on the availability of empirical data. The statistical data published by communist regimes was notoriously unreliable, and Romania represents probably one of the most relevant examples in this matter. Moreover, the data still available for study is qualitative rather than quantitative. In the case of this research, with the exception of one archival document regarding the Carbochim enterprise, which permitted a quantitative analysis, all other sources of information require understanding and interpretation.

The research methods

Two main research methods were used in the empirical investigation: the interview and document analysis. The main sources of information investigated for the purposes of this study were: statistical data, documents found in national archives, monographs, transcripts of discussions between managers and students, and interviews with former employees of the selected enterprises and with other relevant persons involved in the economy during the communist period.

Unreliability and inconsistency represent the most important problems of information from communist Romania. Being aware of these problems, the researcher carefully analysed the sources and whenever was possible tried to verify the collected data using another source. Former employees of the investigated enterprises were identified and they were interviewed for a better understanding of the processes, relationships and phenomena described by the documents found in the archives. Their memories provided personal insights and information that would not have been recorded in official documents, views that could not have been freely expressed during the time of their employment, and also confirmed the accuracy and meaning of the archival information. Other individuals involved in the communist economy were interviewed using the same research instrument.

The interview

The interview was used because a significant number of former employees of Unirea and FMR had been identified as being available to share their consistent experience in the communist regime economy. Each participant was interviewed using a semi-structured list of issues for discussion. The ethical procedures of University of Glasgow were strictly observed and university's ethics committee approved the interview procedure. In the case of a few respondents, multiple sessions were required to clarify all relevant aspects of the respondent experience. The interviews were focused on the following topics:

- The managerial practices used in industrial enterprises during the communist regime.
- The planning methods used at enterprise level.
- The negotiation of the plan targets with ministers and other central structures.
- The human resources management principles and practices.

However, in many cases the respondents gave accounts of other significant events, relevant for these topics.

The same semi-structured interviews were conducted with individuals who held top or middle management positions in other organisations, and with academics who studied the economy during the communist regime. The main objective of these interviews was to verify if the accounts collected from former

Unirea and FMR employees could be confirmed, to get a wider description of the economic activity, of the relations between the enterprise and other state agencies – especially the State Planning Committee, and of the relations among different departments of other enterprises.

Also, since the National Archives only have holdings of documents until the 1970s, another objective of the interviews was to get a description of the evolution of all of the above-mentioned aspects in the last two decades of communism.

Document analysis

Three categories of documents were analysed in depth in this research:

- Archival documents produced by Unirea and Carbochim found in the National Archives deposit, Cluj branch.
- The monographs of Unirea and of FMR.
- The transcripts of more recent discussions between communist era managers and students.

The main and most extensive and original source of information was found in documents stored by the National Archives of Romania, Cluj branch. Extensive archival investigation was focused on documents regarding three enterprises. The main criteria used for selecting these enterprises was the availability of rich and relevant documents in the archives, and the representation of different industrial sectors. In addition to this, in the case of two enterprises (Unirea and FMR) a significant number of former employees were sought and identified in order to be interviewed. Moreover, each enterprise published a *monografie* (in English – monograph). The monographs included extensive descriptions of those enterprises' history and evolution, and a significant amount of statistical data. The data published in the monographs was identical with the figures reported under the communist regime; therefore there is no reason to consider it more reliable than the official statistics. However, the data regarding staff numbers was probably quite accurate.

The archival documents include correspondence between enterprise managers and government structures – planning committee and the ministry, personnel records regarding appointments, promotions and complaints.

In order to analyse the archival resources, the most relevant documents were selected after an overview of more than 10 dossiers with hundreds of documents each. The selected documents are spread over more than a decade of the communist regime, from 1951 up to 1962. The documents undoubtedly show the main problems of the Romanian centralised planning system.

Appendix 1 includes all archival documents selected for in-depth analysis in this part of the study. Appendix 2 includes the list of the former employees of Unirea and FMR that were interviewed with a brief description of each one's position, and the list of other interviewees and the managers that were recorded discussing with students in the first decade of Romanian post-communism. The respondents' anonymity was secured according to the accepted ethics regulations and procedures. They are identified with a code, and just the information relevant for this study purpose is disclosed.

The archived documents were usually produced and stored starting from 1945. Almost all documents identified in the archives can be grouped into three main categories: production and plan, personnel and development plans. The first category documents usually contain the main indicators of the plan transmitted by the state authorities, the periodical reports of the enterprise and a continuing correspondence aiming an almost continuous negotiation of the plan targets. The personnel documents contain periodic reports on the personnel structure of the enterprise, some of them in a very synthetic form, but other reports include name, position, education and salary. A smaller number of documents contain correspondence of the cadres department with other organisations. Files describing sensitive cases in which hiring was denied because of political reasons, or documents regarding the cadre reserve were also identified in the archives. The third category of documents contains mainly technical files regarding innovations or investments to be realised in the enterprise, according to the general development plan.

Finally, the perspectives of Romanian managers on the communist regime, and the values and principles that informed their behaviour were also subject of research. The study aimed to focus on the worldview of the Romanian managerial elite, its perspective on the communist period, and on the values and principles that lie behind its behaviour. The study was focused on the discourse of the Romanian post-communist managerial elite, and on the way the managers behaved as an interest group.

The study consisted in qualitative analysis of discussions between 143 leading managers of Romanian organisations and undergraduate students specialising in management studies from October 1994 until March 2000. The main objective of the meetings was to give students feedback from real-life management practitioners, from managers confronting real problems. The official topic of the meetings was 'The Management Paradigm'. Every meeting was moderated by a faculty member whose task was to keep the conversations focused on the topic. All meetings were video-recorded in order to be analysed later from various points of view. The transcriptions of the meetings formed the basis of this study. The findings represent a narrative regarding how Romanian managers 'produce, and reproduce, a specific interpretation of change which has operational and behavioural consequences' (O'Connor 1995, p. 774). The study aimed to identify the outlook and perspectives of the Romanian managers through a 'narrative about some narratives' (O'Connor 1995, p. 795).

A total of 98 per cent of the participant managers were leaders of private, state-owned or public organisations from Transylvania (the Western region of Romania). Thirty-eight managers (26.6 per cent) had not held any management positions before 1990, while the other participants (105 managers) had held management positions during the communist regime. All this latter group (with one exception) had held lower positions before 1990. All of them were deputy managers, or they held middle-level management positions under the communist regime, and after 1990 they advanced to higher positions. The results and conclusions of this part of the research were published in *Europe-Asia Studies* (Sucală, 2015).

Three enterprises: Unirea, FMR and Carbochim

The first enterprise selected for this empirical study was *Intreprinderea Unirea*. The archived documents of this enterprise were the richest source of information. The history of Unirea was summarised based on the information included in its monograph authored by Mercea (1990). Although *Intreprinderea Unirea* represents a particular case, the enterprise has an important level of relevance for the Romanian version of the communist industrialisation because of several reasons.

First, Unirea was part of the machine building industry, one of the main pillars of the communist industrialisation. This industry together with metallurgy, chemical and extractive industries accounted for more than 83 per cent of the total investment in industry in every single year between 1950 and 1989 (Tismăneanu, Dobrincu and Vasile, 2007, p. 224). These industries were grouped in the so-called Group A – investment goods producing industries, in contrast with the Group B – consumer goods producing industries (e.g. the textile, food industries).

Second, Unirea brought together the tradition of a nineteenth-century established workshop with the extensive development of the communist regime. More than that, at the end of the 1970s, a new enterprise was born out of a section of Unirea – the new FMR (*Fabrica de Maşini de Rectificat*). The monograph of FMR includes a collection of relevant memories of former employees – from workers to managers. The FMR case shows how a highly technologically important investment was planned and managed by the central authorities.

Third, the place Unirea and FMR occupied in the local economy was very important. The book *Istoria Clujului* (The History of Cluj) was edited by the historian Ştefan Pascu and published in 1974 by the local authorities. A few relevant data were selected in order to support this argument. Although the low level of reliability of Romanian statistical data is well known, the figures offer a significant perspective on the local industry. According to this book, the population of Cluj had increased between 1948 and 1974 from 121,753 to 214,812 (Pascu, 1974, p. 447). In 1973, the volume of the all industrial global production was 17 times higher than in 1950, while in the case of the machine building industry it was 38 times higher over the same period (Pascu, 1974, pp. 469–470). In another part of the book it is argued that the weight of the machine building industry in the total industrial production had increased from 17.7 per cent in 1950 to 34.7 per cent in 1973 (Pascu, 1974, p. 457). Among the enterprises of national importance (*importanţă republicană*) in the machine building and metal processing industries, Unirea is the first one mentioned and described. All these data suggest that Unirea was at the forefront of the industrialisation process, a relevant example of how this process was planned and implemented by the central authorities.

The third investigated enterprise was Carbochim Cluj-Napoca. This enterprise was established in 1949 as a producer of professional abrasive products. Initially it was named *Electrocarbon*, but in 1951 the name was changed to Carbochim. The enterprise was developed as the only Romanian producer of professional abrasive products during the communist period. The documents stored in the archives regarding this enterprise are not as rich as in the case of *Intreprinderea Unirea*. The exception represents a register (*Registru de personal*) with a detailed description of all hired employees from 1949 until 1963. During this period, 1,625 persons were hired, and the register records their education, nationality, marital status, political affiliation and military training. All these elements allowed a simple statistical analysis of the industrial workforce evolution over 14 years of the enterprise's development, in a case of a green field industrial investment.

The monographs

The brief histories of Unirea and FMR presented below summarise the information included in the monographs authored by Mercea (1990) and Savu (2013). The monographs provide detailed descriptions of the enterprise's history. The monographs were written not by historians but by former employees. Both authors were directors of Unirea, respectively FMR: Mercea was appointed as director of Unirea on 16 January 1990, and *Savu* was director of FMR between 1976 and 1990 (from 1976 to 1980 as a factory included in Unirea, and from 1981 to 1990 as an independent enterprise).

In order to complete the monograph, the authors had access mainly to the enterprise's archives, but also to other documents (e.g. from the Chamber of Commerce for the period before 1948). The monographs provide important information related to the evolution of production, the number of employees or the development of the enterprise. They also provide lists with the names of management staff during the investigated period.

The history of Unirea and FMR

Unirea was founded as a small mechanical shop in 1840, and it was developed by the Second World War into a mechanical factory. After the 1948 nationalisation it was named *Intreprinderea Unirea*.

What today is known as Unirea was founded as a small workshop producing agricultural machinery, and it had remained a small workshop until 1869 when it was taken over by a bigger company. At the beginning, it had produced ploughs, seeders, cutting machines and other machinery for agriculture. In the mid-nineteenth century, Cluj was in the process of industrialisation. The number of industrial companies was increasing and events such as industrial exhibitions were often organised. At the end of the century, the development process of the company was in progress. The *Law for the Industry Protection* adopted in 1881 had helped the industrial companies to develop at a faster pace. The company produced at that moment steam engines, pumps, mechanical mills, weighing machines, etc. Another law, which was issued in 1890 with the same objective of industrial development, had granted more incentives. Nevertheless, in 1901, the company went bankrupt and it was taken over once again. After 1908, the company started a new development process and the number of workers increased to 50. The range of industrial products had widened, with more sophisticated machines and equipment being produced. World War I had a strong impact on the company's activity. Because the owner refused to execute military orders, all the employees were called up into the army. After the end of World War I and the union of Transylvania with the Romanian Kingdom in 1919, the company changed hands again. The peak of the company's activity was 1929 when it had roughly 600 workers and 3 technical managers. The 1929–33 economic crises, however, significantly affected the company's activity. At the end of 1933, the number of workers dropped to 402. However, between 1933 and 1939 the company resumed the development process and it started to produce industrial elevators, heating systems, vacuum systems, cranes, railway equipment, a wide variety of pumps, etc. In that period, the company began to produce machines and equipment for the textile industry.

In 1940, Nazi Germany and Fascist Italy arbitrated the territorial dispute between Romania and Hungary. The result of the arbitration is known as the Second Vienna Award by which the Northern Transylvania including Cluj was given to Hungary. Therefore, the company was militarised and it started to work for the Hungarian army. After 1945 the company was administered by the State Committee for the Administration of the Enemy Assets until 1948 when it was nationalised.

Starting in 1949 the company was named *Intreprinderea Unirea* and it was fully integrated into the planned economy. After nationalisation, Unirea was transformed into an industrial complex aiming to produce machines and equipment for the textile industry. In the spirit of the communist perspective on industrial development, the enterprise included almost all phases of the technological flow from the metallurgical section (*secția turnătorie*) to final assembly (*secția montaj*) including a shop for tools production and maintenance. Unirea considerably benefited from the new regime's pursuit of industrialisation. In the first decade of communism the number of employees increased from 745 in 1959 to 1,158 in 1960. According to Mercea (1990, p. 62), the value of the annual production almost tripled in the same period. By 1975, the total number of the employees had increased to 3,949. However, the total number of the employees in industrial activity shows an interesting evolution. According to the same source, the highest number was reached in 1980 – 3,860 employees – and then the number decreased to 3,272 employees in 1987. The work productivity had reached its peak in 1980 (Mercea, 1990, p. 87). Starting with 1973, Unirea began to export industrial machines to different countries on both sides of the iron curtain. The main destinations for exports were the USSR, Italy, France, Germany, Poland, Bulgaria, Bangladesh, Cyprus and Greece. However, the figure for exports as a percentage of total production varied considerably – 3.1 per cent in 1973, 10.8 per cent in 1974, 22.3 per cent in 1975, 16.4 per cent in 1976, 20.5 per cent in 1977, 2.3 per cent in 1978, 2.5 per cent in 1979, 7.2 per cent in 1980, 33 per cent in 1983, 53.3 per cent in 1984 and 23 per cent in 1988 (Mercea, 1990, pp. 70–82). Although Unirea represents a particular case, and the evolution of the numbers of employees and of productivity could be related to many specific factors such as the development plan of the enterprise or the evolution of the textile industry at the global level, a similarity with the overall evolution of the Romanian economy can be observed.

According to Savu (2013, p. 9), the idea to produce grinding machines in Cluj was the result of the friendship between a professor of mechanical engineering of the Cluj Polytechnic Institute and the ministry of Machines Building Industry. Because of this friendship significant investment funds were allotted in 1971, and the construction of FMR as a section of Unirea had begun in the same year. Because of lack of tradition, human resources and academic knowledge in the field of grinding machines (*maşini de rectificat*), the whole project was a challenge. At that moment Unirea had the most advanced technology in Cluj, and consequently it received the new task to build and manage the new factory of grinding machines. Since Unirea activity had been focused on textile machines, the task to develop the grinding machines section was perceived as an excessive burden, and whenever possible was neglected and marginalised. The formal separation occurred 10 years later and was a relief for both enterprises.

The production had started in June 1973, and in 1974 the construction of a new section for hydraulic equipment was decided. In July 1973, the first 79 workers were transferred from Unirea to FMR. They then began to install the machines and started the production. At the end of 1973, 254 employees were recorded as working for FMR (Savu, 2013, pp. 46–47). Starting in 1973, the number of employees and the global production constantly increased. Relatively similar to Unirea, the highest number of employees was recorded in 1986 – 1,713 employees, followed by a decline to 1,575 employees in 1987. The number of workers employed in 1987 (1,279) was lower than the figure recorded for 1981 – 1,412 workers (Savu, 2013, pp. 26–36). While in the period, 1976–80, the exports were under 10 per cent (Mercea, 1990, p. 75), a significant increase was visible after 1983: 13.21 per cent in 1984, 16.28 per cent in 1988 and 42.09 per cent in 1989 (Savu, 2013, p. 31).

The managers' perspective

For the first decade after the end of communist rule, managers were drawn mainly from the second level of management of the state-owned enterprises of communist times. As a group they had been educated, selected and formed in late communism. Among the main advantages of this social group were that they demonstrated considerable survival capacity, ideological neutrality and an ability to manoeuvre in a turbulent environment. On the other hand, they had to adapt to their new environment drawing on the skills and mentality they had developed under the old regime.

The empirical research was focused mainly on individuals who had held management positions before 1989. The analysis was structured into four major categories: career, management or organisational context before 1989, the transition process and future expectations. This book makes use of the relevant quotations and conclusions regarding the industrial organisations' context in the communist regime. The methodological approach employed in the investigation was discourse analysis. There were three major assumptions implied in this investigation. First, the analysed managers represented only the 'successful' part of the communist organisational elite. Those managers who did not survive the transition and keep their positions of power in organisations, or who retired just after 1990, were not invited to take part. As a consequence, all results, conclusions, assumptions or hypotheses generated by this investigation are relevant only for a part of the communist managerial elite. Second, it was assumed that the level of accuracy of managerial discourse was reasonable. Third, the managers' views on the Romanian organisational context represented only one version of reality. This version belonged to a part of the communist technocratic elite, to people who succeeded in the last part of the communist regime, but who also succeeded in the first decade of the transition to capitalism.

The study's conclusions reveal that while, at the time of the research, the managers shared a focus on privatisation as a solution for the problems of an economy that had been dependent on state structures, and they displayed a consistent ideological neutrality, a short-term approach to managerial activity, and a lack of any pronounced ideological or political issues in their discourses. It should be observed that all the comments of the managers quoted in the following chapters were very pragmatic in their focus – concerned with the advantages and disadvantages of the planned economy for the daily managerial activity, and were not related with communist or liberal ideologies. They did not adopt the language of some post-1989 politicians or intellectuals in seeing the transition in terms of dichotomies between communist serfdom and freedom, socialism and capitalism, planned economy and the free-market economy, or collectivism and individualism.

This conclusion contradicts to some extent the argument made by Fotaki (2009, p. 217) that the managers' behaviour during transition was driven by 'a shared belief in the market's superior ability to deliver economic growth, to create wealth and contribute to the well-being of the population after the demise of the defunct socialist ideology'. And it also contradicts the suggestion of Farazmand (1999, p. 322) that behind the Western-oriented changes exists 'a strong ideological, market-based, conservative trend'; the findings show the managers taking a pragmatic approach behind the chaotic ideological, political and economic evolution of industrial organisations in post-communist Romania. The Romanian managers' perspectives on the communist period can be structured into three main areas: the advantages of the communist system, the shortcomings of the system, and the expectations they had for the system's failure. This study has been published by the author earlier (Sucalã, 2015), but the most relevant findings for the subject of this book are presented in the next two chapters.

References

Burrell, G. and Morgan, G. 1979. *Sociological Paradigms and Organisational Analysis*. Aldershot: Ashgate.

Farazmand, A. 1999. The Elite Question: Toward a Normative Elite Theory of Organization. *Administration & Society*, 32(3).

Fotaki, M. 2009. Maintaining the Illusion of a Free Health Care in Post-Socialism: A Lacanian Analysis of Transition from Planned to Market Economy. *Journal of Organizational Change Management*, 22(2).

Gioia, D. and Pitre, W. 1990. Multiparadigm Perspectives on Theory Building. *The Academy of Management Review*, 15(4).

Mercea, G. 1990. Unirea Cluj-Napoca. 150 de ani. 1840–1990. Cluj-Napoca.

O'Connor, E.S. 1995. Paradoxes of Participation: Textual Analysis and Organizational Change. *Organization Studies*, 16(5).

Pascu, A. Ed. 1974. *Istoria Clujului*. Cluj: Consiliul Popular al Municipiului Cluj.

Savu, D. 2013. Fabrica de Maşini de Rectificat. Oameni, fapte, amintiri. Cluj-Napoca: Editura Mega.

Sucală, V.I. 2015. Managers of Transition – Leadership in Post-Communist Romanian Companies. *Europe-Asia Studies*, 67(4).

Tismăneanu, V., Dobrincu, D. and Vasile C. 2007. *Raport Final al Comisiei Prezidenţiale pentru Analiza Dictaturii Comuniste din România*. Bucureşti: Humanitas.

5 Plan and enterprise in communist Romania

As noted at the end of Chapter 3, while Romania had developed its own distinctive national form of communist economic management, in doing so it also retained many aspects of the Soviet model, including state ownership, a centrally managed economy, and one-party, communist government. According to authors such as Jowitt (1974) and Berliner (1957), this has meant that in adopting versions of the Soviet model, communist regimes generally displayed many of the characteristics and problems of the Soviet command system, including hoarding of resources, and dissimulation in attempting to influence plan targets. A central concern for this research, therefore, in examining questions of planning and enterprise management in the Romanian economy is the question of how distinctive or how similar were the characteristics, problems and attempted solutions adopted by managers and planners in Romania under communist rule.

The empirical investigation presented in this chapter aims to reveal the main organisational practices in Romanian communist enterprises. It focuses on the relation between the enterprises and the planning structures – mostly industry branch ministries. This part of the study is based mostly on documents identified in Romanian National Archives, and on additional information collected through interviews with former employees of Unirea and FMR. In its argumentation, it also draws on other sources of information such as interviews with persons involved in the economy during the communist regime and newspapers interviews, and the discussions between students and managers leading Romanian companies in the first decade of the transition period.

The Soviet industrial enterprise

As noted in Chapters 1 and 3, the theoretical framework for studies of relations between enterprises and planning structures under communism draws on the studies of the Soviet industrial enterprise beginning in the 1950s. The first main empirical research on the Soviet industrial system was produced within the framework of the Harvard Project on the Soviet Social System. Joseph Berliner, whose book *Factory and Manager in the USSR* (1957) presented the results of a significant number of interviews with former Soviet managerial officials, and a general overview of the project, of which the Berliner's study of the Soviet industrial enterprise was only a part, was provided by Raymond Bauer, Alex Inkeles and Clyde Kluckhohn (1956).

According to Bauer, Inkeles and Kluckhohn (1956, p. 44), over-control and over-centralisation were the main vulnerabilities of the Soviet economic system. The centralised bureaucracy generated a rigid control apparatus and many illicit methods of getting things done, while at the same time managers largely were committed to the system and tried to find ways of making it work. The authors considered that managerial acceptance of the Soviet system was one important element of the system's strength. The investigation showed 'the apparent competence and vigour of the Soviet industrial managers' as well as 'the degree to which the managerial group accepts the main structure of Soviet society, particularly the organisation of such realms as industry, and regards it as worthy of respect and emulation' (Bauer, Inkeles and Kluckhohn, 1956, pp. 227–228). However, alongside the managers' desire for mainly ameliorative measures of the managerial world, the study also revealed problems of lack of trust and confidence, and political interference in day-to-day activity.

Looking ahead, the authors forecasted, there would be an increasing pressure of the Soviet elite towards better morale in organisations while the introduction of more modern technology would require a more educated work force with a higher degree of autonomy, and therefore performance would depend on the workers' morale. It may be presumed that some of these characteristics were based on the mechanism of mutual confirmation of value and competence. In the absence of a real competition for management positions based on transparent criteria, promotion decisions were usually taken behind closed doors, under the strict supervision of apparatchiks, and usually manipulating ambiguous criteria. Therefore, it seemed somehow natural for managers to think that the system was worthy of admiration and respect since it selected them to manage a part of it. This was reflected in the 'wooden' language used under the communist regimes, such as, taking a Romanian example, using the expression 'to be entrusted with the position of' (*i s-a încredinţat funcţia de*) as synonymous for 'to be appointed as'. The expression meant that the respective person was considered reliable enough to hold that position, while the criteria for being reliable were usually decided by a selection's or a panel's subjective judgement. In this way, the whole structure of the managerial elite was altered by subjective judgements, and every director was a 'little Ceauşescu' in his own domain. Every person within the power structure had to be 'entrusted' by the higher authorities, and had to entrust his subordinates. This system may explain the characteristics identified by Bauer, Inkeles and Kluckhohn' (1956) – the admiration for the system that decided that they are competent managers, the desire to limit any change that may alter the rules according to which they were selected and which they used in the management processes, and the lack of confidence since they had to perform in a highly subjective environment in which the reality was altered to fit the ideological imperatives and the plans.

Managerial practices in Soviet industry

The most detailed report of the Harvard project's findings regarding the Soviet enterprise viewed through the eyes of former managers was provided by Berliner (1957). The main conclusion of the study was that 'managers follow an entirely different set of rules which have no officially recognised existence and which, moreover, sharply contradict the official rules' (Berliner, 1957, p. 318). These practices were constantly criticised in the official discourse, but their persistence showed their important role in the Soviet planned economy.

According to Berliner these managerial practices fell into three groups:

1. The 'safety factor' – the tendency to hoard various kinds of reserves. This could take different forms – from manipulating the planning process in order to obtain targets smaller than what could actually be produced, to hoarding materials, spare parts and workforce.
2. Simulation – producing a degree of quality of outputs, or producing a different range of quantities than those planned.
3. *Blat* – 'the use of personal influence to manipulate ministry officials into giving the enterprise an easy production target, or to persuade a bank official to overlook an unplanned use of enterprise funds' (Berliner, 1957, p. 319). The *blat* practice was connected with the invisible occupation of the *tolkach* – 'the specialist in obtaining all manner of scarce commodities through a combination of influence and gifts' (ibid.).

All these practices conflicted with the laws, regulations and official Party's discourse, and therefore the question Berliner tried to answer was why the Soviet manager engaged in such practices. Berliner concluded that the manager 'feels compelled to do so, that the pressures exerted by the economic environment leave him no other way in which to achieve his goals' (Berliner, 1957, p. 320). The unreasonably high level of the plan targets combined with constant shortages and delays in deliveries were the two dominant features of the Soviet economy that generated the managerial practices described before. Berliner synthesised the phenomenon as follows: 'the manager with good *blat* in the proper quarters and the services of a competent *tolkach* is a step ahead of his colleagues in the competition for scarce resources' (ibid.). The control system also contributed to the survival of these practices. The control agencies focused on special problems such as repeated plan under-fulfilment. Therefore, the best strategy to avoid control was to report plan fulfilment regularly. On the other hand, a strict control would show the large scale of these irregular practices. Consequently, a 'looking the other way' attitude of control officials was often mentioned by the interviewed managers. Moreover, a 'family relationship' between Party secretary, chief accountant and manager often appeared, all of them sharing the rewards and prestige that came with regular plan fulfilment.

Finally, Berliner analysed the reasons why the Soviet state tolerated these practices. The author considered that the high rate of industrial growth required that people be pushed beyond the limits to which they would voluntarily go. Therefore, these managerial practices were 'the price the state has been willing to pay for the achievement of its objective' (Berliner, 1957, p. 329). On the other hand, Berliner argued that these practices had some advantages, serving as counterweights to forces which, if uncontrolled, would result in greater dysfunctionalities in the economy. For example, the plan negotiation compensated for the 'constant bias in the planning system toward unrealistically high targets' (Berliner, 1957, p. 326).

In 1976 Berliner published a further book entitled *The Innovation Decision in Soviet Industry*. Focused on innovation processes in industry, the book provides a detailed account of the structure of the Soviet economy, economic planning, research and development organisations, prices and profits, and incentives and decision rules. According to Berliner, there was a significant degree of bias against innovation generated by the structural uncertainty over the supply of materials and equipment (Berliner, 1976, p. 92). The author considered as a sufficient explanation of this problem the state of disequilibrium that characterised inter-enterprise transactions. The policy of excessively taut planning, the imperfections of pricing methods and centralised planning were the main reasons for this disequilibrium (Berliner, 1976, p. 62).

Then in 1988, Berliner published a book entitled *Soviet Industry from Stalin to Gorbachev*, in which the concluding chapter was based on the findings of the Soviet Interview Project (SIP). The author also cited a few SIP project reports authored by Susan Linz (1985, 1986 and 1987). The chapter describes the continuities and changes in industrial management along almost five decades of development. While the economic structure had faced significant changes, and national planning was more sophisticated and based on computers and mathematical modelling, 'many of the practices of the past have survived virtually unchanged' (Berliner, 1988, p. 277). The most important change identified by the author was in technology, 'the fruits of the arduous industrialisation drive' (Berliner, 1988, p. 271). In the same period the labour force had changed dramatically. Most of the workers were urban-born, with a consistent technical education, living in far better conditions than their predecessors. The new managers were also better educated, more self-confident, with a higher social status and with a far better living standard.

But while so many aspects of the industrial realm had improved in three decades of industrialisation, many others had remained constant in the discourse of interviewed managers: 'portions of the SIP interviews read as if they came right out of the Harvard interviews' (Berliner, 1988, p. 277). Berliner identified and discussed ten practices that had survived virtually unchanged during that period.

1 The 'ratchet' principle consisted in raising the target for the next period to the level realised in the current period if this level over-fulfilled the plan. This practice was one of the main sources of plan tautness.
2 There was a persistent practice of obtaining plan targets lower than the production capability.

3 The hoarding of materials was also a common practice due to the chronic supply problems. Hoarding of labour was a practice less present in the responses of SIP informants than in the Harvard study. The reason for this evolution was a stronger control of authorities.
4 Related to materials hoarding was another practice – barter and resale. The SIP informants reported that barter and resale were more often practiced than in the past.
5 Enterprise autarky was also a persistent practice used for minimising the risk of dependence on uncertain deliveries.
6 Lower levels of enthusiasm for innovation and new technologies had also been a persistent feature.
7 The managers' preference for producing established products using existing technology was another form of the safety factor.
8 A side effect of the planning system was a lower concern over the quality of products. In spite of strong official propaganda and even of criminal penalties imposed on persons guilty of producing sub-quality products, this poor-quality production had persisted in Soviet industry.
9 The uneven pace of production, with a lower rate during the first part of the plan period followed by storming in the last part was another practice almost impossible to eradicate in Soviet industry.
10 Finally, the constant focus on relating wages with performance was identified among the persistent practices. Almost all Soviet leaders from Stalin to Gorbachev expressed the need to connect salaries with workers' contribution.

The shortage syndrome

According to Berliner, the *shortage syndrome* was the main reason for most of these practices. The *shortage syndrome* included 'quality deterioration, hoarding, barter, supply expediters, gifts and bribery, organisational autarky and so forth' (Berliner, 1988, p. 286). Berliner argued that a *shortage syndrome* occurs whenever an economy functions under conditions of persistent shortage, regardless of the political system in which it exists. But in the case of Soviet industry, the practices described above derived from particular features of the Soviet system of planning and its relationship to state enterprises: the Soviet economic system's 'mandatory quantitative output targets and centralised distribution of intermediate products' (Berliner, 1988, p. 291). The centralised economic planning had generated the persistence of these managerial practices, in spite of successive attempts to reform the planning system, and in spite of technological development.

As Trotsky had argued in 1937 regarding the Soviet Union society:

> an *a priori* economic plan – above all in a backward country with 170 million population, and a profound contradiction between city and country – is not a fixed gospel, but a rough working hypothesis which must be verified and reconstructed in the process of its fulfilment.

Trotsky also suggested that for a successful implementation of economic plans, two levers were needed. The first lever would be the real political participation of the working class in all decision-making processes. The second financial lever would take the form of 'a real testing out of a priori calculations with the help of a universal equivalent' which would require a stable monetary system.

Thus, drawing on Trotsky, it is important keep in mind that the Soviet system was a particular form of planned economy that developed in adverse political and monetary conditions, while according to Berliner, there were particular features of the Soviet planning system from the longer list of features of a planned economy, that were responsible for its problems. Mandatory targets and centralised distribution of components and materials were major factors responsible for the particular practices entailed in the shortage syndrome: managerial practices based on poor-quality production, hoarding of materials and labour, and informal bargaining with planners and between enterprises. These points should be kept in mind in discussing the detailed character of planning and enterprise behaviour in the Romanian planned economy and the degrees to which it was similar or different from the Soviet model on which was based.

The plan – from theory to Romanian practice

Examining the planning process and its consequences at the enterprise level in Romania, my investigation aimed to identify the enterprises' practices related to the plan and planning system, and to understand the main reasons behind these practices.

However, a brief description of the main characteristics of the Romanian planning system is necessary before analysing the empirical evidence. The main indicators used by the authorities and the enterprises were: the global production (*producția globală*), productivity and the salaries fund (*fondul de salarii*). The communist regime and consequently the planning authorities had always pushed enterprises for an increasing global production, this being considered a fundamental indicator of the industrial development, which would validate the Party's policies and directives. In addition, the planning authorities used the salaries fund to control a gradual salary increase according to the Party's strategy. Both indicators were considered the most important measures of success.

Global production can be increased in two basic ways: by increasing the number of employees, which would also increase the salaries fund proportionally and therefore keep productivity constant; and by more efficient processes, which would reduce the norm of time spent for technological operations. In this way, a constant number of workers will produce a larger quantity of products, and therefore the productivity will increase and the cost per unit will decrease. In order to increase the overall economic efficiency, the global production should rise faster than salaries, and therefore the productivity should permanently be on an ascendant trend.

A more efficient technology is based on a mix of three components: more efficient equipment and machines, better trained workers and a better organised production flow. The practical expression of technology's efficiency is the norm of time (*norma de timp*) – the standardised time required for a technical operation. Norm of time is a very important element in production management and based on it, the total amount of labour required to produce a certain quantity of products can be calculated.

On 19 February 1953, the Political Bureau of the Central Committee of PMR held a meeting with a new system of norms and salaries in the economy as the main item on its agenda. The verbatim record of the meeting shows the Party's approach on these particular issues (Moraru and Moraru, 2012, pp. 118–132). As it was argued in the previous chapters, the norm of time (*norma de timp*) is the practical expression of the efficiency of technology – the standardised time required for a technical operation. The norm of time is a very important element in production management and based on it, the total amount of labour required to produce a certain quantity of products can be calculated. More efficient equipment and machines, better trained workers and a better organised production flow are the main factors contributing to the increase of efficiency and reducing the time required for certain technological operations. While in a market economy, each company is focused on increasing efficiency, in order to reduce the costs and to be more competitive, in communist Romania the centralised system created a strong incentive for enterprises to make all efforts to increase the norms of time, because bigger norms produced a bigger salaries fund. Usually, the norms were proposed by the enterprises and verified and approved by the ministry's authorities. For most usual technical operations, the norms were standardised. But in the case of new products, enterprises had the opportunity to artificially inflate the norms of time in order to increase the salaries fund. This practice was identified as early as in the first year of the first five-year plan. Hoarding labour time was a very important method used by enterprises to avoid disruptions of the production process.

In a centralised economy the technology, machines and equipment are under strict control through investment plans (*planul de investiții*). The number of employees is also controlled, subject of detailed and periodic reports. In a market economy, each company is highly interested in being more efficient, in order to reduce the costs and to be more competitive. Therefore, each company will strictly supervise its operations and it will try to optimise the production flow. The reduction of the time spent for different technological operations of time is a natural and logical objective for each productive company.

The main principles of the planned economy had a contrary effect, with bigger norms of time generating bigger salaries fund. In the Romanian case, this system created a strong incentive for enterprises to make all effort to increase the norms of time. Usually, the norms were proposed by the enterprises and verified and approved by the ministry authorities. For most usual technical operations, the norms were standardised. But in the case of new products, enterprises had the opportunity to artificially inflate the norms of time in order to increase salaries fund. This practice was identified as early as in the first year of the first five-year plan. Hoarding labour time was a very important method used by enterprises to avoid disruptions of the production process. Usually, these disruptions were: the interruption of production due to lack of supplies; unexpected changes in plan targets; challenging investment plans; the constant pressure to increase productivity, which was easier to accomplish using hidden resources of labour time; and intervals of intensive work, usually at the end of each reporting period.

In the Romanian centralised economy, the salaries fund was calculated by multiplying the average hourly salary with the number of hours of work required for the planned production. Therefore, the specific norm of time for each operation was the key element for the calculation of the total number of hours. Due to the Party's push for extensive and also intensive development, the planning authorities also pushed the enterprises for a constant and significant increase of global production and productivity. While for global production the planning authorities had assured, in most cases, the required resources and the clients, the productivity increase was considered the enterprise's task.

According to the statement made by Miron Constantinescu:

> last year the norms were revised, but most of them were improved in practice by 40–50–80, even 100%. This happened because of the new Soviet equipment and machines, because of the machines our country has produced, and because of the increase of the political and technical level of our workers. Therefore it is required a new correction, according to the new industrial potential.
>
> (Moraru and Moraru, 2012, p. 122)

Since the plan for 1953 was based on an increase of productivity by 14 per cent, and of global production by 19 per cent, it resulted logically that the norms should have been smaller. Consequently, the Party's leadership issued a directive regarding this reduction. Another important issue was decided in the same directive: corrections of salaries in some industrial branches such as metallurgy, machines building, oil and gas exploitation. Basically, the new system increased the hourly salary in heavy industry. In the language of that time 'it gives a better settlement to salaries' system and to workers' income' (*dă o așezare mai bună a sistemului de salarizare și veniturilor muncitorilor*). According to Gheorghiu-Dej, this new salaries' system would bring a considerable improvement, and would prove the superiority of the communist regime. While a small part of the meeting was dedicated to the description and analysis of the new salaries' system, a significantly longer part was dedicated to discussing the means through which this directive should be promoted and communicated to workers. As Gheorghiu-Dej concluded:

> It should be made a synthesis on a page, describing the new norms, the need for change, the objective, the basic principles, and the workers' advantages. So a directive should be issued for Party's organisations, unions and youth communist organisations. It is their business how would they proceed further. (…) We have this opportunity to verify the Party rank and file, the political level of our members.
>
> (Moraru and Moraru, 2012, p. 125)

The only technical clarification regarding the directive was made by Miron Constantinescu, who said that the exact figures will be calculated in each enterprise based on the principles, instructions and industrial branch appendixes. The verbatim record suggests a notable disconnection between the real problems faced by enterprises and planning authorities, and the approach and solutions dictated by the highest political echelon.

It must be also noted that this Political Bureau meeting had been held only a few months before the meetings with Soviet leaders held on 8–14 July 1953 in Moscow, described in Chapter 3. At that meetings Romania was represented by Gheorghiu-Dej, Miron Constantinescu and Chivu Stoica. The Soviet Union was represented by Khrushchev, Malenkov, Molotov, Mikoyan, Pervukhin and Lavrentiev. The Soviet representatives were highly critical regarding the Romanian planned economy, especially regarding the Danube-Black Sea channel, the excessive development of heavy industry and the underinvestment in agriculture and the consumer goods industries. Molotov summarised their criticism (Berindei, Dobrincu, Goşu, 2009, p. 430): 'You feel safe under Soviet protection. Without our support you would be overthrown in less than two weeks. If you won't bond with the people, even we won't be able to help you'. Malenkov described Romanian economic policy as 'erroneous, illiterate (*agramatnâi* in Romanian transliteration) and even dangerous' (Berindei, Dobrincu, Goşu, 2009, p. 428). A few months after these meetings, the Romanian leaders decided to embark on a new pathway towards economic development, which was also described in the Chapter 3. As Ţãranu (2004b, p. 168) argued, this new path was the exclusive the result of the Soviet pressures. One important aspect discussed by the Political Bureau was related to salaries and norms. According to the Report presented by Miron Constantinescu at the meeting of Political Bureau on 5 August 1953, the salaries system had to be fairly reset (*justa reaşezare a sistemului de salarizare*) 'according to the political and economic importance of each economic branch' (Ţãranu, 2004a, p. 157). In the same report, the Party leadership decided on the liquidation of salary equality (*lichidarea nivelării în salarizare*), an aspect mentioned and enforced in the labour law issued in 1949. As well, the report mentioned the need for motivating forms of salaries such as the *acordul progresiv*, *acordul premial* and other reward forms, both for workers and for management positions. This report was the first document in which a controversial form of remuneration – *acordul global* was also mentioned. The Party leadership decided to implement this form of remuneration in a narrow industrial branch – *construcţii montaj*.

The production norms were also subject of this report. In this case, the Party leadership decided to 'improve the norms only in the enterprises where the organisational measures had been successfully implemented' and to waive the annual recalculation of the norms.

An interesting discussion regarded the main reasons for all these mistakes. According to the verbatim record of the meeting of the Political Bureau which was held on 3 August 1953, Bodnãraş identified the first reason, or the first culprit, as the Political Bureau itself (Ţãranu, 2004b, pp. 168–188): 'We met too seldom to discuss the economic problems, we let too much responsibility on CSP [State Planning Committee]. Moreover, we did not control the CSP enough'. Basically, the CSP managed the economy incorrectly, it pushed too much onto heavy industry, and it neglected agriculture and the consumer goods industries. The Party general secretary, Gheorghiu-Dej concluded:

> The economic policy is not CSP's responsibility, it is our responsibility. CSP's fault was the lack of attention, the lack of feedback, and when they give us feedback, they are not convincing enough. We considered that the economists are there, and so we don't have to supervise them. But it is our responsibility to guide them, to help them. CSP should study thoroughly all economic aspects, they should apply scientific methods. CSP is the most important institution in the process of building the socialism in our country.

However, among many decisions to reduce the investment in heavy industry, in the machine building industry, to invest more in agriculture or in retail distribution network, Gheorghiu-Dej also stated the fundamental principle of Romanian development: 'heavy industry remains the base of the basis (*baza bazelor*) for building the socialism'.

Apparently, the *Noul curs* meant a step back in the strategy of pressing the enterprises through plan targets, especially by using productivity and salary funds as the main constrictions. But as it was argued in the previous chapters based on the analysis of the correspondence between *Unirea* and the planning authorities, all measures included in this report had mostly a propagandistic character, and the industrialisation process had been resumed following the same principles. Just three years after this meeting, Brucan (2012, p. 77) recalls Gheorghiu-Dej saying, 'if we don't turn 180 degrees in our relation with the Soviets, we are lost'. From that moment on, the extensive industrialisation had been perceived by Romanian leaders not only as a symbol of the correct communist strategy, but also as a symbol of independence and nationalism.

Any failure in fulfilling the plan targets would have resulted in a reduction of the salaries fund. Therefore, managers had few possible strategies: first, to reduce the targets at a realistic level; second, to create buffers of labour time to compensate for an eventual salaries fund decrease; and third, to dissimulate targets un-fulfilment. Probably these strategies were combined by the managers depending on the specific context of each industry or period. The ultimate strategy identified in a few cases was blackmailing the authorities with possible social unrest because of reduced salaries.

Results of the empirical study

In order to identify the enterprises' practices related to planning and managerial practices in communist Romania, six main practices existent in the industrial realm have been identified in this empirical study of selected industrial enterprises. Each practice is presented below together with its supporting evidence.

Taut plan and shortage of resources from the beginning

The plan's tautness and shortage of resources characterised Romanian industry from the very beginning of communist rule. While in the first decade of communist regime labour was the predominant insufficient resource, at the beginning of 1960s the shortage of raw resources had become endemic in Romanian enterprises.

Even in 1951 which was the first year of the first five-year plan, the correspondence between Unirea managers and the Planning Department of the industry's branch ministry shows a consistent shortage of labour force at all levels – from workers to engineers. Many documents have been found in the enterprise's archive supporting this conclusion, but this aspect will be discussed in the next chapter. An example is the document D2, which starts by acknowledging the receipt of the plan of work and salaries for the fourth quarter of 1951, but it also states that the plan 'is not enough given the present and future tasks and this requires a supplementary number of employees and an increased salaries fund'. On the document's three pages, the author presented in detail the enterprise's case for more workers, technicians, engineers and clerks, as well as for an increased salaries fund.

The chronic shortages of raw materials in the Romanian economy had begun to be officially mentioned as early as the beginning of 1960s. As the document D12 shows, the ministry had decided to form a special working group to decide measures across the whole industry in order to reduce the consumption of specific elements. The group had to include specialists in design, heat-treatment, tools and metallurgy. The group's main tasks were to reduce the consumption of steel and cast iron alloyed with scarce elements, by using alloys with less of such elements, by improvements of technologies, by reducing the material losses and by re-designing the products in order to reduce these alloys. The recovery of such materials from metallic waste and scrap was also an objective of this group. The group had to produce an impressive bureaucratic package of technical regulations, records and plans for all enterprises. More than that, each enterprise had to submit its technical documentation to be approved by the group, which was also in charge with 'approval on a case by case basis and for a limited time only, based on technically and economically justified requests, of the use of steel alloyed with scarce elements and cast iron beyond the planned quantities'.

The group also monitored the designers of design institutes and design bureaus regarding the rational use and replacement of alloys with scarce element steel and cast iron in the design of machinery and equipment. As a result, the group had an extensive list of tasks and responsibilities, and it had also to 'ask for the help of specialists from research and design institutes, production directions and may ask for any technical documentation from the ministry's enterprises and directions'.

No later than five days after the document was issued, it was decided that each production direction of the ministry should allocate responsibility for the problems of rational use and consumption reduction of these alloys. The order stated that groups of specialists charged with this objective had to be established in every enterprise and research and design institute which used scarce elements from all industrial branches of the ministry. The groups had an objective to create a record of all parts made of alloyed and scarce elements of steel and cast iron, which would be sent for approval to the Technical Direction department of the ministry, together with proposed measures to reduce the consumption of scarce elements.

In less than a year, another government directive (D16) was issued focusing on the shortage of cast iron. The order begins stating that 'Since the balance of iron foundries is tautened for 1962, it is necessary to take measures in order to ensure the fulfilment of the production plan based on the actual supply of iron foundry production allocated through state plan'. According to D16 all ministry deputy general directors and directors of enterprises had to take measures to fulfil the production plan, using the strict quarterly quotas allocated for cast iron, ensuring strictly the necessary stock for the end and beginning of each period, being aware that no additional quantity would be available. They were also required to replace some of the parts made out of cast iron, with parts made from metallic profiles and welded board. For this purpose, the enterprises had to make concrete proposals indicating the resulting metal weight savings.

A further document, D17, clarified the political directives behind the pressure for consumption reduction of some raw materials. It called from the very beginning 'for the fulfilment of the directives of the 3rd Congress of PMR providing the reduction of specific consumption of ferrous rolled metal in machine building by 22% in 1965 compared to 1959, and by 30–33% of non-ferrous metals'. It went on to state that:

> Having found that in 1961, the scheduled task to reduce the specific consumption of metal by 5% compared to 1960 was not fulfilled, in order to prevent the infringement of consumption norms and to fulfil and to exceed the average planned metal savings, as well as for a better standardisation of the metal use in 1962 and beyond, the following measures are decided.

A list of 15 measures followed, all of them based on directives such as:

- The enterprises' management will immediately take measures to enforce the new consumption norms.
- The activity of the service in charge of computation and supervision of the consumption norms will be reinforced.
- The best designers and technologists in every enterprise will form groups which will analyse and complete the plan of technical and organisational measures for metal and other raw materials savings.
- Specific deadlines will be established for design improvements in order to reduce the weight, to apply new and more efficient technologies and to start the production of maximum efficient machines and equipment.
- The planned measures for consumption norms reduction will be controlled and improved permanently.

For each directive, a specific deadline was set, most of deadlines being between 30 March and 15 May 1962. All industry structures, from the ministry's directions and departments to enterprises, and design and research institutes were held responsible for the fulfilment of the reduction task assumed by the Party's leadership. This order had two main objectives in practice: on the one hand, it tried to press enterprises to reduce metal consumption through various methods, such as re-design, technology improvement, materials replacement and better metal waste management; and on the other hand to discourage the use of such materials in the process of design. Whenever a designer recommended the use of such material, he or she had to obtain approvals from different structures submitting a detailed memo explaining why those materials were strictly required.

Very soon this policy had an impact on current activity. A former FMR foreman recalls that 'there were a lot of shortages of materials and tools used in our current activity. We had to improvise, to experiment in order to accomplish our tasks' (Savu, 2013, p. 97). The practice of improvising in the current activity was one the most mentioned effects of the shortages in industry.

An interesting example was related by the Unirea chief-engineer (respondent I1) regarding a number of pieces of complex textile machinery which were planned to be produced in 1983. The machinery was made based on a patent bought from a Western country, and the design required an important quantity of aluminium – roughly 250 tonnes. Since up to 1983 the shortage problem of the Romanian economy had become more dramatic, the chief engineer had to personally present the actual parts made of aluminium for inspection by the country's prime minister. Consequently, he had to arrange transportation from Cluj to Bucharest of the aluminium parts, and he had to argue in the case of each part that it was impossible to replace them with other materials. Finally, he got an approval for 76 tonnes of aluminium. Based on that approval for 76 tonnes, the enterprises' supply department managed to obtain the whole necessary quantity, and at the end of the year the plan was fulfilled. The techniques used to obtain the whole quantity included mostly influence and personal connections. It was very important to obtain the prime minister's approval for an initial quantity. Based on that approval the suppliers were able to use hidden reserves to help Unirea. This example confirms indirectly the third practice observed by Berliner – the hoarding of materials. Probably this practice was used to some extent by Romanian enterprises due to the chronic shortage problems. The example also shows how important this practice was for plan fulfilment, especially in cases when dissimulation could not be used. It also shows the impossibility to keep accurate evidence of all available resources in a centralised economy even in conditions of shortages.

Poor planning

The Document D1, issued in 1951, which is focused on the production norms – the amount of time spent by an operator on a technical operation – undoubtedly proves the poor knowledge of planning procedures at enterprise level. The enterprise's director was informed that

> During the fourth quarter of 1950 your enterprise received the task of reducing the norms by 20%. This norms reduction should have resulted in raising labour productivity per worker and employee at least by a sufficient rate, so that average salaries would not decrease.

But the enterprise did not follow this task when it proposed the productivity target for the third quarter of 1951:

> You have communicated that in the third quarter of 1950 the productivity realised was 119,601 lei and the average monthly salary was 7,527 lei per worker. In order to follow the norm reduction rate, in the fourth quarter of 1951, the productivity per worker must be at least 143,521 lei, not 138,686 lei as you put into the proposed plan for fourth quarter of 1951.

More than that, the document criticised the enterprise for artificially increasing the norms for new products, so the salaries would remain constant without a corresponding increase of productivity. Finally, the document required a bureaucratic solution of the problem:

> In order to fix this shortcoming and to successfully achieve the target set initially, you have to fill Appendix 1 as indicated, from which will result in productivity and average salaries for the fourth quarter of 1951 comparable with the third quarter of 1950. In addition, you have to take into account the labour productivity growth from quarter to quarter, and socialist accumulations which should underpin the average salaries (index of growth of salaries should be below the growth rate of labour productivity).

The enterprise's director, chief engineer and the heads of the planning and salaries departments were held responsible for fulfilling this requirement. The deadline was set for three months later, on 1 December 1951.

This document shows very clearly that very important economic indicators such as norms, productivity or salaries were set arbitrarily, probably following Party directives. It is a matter of basic micro-economics and industrial management knowledge that productivity increases as a result of significant innovation either in technology or in production management. A requirement of a 20 per cent rate of increased productivity from one year to the next one without any other technological improvements shows a poor understanding of economic and industrial management principles.

Another relevant aspect regards the form of the document D1. As it can be seen in Appendix 4, the document was a template in which the enterprise's name, the norms reduction task, the productivity and the average salary were filled in by hand. This suggests that in the first year of the first five-year plan, the case of Unirea was not an exception, and the planning authorities had to face similar problems in many other cases.

Document D1 also shows the usual method used by the enterprises to respond to irrational demands – dissimulation – by inflating the norms whenever possible, especially in the case of new products or for other special labour tasks. The inflation of norms for special technological operations was one of the most widespread practices in the Romanian planned economy. An investigation performed by a former researcher (R3.1) identified an outrageously high number of labour hours in a mining enterprise he investigated in 1980s. Usually, that high norm was allocated for unusual operation such as tyre replacement for huge vehicles used for transportation within the enterprise. The director explained that such an operation took place rarely enough to be unnoticed by the control bodies, but it could be done in reporting documents occasionally to reach a sufficient number of labour hours so the salaries could be paid.

In the case of Unirea, document D3 offers a similar argument: 'Because of the cooperation plan, we are required to supply different metal spare parts for the Enterprises *Semănătoarea*, *Steagu Roșu* and *Sovrommetal*, small but complicated parts which require 3.5 times more labour time than other average spare parts'. In this case, Unirea planners used the opportunity of having to supply unusual and probably no-standardised spare parts to request 3.5 times more labour time than usual. There were no other technical arguments –such as time measurements – supporting this figure attached to this request.

All of this evidence suggests that central planning was usually aiming to fulfil overall political targets rather than employing rigorous methods and techniques, and the enterprises' planners were using this lack of knowledge to hoard extra labour time whenever such opportunity was available.

Salaries first

Regardless of the main topic of each correspondence with planning authorities, one of most important elements in the negotiation was the security of the salaries fund. All possible arguments were used to support requests for a bigger salaries fund, from extensive and very detailed calculation, to general statements such as this, included in D3:

> Producing textile machines and spare parts for agricultural machines definitely requires more labour time, consequently an increased number of workers at a higher category of qualification, therefore a higher hourly salary and a bigger salaries fund for the enterprise. All these arguments support the increase asked for by our enterprise.

Document D4 reveals the mechanism put in place to force enterprises to fulfil the plan. Because the global production indicator was not fulfilled, the planned salaries fund became excessive in connection with the planned targets. Consequently, the bank had to pay salaries only at the realised production level, which was below the required salaries fund, as a result of multiplying the number of employees by the average salary. Therefore, the only solution enterprises had was either to pay lower salaries, or to ask the ministry to change plan targets to the levels that were actually realised. Also, it can be observed that the bank had a 10 per cent margin for plan un-fulfilment, and the enterprise had to look for a solution only if the un-fulfilment exceeded this margin. Therefore, according to the document D4 Unirea had to request the ministry's approval:

> We kindly ask you to send us your consent to obtain from the bank the amount of money needed, in order to pay the salaries, because the 10% quota granted by the bank does not cover the required amount. If you need further explanation, please ask us for it.

Document D4 offers evidence of a widespread strategy in planned economies: when the plan could not be fulfilled for a specific range of products, other products were produced in excess in order to compensate for the un-fulfilment and to attain the global plan indicators so that the payment of salaries would not be jeopardised.

A decade later, the communication process was more sophisticated, but the main argument used by the enterprise remained the same: the need to assure that salaries were paid at the established level. The planning authorities' replies seem to suggest a better level of competence and control over detailed indicators than it was at the beginning of the communist industrialisation. Apparently, the most disputed indicator was that for productivity, but as it has been argued above, this indicator had a direct impact on the financial resources available for salaries.

In October 1960, Unirea sent to the ministry's planning departments the document D7 regarding the labour plan and salaries planned for 1961. This document is presented here in detail because it is relevant for an understanding of the negotiation process. After a detailed analysis, Unirea management concluded that the salaries fund had to be increased according to the new global production target, the quarterly breakdown had to be calculated according to the global production figure, and the task of achieving an increase in productivity was beyond the enterprise's possibilities. These conclusions were supported by detailed calculations based on the previous year's productivity, numbers of workers and average salaries. The paragraph below illustrates the way Unirea management argued for a change of the plan indicators.

> The global production indicator we proposed for 1961 is higher now to the level of 76,000 thousand lei, so it follows that gross salaries for workers must be increased accordingly. As a result the salaries fund for employees working for the proposed global production target is 14,370.8 thousand lei. This fund will be used to pay the salaries of workers who contribute to achieving the global production target.

While the salaries fund was the first issue on which Unirea asked for a change of a roughly 4 per cent increase, the second important indicator was productivity:

> For 1961 the rise of productivity is planned at 127.5% in comparison with 1960. The global production presumed for 1960 is 53,000 thousand lei, which will be accomplished by 900 workers. In this case in 1961 we would realise 58,888 × 127.5% = 75,082 lei and this would correspond to an average number of workers of 975 at present and 1000 at year's end. This is an almost non-existent increase in comparison with the current number and an increase of 12% in comparison with the average of 1960. We estimate this task is too ambitious for our capacities in view of the following reasons:
>
> - The new mechanical workshop will go into service after the equipment and machines is moved from the old workshop. During the movement and adaptation period, the machines cannot work at full capacity, and therefore productivity will decrease;
> - Because of the investment plan, the foundry refurbishment will be carried out without an interruption in production, but productivity will be certainly affected;
> - The roads will be affected by the works at utilities networks, therefore additional staff will be required;
> - The task of preparing the production of 6 new textile machines requires supplementary workers in different workshops.
>
> All these reasons affect and diminish the possibility of increasing productivity. In our workload plan for 1961 we have already prefigured 5–15% lower labour costs based on technical and organisational measures which will be applied, resulting in 753 workers and 331 auxiliary staff. By the extension of these measures we prefigure an increase in productivity of up to 122%, a figure we ask you to accept as the enterprise's target, instead of 127.5%.
>
> Considering the above arguments, please change our workforce and salaries plan by:
>
> - Raising the salaries fund according to the global production proposed;
> - Changing the quarterly breakdown for salaried funds as we proposed, according to the global production figure;
> - Decreasing of our productivity target from 127.5% to 122%.

Two aspects can be observed in this letter: a more detailed and technical argument had been made supporting Unirea's requests, and the extensive development plan had become an argument supporting the decrease of the plan indicators. The efforts required by the investment plan were a significant burden on the regular production activities, and it was 'politically acceptable' to use this argument in the enterprises' requests.

Document D10, received in January 1961, communicated to the Unirea management that following the enterprise's request for plan adjustment, and 'Considering the average salary realised in 1960, and its planned evolution in 1961 in relation to the production tasks, you will adjust the salary fund plan for 1961. The productivity indicator remains the same'. Thus, as a result of its arguments to the planners, Unirea had been successful regarding the salaries, but unsuccessful regarding the productivity indicator. In simple economic terms, it meant that the cost of salaries had been increased in order to obtain the same production value, while the number of employees remained constant.

A few days later, the ministry transmitted to Unirea the actualised plan in document D11:

> Here are detailed the work and salaries plans for 1961 and the quarterly breakdown, including the salaries fund adjustment. This plan cancels and replaces the previously submitted plan. The labour productivity indicator for 1961, compared to actual achievements of 1960 per employee, calculated on the basis of global production is 127.5%. The bonus fund for technical and administrative staff is included in the salary fund.

Therefore, it seems that at least partially, the enterprise successfully achieved a plan adjustment, obtaining at least an increase of the salaries fund. Because no other correspondence was identified immediately after the receipt of the latest plan version, it can be reasonably concluded that this adjustment satisfied Unirea managers. Moreover, a message received from the ministry in April 1961, document D13, announced an additional bonus fund:

> This is to inform you that Comrade Deputy Minister Actarian approved a bonus for your employees mentioned in the attached list, because of the successful installation of textile machinery. Consequently your salaries fund is increased by 17,700 lei from the ministry reserve fund for first quarter of 1961.

But in May 1961 document D14 arrived from the ministry with a new and higher productivity target because of an increase in the global production without direct labour involved:

> Because you will receive this year the remaining parts from *Cugir* Enterprises, your global production will increase by approximately 5,350 thousand lei without any labour cost. Consequently your productivity target for 1961 is adjusted accordingly from 127.5% to 136%, compared to the final achievements in labour productivity per employee in 1960. This also adjusts the average salary per worker and your salaries fund.

This significant increase of the productivity target produced a strong reply from Unirea. Document D15 was sent to the ministry by the enterprise's Planning Department. The document begins indicating an attached brief of the current status of the enterprise's achievements and the estimations of the whole year achievements. According to the current status of achievements presented, Unirea had accomplished the plan for the first quarter only because of the additional parts received from *Cugir*. If the value of remaining parts was deducted from the global production value, it resulted in 104.8 per cent for the global production indicator and 96.5 per cent for the productivity indicator. For May, these indicators were 101 per cent for global production and 95.8 per cent for productivity. More than that, the enterprise argued that:

> For the next quarters of 1961 we foresee global production just at the planned target, hampered further by investment works in the foundry and the movement of the mechanical workshop in the new hall without stopping production. The planned labour productivity appears constantly unfeasible, the current average number of employees cannot be reduced but on the contrary it will increase. As a result, the overruns of labour productivity will be compensated for by the end of the year 1961, and we forecast a final year indicator of productivity of 98.5% in comparison with the realised value in 1960.

Unirea also argued that the initial target for productivity of 127.5 per cent was unfeasible, because the remaining parts from *Cugir* were already included in the production plan: 'As we argued in our previous letters, we consider that a productivity indicator of 122% is feasible, considering the remaining parts from *Cugir* included in our global production'. More than that, as a result of another government directive, a new department had to be established, requiring 50 new employees. The hiring of supplementary personnel was not included in the previous labour plan, and it would add pressure on the productivity indicator. The conclusion of Unirea's argumentation was sharp:

> Based on these arguments, we cannot accept the productivity indicator increase requested in your letter mentioned above. We ask for a reduction of the productivity indicator from 127.5% to 124.5% based on the fact that the plan already included the parts received from *Cugir*. We also ask for additional salaries funds for the third and fourth quarters. Considering the measures we took in order to increase the average salary, and the average number of employees required to fulfil the plan, we need additional 135,000 lei, and 364,000 lei respectively. Please analyse the above arguments and the details presented in the annexed memo, and resolve the raised problems as we required. We ask this in order to avoid serious disturbances which may appear in the salaries area of activity, because of the apparent inappropriate salaries fund overruns, in our case the overruns being only formally inappropriate.

This illustrates the constant bargaining over productivity and global production in exchange for the salaries fund. This latter element seems to be the enterprise's last resort of negotiation.

No other documents regarding this dispute have been found in the archives. However, the final report for 1961 indicates the fulfilment of a productivity indicator of 127.5 per cent. Also, all plan indicators were formally fulfilled, including the production capacity increase as a result of the investment plan, the average salary and the global production. This suggests that a sort of trade-off between Unirea and the ministry had been achieved, probably based on a salaries fund increase above the initial target.

Permanent negotiations

The correspondence also suggests a tense relation of negotiation with the planning authorities, with a significant power of negotiation for the enterprise. For example, the document D3, issued by Unirea in December 1951, contained the following statements:

> The required numbers of workers you have set based on the productivity index for the second, third and fourth quarters are 571, 575 and 550. These figures seem completely discordant with the planned work load, especially for the third and fourth quarter;

and 'the productivity indicator can be used only in the mass production case, and for similar products. It cannot be imposed in the case of very different products as is clear from the table above'. These phrases suggest an important power position for Unirea in the process of negotiating the plan indicators. It can also be observed that these arguments were communicated in the middle of the last month of the quarter for which the plan is negotiated.

Document D9 is also relevant for evidence of the tense relation between enterprises and the planning authorities. In this document, the enterprise was reminded about the imperative need to report on time to the ministry the exact performances in fulfilling plan indicators in the previous quarter and the whole year of 1960. The letter stated:

> You will give special attention to the measures taken with regard to achievements in labour productivity and average salaries (in case of failure, describe the causes). The reports should outline the resulting productivity indicator according to the planned task. You will also take care that all reported dates are identical with dates reported on separate forms.

Thus, the enterprise was reminded not only to report on its performance on time, but also to take care to report the planned targets, or to fully justify the eventual failure to fulfil the targets. Again, the only mentioned indicators were productivity and the average salary. Both indicators seem to represent the core elements of the Party's policies, other significant indicators for any developing economy such as costs, profit and return on investment never being even mentioned in the identified correspondence.

In document D4 a slight change could be seen in the communication tone, the enterprise kindly asking for the approval, but the main culprit for plan un-fulfilment was considered planning authorities who did not perform a detailed analysis of the plan's structural change. Unirea argued that the main reason for missing the plan target was the change in the plan structure:

> The global production in July was realised at only 87% of the plan target, because of the change in plan assortment by part replacement of textile machines with new and unknown products. The plan change made impossible the fulfilment of the global production indicator which was set without a detailed analysis. The rest of the plan structure was based on unique products and this did not allow us to compensate for the plan un-fulfilment.

Document D5 explicitly described the issues faced by Unirea as difficulties (*greutăți*) related to the shortage of labour. Also, the permanent need for plan adjustment and correction is acknowledged in this document:

> By Order No. 384825/20 February 1952 the General Direction sent us the annual labour plan and the corresponding quarterly plans. However, in each quarter we were forced to make interventions to correct it, especially regarding the average and total salary which was not consistent with the approved number of employees.

This undoubtedly shows a disconnection between the salaries required by the official work contract of the employees, and the salaries resulting from plan calculations. The plan calculations expressed the political will to correlate salaries with the demands for an increased productivity and global production. These interventions suggest a systematic failure of the pursuit to increase productivity and production, so the enterprise's management had to intervene in order to guarantee the salaries. Probably these dysfunctionalities may be explained by the lack of experience in planning a centralised economy, especially in a period of extensive industrialisation. D5 also shows dysfunctionalities in the communication process regarding the production and labour issues:

> In the message no. 22024/28 October 1952 we sent to D.G. our observations regarding the need to keep the original figures, but so far we have not received any response. Other interventions we made to the Department of Labour Norms and Salaries were also unanswered.

The most important strategy used by enterprises to manage the planning constraints was the negotiation of the plan targets. The negotiation of the plan indicators was a continuous process that had started from the first year of the first five-year plan. The most important argument used by the enterprise was the need to pay the employees as agreed in the functions register. Ten years later, the labour force seemed to be the main mechanism used by Unirea to increase productivity, but at the same time to bargain for a reduction of the productivity indicator. Therefore, it can reasonably be concluded that salaries were considered more important than the plan indicators. The labour laws discussed in the previous chapter support this conclusion. A significant change began to take place in 1972 with *Codul Muncii*, and it took almost another decade to institutionalise the possibility to reduce salaries if plan targets were unfulfilled.

As the managers in a centralised system had always focused on the safety factor and had tried to hoard resources, individuals were motivated to develop and hoard connections that were the most important resources. The communist system had created an incentive to develop informal adaptive mechanisms (the Russian term *blat* and the Romanian term *pile şi relaţii*) that had improved to some extent the stability and certainty in an uncertain and threatening context. Both *blat* and *pile* refer to relationships that obstruct the development of a culture based on public, cooperative and rule-based relationships. Instead they reinforce the traditional culture based on covert, personalised, hierarchical relationships involving complicity, informality and political patronage. Many of the respondents admitted that the last resort solution in various plan-related crises was the ability of the general director to use his political connections. What in common language was widely known as '*PCR is the abbreviation for pile, cunoştiinţe, relaţii*' (*pile*, acquaintances, relations), in the economic realm had the significance of being a part of the proper circle of connections, being able to offer and receive favours, and finally being trusted (*a fi de încredere*). An important characteristic of *blat* and *pile* was the normative aspect. Officially, target adjustments were accepted as an exception to the general rule. The widespread shortages and plan tautness transformed negotiation into an unwritten norm. And the more developed and sophisticated the economy was, the more complex negotiation became. I2 and I4 described extensively the ritual of plan negotiation, including laborious calculations, extensive documentation used in multiple stages of the process. This negotiation ritual is presented in the following chapter. However, it is beyond doubt that the documents identified in the archives represent only a part of the never-ending negotiation process.

Irrational investment plans with unlimited resources

Document D6 represents an example of the investment policy after a decade of centralised planning. The information included in it shows how the government decided on 10 December 1959 to take important investments decisions at enterprise level, with sufficient resources (in fact, unlimited financial resources), but without complete plans, and a fixed deadline of 31 December 1960. The deadline and the production capacity of the new investment to be the most important concerns for all central authorities involved. Unirea was supposed to increase its production capacities fivefold in less than 12 months. Unirea received the document on 11 January 1960. The relevant part of the document D6 is cited below.

> Your enterprise has a particularly important task in increasing its production capacity five times until 31 December 1960. The investment must be

> executed unconditionally, until 31 December 1960, when your enterprise's capacity should reach 4100 tons/year of textile machinery.
>
> In order to ensure the projects required for the investment plan and to start the works at the mechanical workshop for which the projects already exist, from the beginning of January 1960 your relevant technical structures should take the following measure:
>
> You and your investment department head will contact immediately IREP Cluj[1] and you will insist on the beginning of the design process based on the design themes that you will receive from ITCME[2] in January 1960 for the foundry – construction and installation, energy networks, plumbing.
>
> Please be advised that in order to be able to execute these projects as well as and other adjustments and changes, the Ministry Technical Department has proposed to the comrade Minister four supplementary positions which will be used exclusively for the investment plan.
>
> As you have been informed by the letter no. 225.836/12 December 1959, the objects breakdown of the total amount approved is only indicative, you can make any proposals for amendments, according to the total plan indicators for investment and construction, and ensuring the unconditional capacity of 4,100 tons/year of textile machinery by the end of 1960. Any adjustments you request should be well argued in a detailed memo.
>
> In conclusion, in order to ensure all conditions for the planned works' beginning and execution and to achieve 4100 tons/year by the end of 1960, you will immediately proceed to take the measures above, which are not exhaustive.

The first point to note regards the timing of the communication: the enterprise had been informed about the investment plan on 14 December 1959, and further details were transmitted on 11 January 1960. The final approval of the government (Consiliul de Miniştri) was issued on 10 December 1959. The planned development was very significant – the production capacity had to be increased by five times up to the end of 1960, which was in less than a year. The projects were incomplete, and the enterprise's director was instructed to insist on the realisation of missing projects. These aspects raised doubts regarding the capability of the planning authorities to manage the Party's ambitions to industrialise the country. The final approval was issued in mid-December, the enterprise was informed in January, the projects were incomplete, and the projects themes were also late. All these delays indicated a systemic delay in the process of industrialisation in comparison with the Party's leadership plans. The availability of resources may have been among the factors that generated the systemic delay.

Another point to note regards the surprisingly important degree of flexibility regarding the resources and measures the enterprise had been granted. As it was repeatedly stated in the document, the delivery date and the planned capacity were the only non-negotiable aspects. These two indicators seemed to result from a Party directive, and seemed to be a part of an overall economic indicator assumed by the Party's leadership for 31 December 1960. While not very relevant, production indicators were subject of continuous negotiation and pressures between the enterprise and the planning authorities, and in the case of this important and costly investment, such details were not considered important.

Another piece of evidence supporting this conclusion is the investment in FMR. According to Savu (2013, p. 9), the idea of producing small and medium grinding machines in Cluj was the result of the friendship between a professor of mechanical engineering of the Cluj Polytechnic Institute and the minister of Machines Building Industry. Because of this friendship significant investment funds were allotted in 1971, and therefore the construction of FMR as a section of Unirea began in the same year. This shows the impressive speed of developing an investment once the decision was taken by the political leadership. At the same time, it shows the prevalence of political decision over any other rational argument. The lack of tradition, of human resources and of scientific knowledge in the field of grinding machines (*maşini de rectificat*) were all arguments worthy of consideration in the process of decision making. But because at that moment Unirea was the most technologically advanced enterprise in Cluj, it received the task of building and integrating the new factory. In spite of the apparent unlimited resources available for FMR development, the deadline was not met completely. According to Savu (2013, p. 13), on 30 June 1973 – the official date for the festive beginning of activity, some machines were not yet started. Therefore, a quantity of metallic waste was brought from Unirea, to give the impression of activity to the high-rank officials present.

Poor performances and quality – the case of exports

As one of the former FMR workers recalls (Savu, 2013, p. 105) the slogan in the 1980s was: 'Let's produce world class grinding machines, and even better'. But in the real competition on the international market, FMR products were much under the acceptable level of quality and reliability. The FMR case offers few examples of technological problems especially in exports. Savu (2013) describes two such cases. Designed to be an example of a Romanian enterprise able to compete successfully with the most advanced countries in the sector of the machine-building industry, FMR failed to perform consistently on foreign markets. Its exports to the UK and East Germany ended with serious reliability problems, and with important additional costs.

In addition to the poorly organised industry, and to the lack of experience and tradition, another aspect contributed to this failure: Romanian enterprises were totally disconnected with the international market. Romanian enterprises were represented abroad by specialised import-export organisations, and local specialists were involved as little as possible in negotiations or operations. The Securitate supervised all contacts with foreign representatives, and in most cases the employees of such import-export organisation were undercover officers. A post-1989 manager (O2) described this aspect during meeting with students: 'State-owned import-export organisations had a monopoly over foreign trade before 1989; consequently industrial companies did not have any specialists in this activity', and another manager added 'there were few export-import companies, the people working there used to travel abroad and to call me saying: "I made a contract for you" ' (O3). This represented another irrational constraint – the pressure to export without any consistent contact with the market. An episode mentioned by Savu (2013, pp. 190–191) describes the challenges faced by Romanian enterprises when trying to develop collaborations with foreign companies. In 1976 the general director of FMR was sent to East Germany to a similar enterprise in order to develop a cooperation programme agreed by Ceauşescu and Honneker a few years before. The general director of the German enterprise bluntly declined the cooperation, stating that:

> If a problem appears during the cooperation, he immediately calls the FMR general director, while if the FMR general director wants to call East Germany, he needs approvals from the Interior Ministry, from the Party … and while getting all approvals, the problem stagnates.

Both Unirea and FMR were able to export mainly to Comecon countries based on bilateral political agreements, or to third world countries. According to I1 and I2, Unirea had a record of solid exports in countries such as Bangladesh or Thailand, where the textile industry was in development and based on cheap labour rather than high technology.

Except for very few industries, Romanian enterprises were unable to build a solid export record, and failed to meet the Party leadership's claims regarding the industry's competitiveness. This represented another constant aspect identified by Berliner in the Soviet economy. Because the plan's focus was almost exclusively oriented towards quantitative indicators, the incentive to improve quality was very weak. In most cases the quality control department had a marginal importance in the enterprise's structure. This attitude was summarised in a brief story by one manager (O4) in his meeting with students: 'We had a director who used to say: "it must pass the test". But we said: "Comrade Director, the engine is not ready yet" and he replied "F … the engine, it just has to pass the test" '. This shows that the enterprise's and the director's responsibility ended once a product was delivered to the customers and the plan target was considered to be fulfilled. Quality control was not only rather formal, but also it did not take into consideration the real performance of the product in its use. Moreover, the extensive maintenance required post-sales – especially in the case of exports, was a source of more labour time useful for the salaries fund.

Another negative consequence of this system was the lack of access to the international flow of knowledge. After 1990, Romanian managers acknowledged this aspect: 'Unfortunately, this isolation deprived us of access to world-relevant information' (O5). This isolation contributed significantly to the technological backwardness of Romanian industry which had a very visible impact after 1990.

Conclusions – the vicious circle of the Romanian planned economy

This was the way Unirea and FMR existed and developed during the communist period. Both were considered in 1990 as the most technologically advanced enterprises in the Romanian machines-building industry. But because they were the result of an unrealistic strategy, the transition period almost eliminated both enterprises form the markets. Unirea and FMR had become the symbols of the important efforts made by the communist regime on the population' expense to develop high technology enterprises in the conditions of total lack of efficiency controlled feed-back from a competitive market. The study's findings summarised above, in conjunction with other information presented in the previous chapters, suggest a possible vicious circle explaining the planned economy failure, depicted in Figure 5.1.

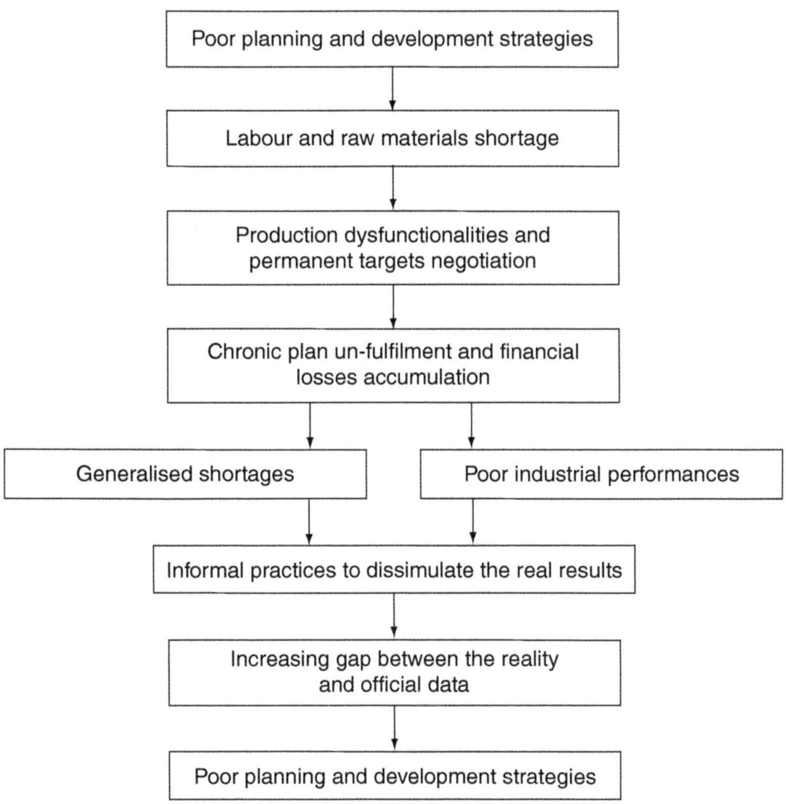

Figure 5.1 The vicious circle of a planned economy.

Shortages from the beginning

Resource shortage started to be officially acknowledged in 1960, ten years after the establishment of the centralised planned economy. The pressure towards reduction of use of certain raw materials indicates either an unbalanced development exceeding the available resources – a hypothesis which is supported by the memoires of Gaston Marin, or a lack of control over resource consumption at enterprise level. Regardless of the cause of the shortage, the solution envisioned by the Party and implemented by the planning authorities was to reduce radically the consumption of deficit resources with an arbitrarily decided percentage. The chronic shortages of raw materials had appeared, probably at the end of the 1950s and it was officially acknowledged at the beginning of the 1960s. In the academic literature, it is usually considered that in the first two decades of communist Romania, the economy performed better than most world economies, and only starting with the years 1975–77 did the economy start to show signs of decline. The statistical evidence presented in previous chapters indicate a visible economic decline in the 1980s, when both macro-economic indicators and consumption experienced a decline. The evidence collected so far shows important economic dysfunctionalities from the very beginning of the planned economy in Romania. While during the first decade, labour was the scarcest resource, in less than 10 years raw materials became the main topic of directives calling for a brutal reduction in consumption. The reductions required defied any technological principles, and created supra-bureaucratic structures in charge of very detailed aspects of industrial production. In many cases, the resources available in reality were far lower than the resources allocated by the plan. In this situation, there was a critical need to develop informal mechanisms in order to acquire all the resources needed for fulfilling the tasks. The bribes, influence, barter and informal networks were examples of such mechanisms.

The impressive number of specialists involved in the process of supervision also raises the problem of a cost-benefit balance. Many groups at almost all levels of the economy were appointed to fulfil bureaucratic tasks, to supervise, re-design, approve and report what in the end proved to be an irrational approach on the very important issue of innovation. The whole pursuit to create new and more productive technologies, and better and cheaper products, failed and resulted in less competitive products, old technologies, low level of employees' motivation and loss-generating enterprises.

Dysfunctionalities from the beginning

Important dysfunctionalities in the planning process had appeared from the very beginning of the industrialisation process in communist Romania. As shown by one of the analysed documents (D1), issued on 28 August 1951, Unirea did not comply with the task of reducing the norms by 20 per cent. This task was communicated at the end of 1950 and it aimed to increase the average productivity by at least the same rate. This document also outlined one of the main strategies used by enterprises to avoid or dissimulate indicators of non-fulfilment: the increase of norms for new products, which can be understood as a labour hoarding strategy, in order to create reserves for further reductions if required. The same document also showed that planning authorities did not suggest practical solutions except for formal requirements:

> In order to fix these shortcomings and to successfully achieve the plan targets set initially, you have to fill Annex 1 as indicated, wherefrom will result the productivity and average salaries for fourth quarter of 1951 in comparison with third quarter of 1950.

It is reasonable to consider that most industrial enterprises had significant potential to increase their productivity at that time. The lack of industrial tradition, an expanding working class, and a political leadership that decided to pursue the country's industrialisation are the basic premises for such an assumption. However, the planning authorities had constantly pushed enterprises to achieve productivity increase rates between 20 per cent and 36 per cent per year, throughout the investigated period. Supported to some extent by new technologies acquired from abroad, by a significant development of polytechnic institutes and technical schools (*şcoli profesionale*), and by extensive investment plans, such rates were unreasonably higher for most enterprises. No matter how modern a technology is, its capacity to induce productivity increases is very limited in time. Even if the education system had been geared to produce engineers, sub-engineers, industrial technicians and workers with good qualifications, this transformation required years if not decades to create a visible advance in the performance. Last but not least, no matter how ambitious an investment plan is, if it is disconnected from a real value chain, if the supplies are non-existent at a reasonable cost, if the market is not available or willing to absorb the products at profit, the investment will generate a loss and it will become a liability to the centralised economy. While in a market economy such investment will soon end up in bankruptcy, or take-over, or it will be abandoned, in the Romanian communist system almost all erroneous investments continued to work at full or almost full capacity, adding more financial burdens to an exhausted economy. Other enterprises which normally would generate a reasonable financial result, were constantly pushed to increase global production and productivity year after year. Very soon probably, the enterprise managers concluded that alternative strategies were a part of the economic game: including plan indicator bargaining, dissimulation, resource hoarding, influence, bribes and even blackmailing the authorities with possible consequences of reducing the salaries. Among these strategies, dissimulation had an important characteristic: it was cumulative. Every overstatement of the production reported at one moment will remain in the records for the future. I2 recalls that in 1990 Unirea production of six to nine months was simply wiped off the enterprise's records, because it simply did not exist in the enterprise's deposits or in the production flow. This suggests the rough dimension of the dissimulation in Romanian economy accumulated up to 1990: between 50 per cent and 75 per cent of one year's total production.

The pressures on enterprises regarding plan indicators were irrationally high – for example to reduce norms by 20 per cent in a few months, to increase the capacity five times in one year, to increase productivity by 27 per cent from one year to the next, or to reduce the consumption of selected materials by more than 20 per cent in a few years. These requirements seem to be the results of political directives aimed to push industrial development far beyond the natural evolution of the economy, and far beyond the available human, material and knowledge resources. Therefore, industry appeared to be a conflicting area between political will and organisational rationality. From the investigated archival resources, as well as from interviews with former managers of industrial enterprises, it is clear that in most cases the accomplished indicators were a trade-off between the authorities' initial targets and subsequent requests by enterprises. Thus, the accomplished plan was systematically below the initial targets set by the Party's leadership. But since neither the Party's leadership, nor the planning authorities ever acknowledged a failure in fulfilling general indicators for the entire Romanian economy, a growing gap between reality and alleged results existed from the very beginning of the planned economy in Romania.

Permanent negotiation of the plan

The plan indicators were systematically changed throughout the whole year. The planning process usually began in the last quarter of the previous year and both parties dispute the values of the indicators. Even in 1951, a period of terror, arrests and deportations, the enterprise seems to have had a significant bargain power with the planning authorities. In the 1960s, the enterprise used two main arguments to dispute the plan indicators received. One argument used was the need to assure salaries at promised level. The other argument concerned the burden produced by the investment plan. The enterprise's main objective was to obtain additional funds either as more money for salaries, or as additional funding for the investment plans. In both cases the national budget had to support additional costs, while the enterprise was still manipulating the final production results.

At least in the first two decades of the command economy, the enterprises seem to have had a stronger negotiation power in relation to the planning authorities from two main points of view: knowledge regarding their industry, and control of the working class through salaries. In a few cases, the planning authorities seemed to be incapable of responding to enterprise's demands. While most of directives received by Unirea simply requested the fulfilment of specific plan indicators, the documents sent by the enterprise argued extensively and using very technical arguments related with production, norms and technology. No correspondence in which the planning authorities would have engaged in consistent technical argument has been identified. The answers were usually brief, setting new plan indicators, and in some cases, it appears to be a sort of trade-off between initial targets and the enterprise's requests. According to the testimony of the former chief engineer of Unirea (respondent I1), in the last two decades of the communist regime, even the planning authorities admitted the impossibility of continuously raising the targets, especially in the last decade when the economic crisis had become acute. The shortage of resources had become so important than even fulfilling export targets, which usually were high priority objectives, was difficult. The solution imposed by the planning authorities for the shortages was to create redundant structures at all levels with the main tasks to record, supervise, propose measures and report the consumption of scarce materials. In the ministry's orders, while the list of tasks, responsibilities and deadlines was long, those structures had no real power or mechanism in place to impose in practice the measures that were decided. More than that, these groups had the right to approve consumption of scarce elements in addition to the planned quantity in 'well-argued cases'. The case recalled by the respondent I1 showed that up to 1980s the list of scarce materials had widened, and shortage had become so important than the prime minister had to approve the use of 250 tonnes of aluminium for a planned production task.

This supports the hypothesis that the planned centralised economy lacked the feed-back mechanism required for corrective measures. And if the prices system was disconnected from real market processes, the errors in strategic planning at the level of the economy mounted up and finally forced the central leadership to find solutions to reduce the losses. In the case of Romania, the Party used salary reductions that had begun to be applied from 1973, and private consumption reduction which had been observed from the end of 1970s as 'valves' to release some of the financial tensions. One can observe that both solutions were in deep contradiction with the basic principles of communist ideology. Both measures were at the immediate cost of the working class, and both were accompanied by discourses around strident nationalism and the personality cult of the leader. The North Korean and Chinese models can be easily identified as continuing examples of this strategy.

Constant loss accumulation

The important change in labour legislation that had begun in 1972 probably had at least one hidden reason – to give enterprises the right to decrease salaries. This was acknowledged by the respondents I1 and I2, and according to their testimonies, was correctly identified as such by the workers. Similarly, Haraszti observed in the case of Hungary in 1972 in the Red Star Tractor Factory: 'the real meaning of piece-rate lies in the incessant increase in production' (Haraszti, 1977, p. 59).

A growing gap between official results and reality, probably created rising tensions in the financial system. At the beginning of 1970s two attempts were made in order to correct this problem: the recalculation of prices (*reaşezarea preţurilor*), and labour legislation reform. Both attempts had as their main target a better understanding and a better running of the economy. But since prices recalculation ended in failure in less than four years, salary reduction was the only available valve which could reduce financial tensions for the whole economy.

Regarding the attempt to recalculate prices, as part of a long and detailed process, numerous phases of prices recalculation were discussed and approved by the Executive Politic Committee, and in 1974 new prices were announced. But the results showed an increase of production costs by 14.1 per cent, a lower national income, significant losses in mining industry and losses made by some exported products. And in order to obtain the improved version of prices, the prices of oil, cement and electrical energy were reduced below 1973 level (the level before the first oil price shock). While more correct established prices would have acted as a correction mechanism in the economy, and probably would have improved the real performance, Ceaușescu decided to end the process and reject the new prices. According to Gaston Marin (2000), Ceaușescu was troubled by two outcomes of the recalculations: lower national income and a lower weight of some industrial branches that he considered pivotal.

Consequently, the only economic mechanisms available to reduce the financial pressure were salaries reduction and hidden inflation. However, moving in this direction raised an ideological problem: it was contrary to the socialist promises of equality and fairness. As was shown in the previous chapter, the process of imposing and generalising salaries *în acord global* took another decade and this payment method generated most of the strikes and protests which started in 1977.

Radu Ghețea, a former bank manager who served for 22 years in the communist regime, provided a relevant piece of information regarding the method of financing. In a video interview for the financial newspaper (Ziarul Financiar, 24 May 2015) he recalled that:

> Before 1989 the banking activity was completely different from now, with one exception – the Romanian Bank of Foreign Trade (*Banca Română de Comerț Exterior – BRCE*). Although *BRCE* had apparently to fulfil Party policies, it had to comply with international norms. But all other banks worked based to the plan, even the credit system was based on the plan, with no risk assessments at all. If the plan allocated credit for one enterprise, the bank provided that specific amount of money for the investment plan. If at a certain moment a bottleneck in the financing system appeared, compensation among banks was the usual solution. But sometimes the budget deficit was so important that compensation was not enough, so the gap was filled by printing money.

It resulted clearly in the usual method of hiding the financial losses generated by the planned economy. According to Ghețea this method was used seven or eight times in the last 22 years of the communist regime. This means that every two or three years of the last two decades of communist regime, the financial losses were transformed into hidden inflation. This phenomenon may also explain the generalised shortage of consumer goods that began in the 1980s. In the conditions of a controlled system of prices, an over-supply of money had the effect of under-valued products. In a market economy, such a phenomenon would generate price increases, but in the communist economy the prices were stable and controlled. In these conditions, many products were produced and sold at a loss, either to internal or external markets. While in the last decade Ceauşescu pushed for an increase in exports at any cost in order to return borrowed money from foreign countries or institutions, the internal market had to bear the consequences of the system. This irrational drive had immediate consequences at enterprise level. While the targets were incessantly increasing, the allocated resources were reduced. A former manager (O6) described the widening gap between resources and objectives in the last decade of the communist regime: 'We were pushed to make 10 million US dollars, but we didn't have access to the money. We didn't have money for imports, so we had to build our machines by ourselves'.

Romanian enterprises in Berliner's frame

As noted above, Berliner identified 10 practices that had survived virtually unchanged for almost five decades in Soviet industry. After the study of similar practices in the Romanian enterprise, it can be observed there were some similarities, but also a few differences.

Perhaps the most striking similarity regards the constant focus on relating wages to performance. In the Romanian case, this focus took two forms: pressure on the productivity indicator and the implementation of the system *salarizarea în acord global*. But since both methods were subject to intense negotiation between the enterprise and the planning authorities, the success was also similar to the Soviet case.

The Romanian version of *blat*, but with a wider and more complex meaning than the one offered by Berliner, was the crucial element in the negotiation process. While Berliner defines *blat* as the capacity to influence ministry officials, the findings of this study suggest that *pile şi relaţii* and *blat* were the proof of an invisible network of connections developed by a part of the state and Party bureaucracy.

Another similar feature was the lower level of concern regarding quality. Because the plan's focus was almost exclusively oriented towards quantitative indicators, the incentive to improve quality was very weak. In most cases the quality control department played a formal role and had marginal importance in the enterprise's structure.

In the Romanian planning system, the 'ratchet' principle was undoubtedly present. Many respondents recalled this practice, and many analysed documents prove it. But in Romanian practice this principle was balanced by negotiation and dissimulation, leading in the end to a significant level of reported but non-existent production. Romanian enterprises preferred to produce established products, but many employees were enthusiastic about the introduction of new technologies and products. Moreover, any new product was an opportunity to negotiate the plan targets and to hoard labour time – a very useful method to ensure the salaries fund. Materials hoarding, barter and resale were probably present in the Romanian industry, although no direct evidence was found either in the archival documents, or in the interviews. Probably the shortage of different materials, parts and tools was too important to be overcome using these methods, and the control system was efficient enough to keep the phenomenon under control.

Notes

1 IREP Cluj was a local engineering design institute.
2 ITCME was a central design and research institute for machine building industry.

References

Bauer, R.A., Inkeles, A. and Kluckhohn, C. 1956. *How the Soviet System Works*. Cambridge, MA: Harvard University Press.

Berindei, M., Dobrincu, D. and Goşu, A. 2009. *Istoria comunismului din România: documente. Perioada Gheorghe Gheorghiu-Dej (1945–1965)*. Bucureşti: Humanitas.

Berliner, J. 1957. *Factory and Manager in USSR*. Cambridge, MA: Harvard University Press.

Berliner, J. 1976. *The Innovation Decision in Soviet Industry*. Cambridge, MA and London: The MIT Press.

Berliner, J. 1988. *Soviet Industry from Stalin to Gorbachev*. Aldershot: Edward Elgar.

Brucan, S. 2012. *Generaţia irosită*. Bucureşti: Editura Teşu.

Codul Muncii. Legea nr. 10. 23 November 1972. [Online]. [Accessed 21 July 2017]. Available from: www.legex.ro/Legea-10-1972-500.aspx.

Gheţea, R. 2015. *Cum se făcea banking în România pe vremea comuniştilor?* 24 May 2015. [Online]. Available from: www.zf.ro/zf-live/video-zf-live-cum-se-facea-banking-in-romania-pe-vremea-comunistilor-14286507.

Haraszti, M. 1977. *A Worker in a Worker's State*. London: Penguin.

Jowitt, K. 1974. An Organizational Approach to the Study of Political Culture in Marxist-Leninist Systems. *The American Political Science Review*, 68(3).

Marin, G.Gh. 2000. *În serviciul României lui Gheorghiu-Dej. Însemnări din viaţă*. Bucureşti: Editura Evenimentul Românesc.

Moraru, C. and Moraru, C. 2012. *Stenogramele şedinţelor Biroului Politic şi ale Secretariatului Comitetului Central al P.M.R. Vol. V. 1953*. Bucureşti: Institutul Naţional pentru Studiul Totalitarismului.

Savu, D. 2013. *Fabrica de Maşini de Rectificat. Oameni, fapte, amintiri*. Cluj-Napoca: Editura Mega.

Ţăranu, L. 2004a. 'Noul curs' în politica economică a României comuniste. August 1953. I. *Arhivele totalitarismului*, 42–43(1–2).

Ţăranu, L. 2004b. 'Noul curs' în politica economică a României comuniste. August 1953. II. *Arhivele totalitarismului*, 42–43(3–4).

Trotsky, L. 1937. *The Revolution Betrayed: What Is the Soviet Union and Where Is It Going?* [Online]. [Accessed 12 July 2017]. Available from: www.marxists.org/archive/trotsky/1936/revbet/.

6 The human side of the communist enterprise

Paraphrasing the title of a well-known management book first published by Douglas McGregor in 1960, this chapter aims to describe the processes and the main actors involved in enterprise activity in communist Romania from the human resources perspective. While McGregor aimed to 'urge management to examine its assumptions and make them explicit' (McGregor, 2006, p. 330), this book's objective is to explore and understand the gap between the official assumptions and the informal practices of a centrally planned and managed economy.

In developing its focus on personnel aspects, the chapter examines the background to these issues in the ruling party's attempts to create a new working, and then examines issues relating to the education and training of a new industrial workforce, the processes of selection and promotion within the enterprise, and the relation between these processes and the Party's strategies, directives and plans.

The chapter is organised in two parts: the first one is focused on general aspects of the personnel policies – the significant increase in employees' number in 1950s and 1960s followed by a more reasonable pace in 1970s and stagnation and slight decrease in 1980s, the strong influence of the social origin in the education system, the hiring regulations and the repartition system. The second part is focused on a particular aspect described in depth based on empirical evidence: the influence of two apparently marginal departments of the enterprise – *serviciul de cadre* and *serviciul plan* – on the enterprises' internal personnel practices, and on the successful negotiation of the upcoming plan targets.

In addition, the analysis of discussions between managers and students that took place in the first decade of transition adds useful details regarding the managers' perception of the planned economy and of their key position in the whole economic and social mechanism.

The central hypothesis of this part of the book is that the human resources management system had a significant and negative influence on the economic performance of the Romanian economy. The intense demand for skilled workers in the first two decades, followed by a significant pressure for productivity, the very limited capability of enterprises to hire the appropriate persons, the permanent prevalence of political criteria over competence and skills, the informal networks of *pile şi relaţii* able to overcome any regulation, and above all, the ideological commitment to assure a job for everyone, all affected the enterprises' efficiency.

Building a working class

As it was argued in previous chapters, the creation of a working class in a predominantly rural country was a complex process, involving many problems to be solved – from an adequate urban infrastructure to developing new personnel processes adequate for industrial organisations. Many authors (e.g. Shafir, 1985, Gallagher, 2005) have argued, while the predominantly rural character of Romania after WWII represented an advantage to some extent, it also posed a serious challenge for the Communist Party. In 1930 'less than 10 percent of the active population was engaged in industry' (King, 1980, p. 20), and Transylvania and Banat comprised the largest part of it. Because these territories had a longer tradition of industrialisation, in 1929 the proportion of total union members of these two areas was 60 per cent, while they accounted for only 23 per cent of the country's total population (King, 1980, p. 20). Once the political competition had been eliminated with the support of the Soviet Army and Soviet advisors, the working class had the Communist Party as its only legitimate political force. On the other hand, the process of transformation of the mass of peasants into an engaged working class proved to be difficult.

Apparently, the Party succeeded in creating a new working class: by 1979 the urban population increased to almost 50 per cent, and the industrial employment grew from 12 per cent to 34.7 per cent (Nelson, 1988, p. 9). In less than four decades Romania was transformed into a relatively urban and industrial-agrarian country.[1] The 'industrial worker with peasant origin became the ideal social basis of the Communist Party' (Brucan, 2012, p. 166) and supported the modernisation process because it provided better living conditions. Moreover, this new industrial worker was neither educated nor willing to exercise the political power granted by communist ideology, and therefore the Communist Party played this role on behalf of the working class. As Brucan argued, the new working class was perfect for revolution from above. For the new industrial worker, 'political freedom seemed redundant, and the freedom of press had never been the dream of the illiterate' (Brucan, 2012, p. 167).

In quantitative terms, the objective of the creation a working class, *the new man* (*omul nou*) in the official language, had succeeded. The percentage of the urban population in Romania grew from 23.4 per cent in 1948 to 53.2 per cent in 1989 (Direcţia Centrală de Statistică, 1990, p. 51). The percentage of the labour force in industry was only 12 per cent in 1950, but grew to 38.1 per cent in 1989 (Direcţia Centrală de Statistică, 1990, pp. 102–105). These significant increases had as their unique source the rural population and agricultural labour force. The drive for industrialisation generated widespread social changes that further influenced the structure of organisations. However, the traumatic experience of collectivisation was a further cause of popular distrust and suspiciousness in the

Party's policies. Various methods were used to increase the workers' engagement – propaganda, involvement in the decision-making process at work (*COM* and *autoconducerea muncitorească*), and relating salaries to performance – but they all failed to convince the new working class to engage more in the process of building socialism. The Unirea's chief engineer (I1) recalled workers' reactions after the introduction of *acordul global*: 'they (the Party) introduced *acordul global* just to be able to reduce our salaries legally'. This reaction led to the beginning of a period of strikes and unrest in the late 1970s, almost three decades after the beginning of the communist regime.

There has been a lot of argument about the Romanian working class. Statistical indicators show the country's backwardness in terms of industrialisation, urbanisation and education. Most of the arguments have been based on the national statistics before and after 1945. The performance of the communist regime in terms of these indicators was largely praised as exceptional, at least up to the end of 1970s. The main official aims of the extensive industrialisation policies were the transformation of Romania into an industrial state with an efficient economy, the reduction of the discrepancies between Romania and developed countries and between country's regions, the intensive use of local resources and the creation of a modern economy. However, the means chosen by the communist elite to achieve these aims were an irrational focus on heavy industry, and a central planning system whose shortcomings had serious consequences. As it was argued in the previous chapter, the system's shortcomings had started to be noticed in the industrial activity from the very beginning of industrialisation. While according to official statistics, the growth of the Romanian economy was impressive, being through the 1960s and 1970s 'among the highest in communist Europe as well as in the world' (Nelson, 1988, p. 7), and many 'key achievements of socialism' (Fotaki, 2009, p. 151) were secured, there was also significant workers' unrest determined by the system's failures to maintain salaries and benefits at previous levels. Workers' protests and strikes appeared when the salaries were reduced because of plan un-fulfilment, when other benefits (such as work conditions, meals and other benefits) were reduced, and when general living conditions significantly worsened.

At the beginning of communist industrialisation the insufficient number of industrial workers was one key problem for enterprises and planning authorities. The request for more workers, technicians and engineers was one common characteristic of many documents identified in Unirea archive.

Even in these conditions, strange political decisions were taken by the Party's leadership. A meeting of the Political Bureau held in 1953 approved the decision to send 15,000 workers, engineers and foremen from industrial enterprises to agriculture. These personnel were designated to work in SMT – *Stațiuni de Mașini și Tractoare* (Workshop for Trucks and Tractors). The rationale behind this decision was based on the conclusion that most of the investment in agriculture technology was wasted. According to Gheorghiu-Dej (Moraru and Moraru, 2012, p. 181):

> In 1953 the tractors capacity was used at most at 50%, and in some regions by less than 50%. Also, according to our information, we use 2, 3 even 4 times more spare parts than the norm. This happens because the employees' qualification level in SMTs is very low.

While the very low level of agriculture's productivity represented a clear danger for the country's stability and leaders' popularity, this measure definitely had a strong impact on the industrialisation efforts.

However, as early as in 1951, which was the first year of the first five-year plan, the correspondence between Unirea managers and the Planning Department of the industry's branch ministry showed a consistent shortage of labour force at all levels – from workers to engineers. Such examples are documents D2, D3 and D5. Document D2 started by acknowledging the receipt of the plan of work and salaries for the fourth quarter of 1951, but it also stated that the plan 'is not enough given the present and future tasks and this requires a supplementary number of employees and an increased salaries fund'. On the document's three pages, the author presented the enterprise's detailed case for more workers, technicians, engineers and clerks, as well as for an increased salaries fund. The same document D2 provided evidence of the poor level of planning of personnel numbers. The planning authority demanded an increase of worker number with 33 per cent (from 550 to 735) in few days, because no salary funds were provided for December 195, but all new employees should be in place starting with 1 January 1952. The planned number of workers for the fourth quarter of 1951 was 550, but in the first quarter of 1952 this number was planned to increase to 735. So, the enterprise argued:

> Since we cannot increase the number of workers on the night between 31 December and 1 January, we need to hire more workers in the fourth quarter of 1951. Therefore we ask for an increase of this number by at least 95 workers.

Just two months later, in December 1951, Unirea complained again (document D3) about the insufficient number of workers:

> In order to respect the productivity indicator set by you, in the Labour Force and Salaries Plan for the fourth quarter 548 workers have been required. This figure proved to be insufficient for plan accomplishment.

One year later, the personnel problems seem to have become more acute:

> In the fourth quarter the situation has become more difficult because the production plan has been greatly increased above the initial target, by adding new products which require more thorough preparation. Therefore we need more technicians, but the approved number of technicians was reduced from initially planned 92 to 83. We face the same problems with

> other categories of personnel, as we communicated in message to D.G.M.U.G. no. 386.644/23 Oct.1952.
>
> (D5, issued on 17 November 1952)

The explosive dynamic of employees' numbers proved by the documents regarding Carbochim suggest that in the 1960s the labour shortage had gradually disappeared.

From archival and monograph data regarding the number of workers in three enterprises in Cluj – Unirea, FMR and Carbochim – it is possible to trace the evolution of the number of employees in each enterprise.

Table 6.1 and Figure 6.1 present Unirea's total number of employees from 1938 up to 1990. They reflect on the one hand the extensive industrialisation in quantitative terms, and on the other hand the crises of the 1980s in the Romanian economy. As Mercea (1990, p. 87) noted in the Unirea monograph:

> 1980 represented the best year in terms of productivity and total production, and it was followed by a period of continuous decline. This was reflected by a significant decrease of Unirea production, due to shortage in raw materials and spare parts.
>
> (Mercea 1990, p. 78)

Note: Since FMR was a division within the organisational structure of Unirea between 1973 and 1980, the numbers of employees of FMR are excluded in both Table 6.1 and Figure 6.1 in order to show the evolution of Unirea only.

The register of personnel (*Registru de personal*) of Carbochim provides a detailed description of all employees hired from 1949 until 1963. During this period 1625 persons were hired, and the register mentions the education, nationality, married status, political affiliation and military training. All these elements allowed a statistical analysis of Carbochim workforce evolution over 15 years of enterprises' development.

In the case of Carbochim, no information regarding the total number of employees was identified. But the analysis of the *Registru de personal* gives an insight on the evolution of the enterprise through the number of newly hired employees in each year.

Both datasets presented above suggest an explosive phase of development of both enterprises that had started between 1955 and 1960. For Unirea, according to the enterprise's monograph, the development peaked in 1980. In the case of Carbochim, a lack of data prevents any conclusion regarding the evolution after 1962. But an important conclusion is supported by this analysis: after 1955 both enterprises were developed at a much more intense rate than in the previous decade. This happened just a few years after the Romanian leadership accepted the Soviet criticism and decided to reduce investment in industry and to develop consumer goods branches. After the U-turn decision of the Romanian leaders confronted with the de-Stalinisation process, nationalism and industrialisation were the main characteristics of the independent path of development.

Table 6.1 Unirea total number of employees from 1938 to 1990

	1938	*1948*	*1950*	*1960*	*1965*	*1970*	*1975*	*1980*	*1982*	*1985*	*1987*	*1990*
Total no. of employees	398	408	754	1,158	1,904	2,752	3,199	3,860	3,673	3,365	3,272	3,288

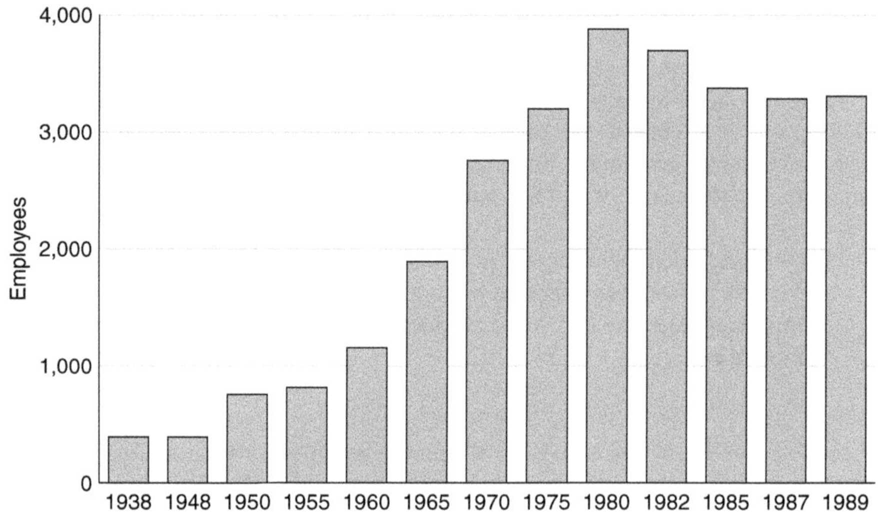

Figure 6.1 Evolution of Unirea's number of employees.

The problem of labour shortage had transformed into its opposite in the late 1970s. According to the informant I5 – who had started his career at FMR in 1979, approximately 15 per cent of the direct productive workforce was redundant in FMR. And this was in addition to the hyper-dimensioned administrative apparatus, with excessive staff in various departments such as personnel, production control and planning. I3 confirmed these estimations. According to I5, a great number of young newly qualified employees with different educational qualifications (from apprenticeship to university level) had to be hired each year, regardless of the real need on the enterprise. Informant I1 also declared that in the last decade of the communist regime, Unirea was able to reach the same level of production using less than 80 per cent of the existing workforce. This illustrates how, in less than two decades, Romanian industry had switched from labour shortage to labour excess. This aspect, correlated with a significant decrease in demand, and with the authorities' pressure to increase the productivity, shows the extent of the real challenges managers had to face.

In qualitative terms, the mentality of *the new man* (*omul nou*) appeared to be significantly affected by the condition in which the working class had been developed. After 1989, the managers blamed this mentality for the very difficult

Table 6.2 Number of hired persons in each year by Carbochim

	1949	*1950*	*1951*	*1952*	*1953*	*1954*	*1955*	*1956*	*1957*	*1958*	*1959*	*1960*	*1961*	*1962*	*1963*	*1968*
Hired persons	13	12	33	67	78	71	44	57	81	85	182	231	355	245	6	1

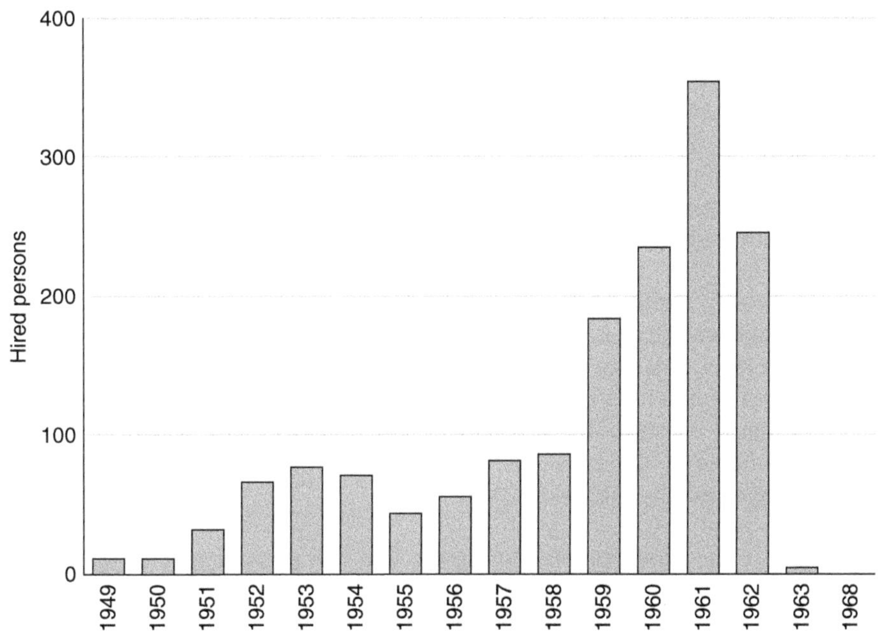

Figure 6.2 Evolution of the number of hired persons in each year by Carbochim.

transition to capitalism: 'Romanians … don't understand that work mentality is very important in life' (O2). The same manager considered the education the main culprit for this phenomenon: '… everybody fought to assure everything for his or her children, but it was an education against work. Those generations are not able to adapt to the new society' (ibid.). The wider prevalence of *pile şi relaţii* in every organisation, dissimulation, corruption and overall the complicity network extending to the highest levels in society have all contributed to this work mentality. The lack of responsibility for work performance and for rule of law was illustrated by one manager's conclusion: 'Generally speaking the concept "if one steals, everybody steals" has been very successfully applied in Romanian society' (O5).

Red versus … not-so-red in education

The communist leaders were well aware of the importance of the education system in order to control society and for the process of the creation of a new working class. Even in 1949, Gheorghiu-Dej declared in a meeting of the Party's leadership that 'the Education Ministry is more important than the Securitate Ministry, because it is about the destruction of our enemy in the cultural field, about training future cadres, about education of the working class' (Moraru *et al.*, 2003, p. 39).

Consequently, the Party had dedicated significant efforts to shape the education system according to ideological imperatives. However, as Tismãneanu, Dobrincu and Vasile (2007) argue, it is not easy to discover the way the system worked with regard to the leadership's aims of building a new working class, because there were no laws relating access to education according to the *social origin* of the candidates. Many directives were secret, or were not published. However, a few reports regarding various measures and personal memories offer a perspective on the significance of social origin for access to education. Tismãneanu, Dobrincu and Vasile (2007, p. 484) described three categories of classification of pupils or students. These categories were:

1 Children of industrial or agriculture workers, collectivised peasants, and small and middle peasants; children of military personnel, engineers, technicians, clerks, cooperative members, craftsmen or of retired parents.
2 Children of small merchants or liberal professionals.
3 Children of *chiaburi* (the Romanian word for kulak), merchants, industrialists; children of war criminals, spies, traitors, saboteurs, those who left the country especially after the WWII.

According to the same authors, during the first two decades of the communist regime, many directives were issued in order to improve the social structure in schools and universities, namely to increase the 1st category intake and decrease the third category. While the primary and secondary education was mostly subject to admission manipulations, in the higher education system multiple methods were used in order to influence the social structure and to promote the *omul nou*. The admissions, the scholarship and bursaries system, and repartition were the main methods used by the Party.

Regarding control of admissions and scholarships, a respondent interviewed by Tismãneanu, Dobrincu and Vasile (2007, pp. 484–485) recalled that the university's admission exam marks of second category candidates was decreased by 10 per cent. The same authors also identified reports regarding the progress in changing the social structure of various schools. For example, such a report dating from 1953 stated: 'the children of the enemies of the popular-democratic state were eliminated from the 6th to 11th years of study, and all the children of *chiaburi*, industrialists and other exploiter elements have been expelled from the pedagogical schools' (ibid.). According to other sources cited by Tismãneanu, Dobrincu and Vasile (2007, pp. 484–485), the third-category children were not admitted to the eighth year of study in schools in the 1951/1952 academic year. The same source reported a decrease of the second-category children enrolled in fifth year compared with the previous year.

A report presented by the Education Ministry indicated that in the 1956/1957 academic year only 9 per cent of the students enrolled at the Bucharest Polytechnic Institute were of 'working class origin' while overall Bucharest higher education institutions this percent was less than 25 per cent. Therefore, in 1957 another directive was issued by the Central Committee of PMR setting the target of 70–75 per cent of enrolled students of first category (Tismăneanu, Dobrincu and Vasile, 2007, p. 486). Apparently, these efforts had better results, a report of the Education Ministry indicating than only 0.1 per cent of the students enrolled in higher education institutions in 1958/1959 being of third-category social origin (ibid.). The same authors mentioned that verbal indications were also transmitted to universities demanding a higher level of attention to the increase of first-category intake and limiting the enrolment of third-category candidates.

According to Tismăneanu, Dobrincu and Vasile (2007, p. 485), the government Decision nr. 2759/17 August 1953 stated that the student's social origin and the political orientation as main criteria for scholarship and bursary. The information provided by the candidates should be verified by the university's personnel department. In this way, the Party tried to increase the access to higher education of the politically loyal allies mostly from the peasant and working classes.

The other important mechanism for controlling the recruitment of young educated professionals was *repartiția* (repartition). Until late 1960s the *repartiția* process for university graduates was managed at university level. Briefly, the whole process was organised as follows: all available places were shared among all universities according to the programmes, the graduates were hierarchised by each university according to their final average mark, and following this hierarchy they chose the enterprise (or research institute, or university in some cases) according to their preference. The graduates would then spend the next three years in the chosen enterprise – the *stagiatură* period. This period was planned as a training period in the industry. After this period, many of them tried by various means to move closer to their native area, or to a bigger city. But at the beginning of 1970s, most of the bigger cities of Romania had become *oraș închis* (*closed city*), which means that it was almost impossible to acquire a *repartiție* or to move legally there.

At the beginning of 1970s, the *repartiția* process was centralised at national level. This means that the graduates' hierarchy was national, as was the pool of available workplaces. The whole process took place once a year, simultaneously for all identical programmes, and in a quite transparent manner. All graduates of a specific programme were gathered in a lecture theatre connected by a teleconference system with the central location. The graduates were informed of the available workplaces, and following the national final mark hierarchy order the graduates selected their desired and still available enterprise. Apparently, this change was done in order to stimulate competition among students, and to encourage mobility at the national level. Respondent I4 recalled that while the graduates were allocated at university level, some arrangements were possible – the manager talked with the dean to get a specific candidate, but when the process became national, such arrangements were no longer possible. So after the beginning of 1970s, all graduates had to go, at least for the first three years, to the enterprise where they were allocated, based on their final average mark. But this change increased the pressure on two other stages: on the struggle for better marks during university education, and on arrangements immediately after the three years of *stagiatură*. It is also worth mentioning that the final mark was a figure between 1 and 10, computed with two decimal places. According to the testimony of I1, the students' political involvement had an important effect on the final mark. For those students elected in a leadership position in UASCR (The Union of the Communist Students Associations), the final mark was increased by 5 per cent (0.5 points out of 10).

After 1948, the students were pressed to enrol in The Romanian Students' National Union (UNSR) and all other students' associations were banned (Tismăneanu, Dobrincu and Vasile, 2007, p. 481). After 1973 the UNSR was renamed The Union of the Communist Students Association (UASCR). The number of its members had increased following the number of students from more than 100,000 members in 1973 to almost 150,000 at the end of 1980s (ibid., p. 155). At the beginning of 1970s, Nicu Ceauşescu – the son of Nicolae Ceauşescu, was appointed the UASCR leader. According to Tismăneanu, Dobrincu and Vasile, 2007 (p. 155), this shows on the one hand how important students organisations were considered, and on the other hand, the regime's tendency towards nepotism, clientelism and dynastic communism. The same authors argued that the will to complete higher education without problems, to have a bursary and canteen access, the fear of being expelled were the main reasons why students enrolled in this organisation. The UASCR structure required a significant number of active and involved students, enjoying a number of benefits for their efforts. While no document was found prescribing how UASCR activists should be rewarded by increasing their final mark, many testimonies confirm this norm (I1, I2 and I4). Therefore, one can conclude that it was not only for better accommodation, bursary, canteen, access to holiday camps that had made many students to compete for becoming UASCR leaders. It also was the possibility to get a better position in the final graduates' hierarchy, so to get a job in a better place. It was also a way to get connected to informal networks which could be useful at later stages of the career.

Hiring in the communist enterprise

In the Romanian planned economy, as in other societies under communist rule in general, the processes of personnel recruitment and selection were quite different from those in a free market economy. In the latter, any organisation aims to attract as many candidates as possible for a specific position, in order to be able to select the candidate who fits best the job's requirements. On the other hand, every person can search for jobs, and can apply for any available position according to their qualifications, skills, ambitions and personal plans. However, in communist society, these basic processes have been consistently different.

The starting point of this analysis is the promise in communist ideology of a society with 100 per cent employment. Unemployment being considered a major dysfunction of the capitalist society, the communist leaders had been very keen to assure a job for everybody. In order to fulfil this objective, a complex human resources allocation system was developed during the communist period. One of the main characteristics of this system was the very limited influence enterprises had over the employment process.

This system is presented below, as it was described by my respondents. According to them, the employment system had a few main sources: universities, professional schools and colleges, and each county's labour agency.

Unskilled workers were allocated mostly by the county labour state agency. Usually they were peasants looking to leave the countryside, but lacking any relevant education. Their normal route was to the county labour agency where they were either sent to an introductory training course for a technical profession and following that to an enterprise, or straight to an enterprise where they were trained according to the enterprise's needs.

In the case of foremen and skilled workers, most enterprises had affiliated colleges and professional schools (*licee şi şcoli profesionale*). These secondary school were integrated into the national education system, but they received additional help in terms of equipment, machinery and internships from the sponsoring enterprise. Not all enterprises sponsored such schools, but most of the significant ones did. For example, Unirea had *Liceul Industrial Unirea* (*Unirea Industrial College*) as its associated college and professional school. Each year a significant number of teenagers graduated with various technical qualifications. Most of them were hired by Unirea, the remaining being allocated to other enterprises. Very few of those graduating from the college applied to university. For the graduates of these schools, the enterprise had the possibility to select the workers to be hired. The selection was based mostly on the internship period the pupils had to spend in the enterprise. In some cases, enterprise staff even taught specific courses, providing an additional source of information for the selection process. I2 recalled a brief experience as a part-time teacher in *Liceul Unirea*, in addition to his full-time job in Unirea.

However, while Unirea had the possibility to select the new employees, the recruitment process – in this case the admission in the school, was completely out of the enterprise's control. In the Romanian education system at that period, the pupils had to pass an admission exam after 8th grade either to the college or to professional school. The better a school was perceived to be by the candidates, the stronger competition for admission was. Industrial colleges and professional schools were considered inferior to colleges providing more academic teaching, where most of the pupils were preparing for university. But especially industrial colleges based in main cities were attractive enough because of the possibility to get a job immediately after graduation in an enterprise with all associated advantages. So most enterprises that were big enough, based in attractive cities, had a constant inflow of skilled workers from their associated industrial schools. While other smaller enterprises based in cities were able to sponsor only specific classes in such industrial schools, hiring skilled workers was more difficult for enterprises based in smaller cities, especially in poor regions.

For university graduates, the employment method was *repartiția*, as described above. Many efforts were made by young graduates to mitigate the consequences of *repartiția* and *stagiatura*. I4 held various management positions in the first decade of FMR's existence. According to his testimony, roughly a third of the number of engineers were hired by various arrangements rather than national repartition. I2 estimated that between 3 per cent and 5 per cent of the university graduates were hired because of Unirea's special interest based on previous experiences with a specific person (usually following internship there). Ninety-five per cent of new employees were hired based on the national repartition process and transfers following the *stagiatură*. I4 described in detail the process of transfer following *stagiatură*. Those graduates who were not able to get a position in Cluj were seeking a position in a smaller city, but in the same *centrală industrială* as a Cluj enterprise. In the case of FMR, a popular destination for such graduates was Baia Mare – a city in the North of Transylvania were another enterprise belonging to the same *centrala industrială* existed. More than that, Baia Mare was not *oraş închis*, therefore there were more available jobs and greater flexibility there. At some point during the three years of *stagiatură*, those keen to move to Cluj tried to arrange six months transfer to the desired enterprise in Cluj. This transfer required the approval of the Cluj enterprise's manager, Baia Mare enterprise's manager and that of the *centrala industrială*. But because both enterprises belonged to the same *centrala industrială*, the transfer did not affect in any way either the total number of employees or the total salaries fund of the *centrala industrială*. Therefore, as long as both managers agreed on the transfer, no opposition was faced from the *centrala industrială*. The six months transfer period was extended a few times, and at the end of *stagiatura* the position was transformed into a permanent one, and the employee was able to settle permanently in Cluj. According to I4, this was the most popular nationwide method used to bypass both the repartition system and the *oraşe închise* (closed cities) policy. This method had a few important consequences, relevant for the efficiency of the whole industry:

- First, it was almost impossible for an enterprise located in a smaller city or in a poorer region to attract the best graduates based on financial rewards, because the salaries system was identical for all enterprises belonging to an industrial branch. The majority of graduates were hunting for positions in main cities, mainly because of the access to better facilities such as infrastructure, schools and hospitals. It can be assumed that most of the best graduates gained jobs in main cities, while graduates having lower marks got jobs elsewhere.
- Second, political activity during university education had also an impact on the student's future career. On the one hand, political involvement was rewarded formally and informally in the evaluation process. On the other hand, involvement in political activity opened the doors to networks of influence that might be useful later on.

- Third, many enterprises located outside main cities had been transformed into 'training stations' for young engineers keen to move in a better place. Of course, in theory the manager could refuse the transfer requests, but in reality once the destination enterprise's manager requested such transfer, and both enterprises belonged to the same *centrala industrială*, the relations were so complex and based on mutual favours, than such a refusal was improbable. Besides this, if the employee wanted to leave and had enough *pile* to arrange the transfer, it made no sense for the enterprise to oppose. However, the technical capacity and performance of such enterprises were negatively affected.

Consequently, the enterprises' ability to recruit and select new employees according to its specific needs and following candidates' evaluation was almost non-existent. The new employees were the result of a highly-centralised repartition system and of the influence traded along the networks of relations.

Serviciul de cadre: red versus expert – Romanian version

Just as the education and training of the new industrial workforce, and the processes by which it was selected for appointments, were all strongly influenced by political and ideological concerns, while at the same time individuals tried to find ways around the restrictions they imposed, so a similar situation was evident in decisions concerning personnel management and promotion of employees after they had been appointed to the enterprise. In order to explore these issues, it is necessary to examine the role of the *Serviciul de cadre* in order to provide a better understanding of the decisional process regarding personnel aspects.

The empirical evidence here is collected from the Unirea archives, from the Unirea monograph and from interviews with former managers and specialists.

Serviciul de cadre was a relatively marginal department in all organisations' structure, in charge with the employees' dossiers (*dosarul de personal*) and with the strict observation of all human resources policies and regulations. It had various names along the communist regime such as *Serviciul de cadre*, *Serviciul Personal şi Formarea Cadrelor*, *Serviciul de Cadre şi Învăţământ* or *Serviciul Personal*. As it results from the multiple *Stat de funcţiuni* (D20-D23) documents, *Serviciul de cadre* of *Unirea* had five or six employees, including its head. In all these documents Serviciul de cadre had an apparently less important position, listed among the last administrative departments.

Many documents were found regarding the activity of *Serviciul de cadre* of Unirea. Most of the activity consisted in collecting information regarding the enterprise's employees, creating impressive dossiers for each employee, and an intense correspondence with other enterprises and institutions. It is clear that the employees of *Serviciul de cadre* had the authority to interrogate not only enterprise's employees or university's students but also other people related to a particular case. Collecting references about a person from former colleagues or neighbours was a regular practice. Each dossier was completed with a significant number of such references.

A document issued on 3 April 1961 (D19) indicates the position, education, salary, social background and political status of all employees of the *Serviciul de cadre*. According to this document, all employees had a working-class background, all were members of PMR, and their education varied between 8 and 11 years of school. The chief of department at that time had eight years of education. This information was produced at the ministry's request (D18). The importance of the *Serviciul de cadre* is evident from the concluding remark to its request for information in which it called on the enterprises' management to be very careful in making any changes to the *Serviciul de cadre* without previously informing the ministry department: 'the Ministry will be informed as early as possible about any change in *Serviciul de cadre.* You will be held responsible for not complying with this rule'.

Serviciul de cadre had also the authority to request information from public institutions such as local councils, or even the Military Court or state prosecutor. For example, *Serviciul de cadre* sent a request dated 22 February 1961 to *Sfatul Popular* (the local council) of Baraolt, Braşov Region, asking for details regarding the wealth, attitude towards collectivisation and political affiliation before 1945 of an employee of Unirea (D24).

On 2 March 1961, *Serviciul de cadre* sent a request to the Military Court of Cluj asking for a brief of a judicial decision regarding the brother of a Unirea employee who was suggested to be promoted as chief of *Serviciul de cadre* in another enterprise (D25).

In another case, an employee of *Serviciul de cadre* studied the dossier of a typist who asked for a transfer to Unirea. The dossier was studied at the office of the city prosecutor. In the *Referat*, dated 11 February 1961, *Serviciul de cadre* did not support the transfer because the applicant intended to leave the country for Israel with her whole family, and she was not a Party member (D26).

It can be also observed that most such requests were signed only by the chief of *Serviciul de cadre*. The impressive amount of work invested in this activity can be observed in the letters attached when individual dossiers were transferred from one enterprise to another. Those letters also indicate the dossiers' number of pages. The number of pages of the letters identified in Unirea's archive varied between 41 and 76.

According to the respondent I1 *Serviciul de cadre* had always been the director's main source of information, it had applied secret criteria and procedures, all its employees were rigorously verified by the Securitate, and there were rumours that some of them were Securitate informants. However, according to I5 the *Serviciul de cadre* was never neither interested, nor competent to help the managers with useful human resources advices, because of the poor qualifications of its members.

A detailed insight into the way the *Serviciul de cadre* operated is offered by the case of Pangraţiu Aurel, a talented student, whose application for a job was refused by Unirea general manager. The Pangraţiu dossier shows in a detailed and descriptive manner the way personnel selection was being managed in

Unirea at the beginning of 1960s. Exactly in the same period, the enterprise had started to implement a very ambitious development plan of increasing its production capacity by five times. This increase also required a significant increase in the labour force, as detailed in Unirea's monograph and from the statistics presented above. This was also a period of chronic raw materials shortages, acknowledged by the authorities in administrative documents and official directives which pressed enterprises and planning authorities to limit the quantities of various materials, to improve the technology, the design and the equipment used in the production process.

Eight documents in particular are relevant regarding the case of Pangrațiu Aurel, documents relevant for the manner in which the enterprise management and departments handled a hiring case in which professional expertise collided with the personal characteristics and an uncertain past of the applicant. All documents analysed below were identified in a single dossier. Five documents were issued in December 1960, while the other three were produced in 1959. The document which shows what seems to be the initial reason for the whole dossier was a transfer request from another enterprise to Unirea (D30). The other four documents issued in December 1960 illustrate the debate regarding this decision. The documents provide a detailed description of the way personal dossiers were produced, the effort invested in personnel activities, the extent of surveillance through personal relations and connections, and last but not least, on how the candidate's personal background impacted on a personnel decision. This particular case is very relevant for illustrating the balance between political trustworthiness and expertise in 1960s Romania.

On 16 December 1960, Pangrațiu Aurel submitted a request to the comrade director of enterprise Unirea to be transferred from another enterprise based on his desire 'to work in an enterprise with a profile closer to my specific education as a graduate of the Mechanical Faculty of the Cluj Polytechnic Institute'.

An autobiography dated 20 December 1960 (D31) was attached to the request. It contained personal details – place and date of birth, parents, school and work experience. A few elements appear to be relevant in connection with other documents from his dossier. His father was an officer in the Romanian Royal Army and he fought both in the Eastern campaign against the Soviet Union, and in the Western campaign against Germany. After the war, his father became a Party member but in 1951 he was arrested and detained without any trial until his death in 1955. Pangrațiu also declared that in 1950 he was excluded from the Party because 'I was considered untrustworthy and because nobody could guarantee I wouldn't flee the country'. According to Pangrațiu's autobiography, this decision was also based on incorrect interpretations of his own previous declarations in which he admitted that up to 1945 – when he was 16 years old, he wanted to leave for the USA. Pangrațiu argued that this intention was a reaction against the German occupation. Pangrațiu was affected by his exclusion from the Party, which hampered his activity. In 1955 Pangrațiu was enrolled by Cluj Polytechnic Institute, but on 15 February 1960, after the final exams, he was expelled.

On 21 December 1960, two documents were issued by Unirea departments, one by the Chief of the Mechanical and Investment Service (*Serviciul Mecanic Şef şi Investiţii*) eng. Cadar Romulus (D33), and the second by the Personal and Cadres Training Service (*Serviciul Personal si Formarea Cadrelor*) (D32).

The first document, which was signed by the chief of the service, begins with the conclusion: 'The applicant was verified by us and corresponds to our requirements in terms of professional competences and knowledge'. Eng. Cadar argued the Pangraţiu knew Russian and German languages, and in addition possessed extensive knowledge in electrical engineering and automation. This was an important advantage for the enterprise because Unirea's machines required a specialist with that knowledge. Pangraţiu additionally knew foreign languages, a fact which made him more valuable for translation operating instructions written in foreign languages, respectively for machines' maintenance as it was required by a specific ministry's order. Cadar also noted that he had been specifically looking for such a person for a long time and therefore he recommended the approval of the transfer required by Pangraţiu. Cadar also mentioned that he was

> ... aware that he is not politically suitable, but today we really need such a specialist and we propose solving the problem by accepting its political situation. If this comrade we already verified will not be accepted, we request the enterprise's management to provide us as soon as possible with another comrade who will meet the professional conditions shown above – specialised in automation and electrical problems and knowing Russian and German languages. We also note that if the enterprise management will not provide us such a comrade, we cannot fulfil the Ministry's Order 258/1960, which we had until 30 June 1960 to fulfil.

The document issued by Personnel and Cadres Training was entitled *Notã informativã*, and it bears the director's hand-written resolution: 'He won't be hired' ('*Nu se va angaja*'). The document begins by stating that:

> Pangraţiu Aurel submitted us a request to accept his transfer from his current employer to our enterprise. His request is supported by eng. Cedar Romulus, who argues that without Pangraţiu he cannot fulfil his department's tasks, because Pangraţiu has deep knowledge in the fields of electronics and automation, and he can speak Russian and German languages.

Then the document briefly describes the main points of Pangraţiu's personnel dossier. His father was an officer in the Romanian bourgeois army, until 1945 he held important positions in the General Staff, Intelligence service. He fought on the Eastern front from 1941. In 1950, he was arrested by the state security authorities and held in prison until 1955 when he died. Pangraţiu Aurel joined the School of Civil Aviation in 1942, and in 1950 was expelled from PMR and from Civil Aviation because of his unhealthy social origin (*originea socială nesănătoasă*), and because of his desire to emigrate to the USA expressed around 1945. The document concludes that

> Because of the above described aspects, our service does not politically endorse the hiring of this person as a technician in the enterprise. We suggest that the Party Committee and the enterprise management should analyse the above facts, the report prepared by Ing. Cadar, and decide accordingly.

These documents clearly show that while such an employee was suitable and desirable for the enterprise's professional requirements, his political background limited the possibilities for his being hired by Unirea. They also clearly show that political arguments were more powerful in comparison with the professional qualities. Even if eng. Cadar showed that he was looking for such an employee for a long time, and that the lack of such qualification limits the fulfilment of an order that had been due to be implemented six months earlier, his request was denied based on ideological reasons. The negative report of *Serviciul Personal şi Formarea Cadrelor* dictated the manager's final decision. In order to create a better perspective over this particular decision, other documents will be briefly analysed below. In the context of that period it is important to understand the negative aspects of Pangraţiu's political characteristics.

On 22 December 1960, Cluj Polytechnic Institute issued a brief hand-written document (D34), without any title, regarding Pangraţiu Aurel. In a list of bullet points are presented the main negative aspects of his personal life:

- In a statement made on 8 April 1960 he argued that … his desired to leave for USA (1945) because he saw the USA as the country of freedom.
- In 1946 he attended 'American culture' courses (Romanian-American Association). Also his father was offered an American passport in order to flee to the USA with the whole family.
- When the American Mission left the country in 1947, he was invited to leave Romania.
- Divorced three times.
- His ex-wife told us Pangraţiu intended to flee Romania in an aircraft to the USA.
- Impertinent, treacherous person with a provocative behaviour.
- Suspicious person, not trustworthy.
- In 1942–43 he was in Cernăuţi. (former Romanian city, today part of Ukraine)
- Impertinent in relations with his neighbours.
- Hired as electrician at Electromontaj.
- Expelled from Polytechnic Institute in February 1960.

The letter is unsigned, but it is dated. It shows clearly the negative intent of this information letter. Only negative aspects are listed, and none of those are supported by relevant information. In spite of the fact that this letter had been issued by the Polytechnic Institute, no comments were made regarding Pangraţiu's professional skills, knowledge or obtained grades. Not even the reasons for which Pangraţiu was expelled were presented. Objective aspects, such as his current workplace and number of divorces, were mixed with negative allegations in the language of that time, for example that he was '*element dubios, nu inspiră încredere*'. The letter had as its obvious objective to create difficulties for Pangraţiu in his professional life.

The other three documents are helpful on the one hand to understand why Pangraţiu was not considered acceptable as a Unirea employee despite his professional knowledge, and on the other hand to understand how personal information was collected, analysed and later on used in such decisions.

The first of these documents in the Pangraţiu dossier, in chronological order, was a paper entitled *Referat asupra studentului Pangraţiu Aurel*, and it was issued on 24 April 1959 by the *Serviciul de cadre* of the Polytechnic Institute Cluj (D27). The document presents a brief account of Pangraţiu's father, without mentioning his arrest and his death in prison without any trial. An important element in this document is the following statement:

> Based on an information obtained from other persons, our service has found out that Pangraţiu Aurel tried in his biography to deceive the management of our institute. After several discussions in our office, he completed his biography accordingly. The following elements were added to Pangraţiu's biography:
>
> - His father was arrested by the Securitate and detained in Fãgãraş prison until 1955 when he died. Until the moment he was arrested, he was a member of the PMR.
> - Pangraţiu was excluded from the Party because of the following reasons:
> - Until 1945 he explicitly wanted to leave the country,
> - He constantly missed Party meetings because during the meetings he used to work,
> - He did not have a healthy social origin (*origine sãnãtoasã*).
> - In 1945 or 1946 he took English lessons at the Romanian-American Association. He could also speak Hungarian, French, German, Italian, Spanish and Russian.

After this list of new elements of Pangraţiu's biography, *Serviciul de cadre* added some conclusions drawn out of its investigations: 'We have to mention that student Pangraţiu represents a negative example for other students. He is an impertinent and untrustworthy person, he doesn't respect and defies our professors. This behaviour is a direct consequence of his family's education'. These aspects seem to be a constant feature of the characterisation of Pangraţiu by the Polytechnic Institute. However, his previous desire to leave the country, his family background, his attitude towards professors, his knowledge of foreign languages were the main arguments used by *Serviciul de cadre* to stop the professional evolution of a promising young student, with practical experience and deep knowledge in fields very important for an industry in the process of extensive development.

Most of the arguments described above were debatable, even in terms of the political correctness of that period. Pangrațiu's family background was non-working class, but nevertheless his parents were not a part of the petty bourgeoisie, nor did they own properties. As an officer in the Romanian Royal Army, his father fought on the Eastern front, but he also fought on the Western front, where he was wounded. His father passed previous Party investigations since he was even secretary of a local Party organisation. No document gives any clue regarding the reasons for which he was arrested and detained without trial, in a period when trials were mostly the legalisation of Party's decisions.

Aurel Pangrațiu's statements about his intentions to leave the country were made at an early time during the German occupation. However, he was later admitted to an aviation school, where if he really had the intention he would have been able to flee Romania. Finally, his attitude towards the Party and in relation with his professors seems to be at based on subjective allegations.

The next document identified gives a useful insight regarding the sources *Serviciul de cadre* used in order to create such dossiers. It is entitled *Notă de relație*, and it was issued on 10 July 1959 (D28). This document represents the account of a meeting between one employee of *Serviciul de cadre*, and one of Pangrațiu's former wives. This woman, a simple railway worker, added a lot of negative aspects to Pangrațiu's characterisation. It must be also noted that the information synthesised in *Notă de relație* was collected a few months before Pangrațiu was expelled from the Polytechnic Institute. According to Pangrațiu's ex-wife, 'he had a violent character, he often cheated on her, he did not allow her to continue her education' and because of all these reasons she became ill. This is the moment when the employee who wrote the report asked the key question: 'Out of all these aspects, one may ask why Pangrațiu got married to this girl?' After he enumerated a few other episodes, he concluded that 'Pangrațiu was not attached at all to this girl, he probably married her in order to hide his social origin, because she is a railway worker.' Other interesting aspects added by Pangrațiu's ex-wife was that 'he often used to say that if he really wanted to leave the country, we would have been able to do it when he was in aviation'.

The last document identified in the archives regarding Aurel Pangrațiu is a *Referat* issued by *Serviciul de cadre* of the Polytechnic Institute on 24 November 1959 (D29). Probably this was the official document which supported the decision to expel Pangrațiu from the Institute. The document provides an extensive résumé of all the personal aspects of Pangrațiu's life: family background, education, his desire to leave for the USA, foreign languages knowledge, aviation school, three divorces and exclusion from the Party. This document is apparently a development of the previous *Referat* issued by the same *Serviciul de cadre* on 24 April 1959. Two main aspects were added to this last *Referat.*

First, the argument that 'he seldom used to say that if he wanted to leave the country, he would have been able to do so when he was in aviation' is taken from his ex-wife's testimony. This aspect was included in the *Referat*, probably as an argument supporting the untrustworthiness of Pangraţiu, implying that the Party, the working class cannot trust such person who openly discuss about leaving the country.

Second, another important aspect introduced in this *Referat* was a brief paragraph regarding Pangraţiu's professional performance:

> From the professional point of view, Pangraţiu is a capable person, he has passed all his exams very well, and he is a prominent member of our scientific students' circles (*cercuri ştiinţifice studenţeşti*). However, his behaviour is not always correct in relation with some professors. He is an impertinent and untrustworthy, he underestimates and defies some professors.

According to the *Referat* author, one of Pangraţiu's most important shortcomings was his lack of involvement in group activities (*activitatea obştească*), especially in patriotic work. Usually in such cases, Pangraţiu missed these activities calling in sick. More than that, he had been heard saying he could do any activity but not political activity. The author concluded that Pangraţiu had deep political knowledge, but his political level (*nivelul politic*) was unsatisfactory. The main conclusion of the *Referat* represents a significant synthesis for all these previous judgements: 'In conclusion Pangraţiu is a very capable person from professional point of view, but he is also a dubious person, untrustworthy, insincere, and he is a negative example for the students'. According to the documents identified in Unirea archives, this was the last document issued before Pangraţiu was expelled from the Polytechnic Institute in February 1960. Also, this document synthesises the arguments for which one year later, his transfer to Unirea was denied, despite the acute need for people with such qualifications in order to fulfil the development plan, and despite the well-argued case made by the chief of *Serviciul Mecanic Şef şi Investiţii*. Although Pangraţiu was a good student he was expelled from Institutul Politehnic. Although he had very valuable knowledge for Unirea, and even the chief of *Serviciul Mecanic Şef şi Investiţii* insisted on this, his transfer was denied. This event happened in the year in which the very ambitious development plan was due to be fulfilled, and according to the letter received by Unirea director in January all efforts had to be made in order to attain unconditionally the planned production capacity.

While the Romanian economy experienced an acute shortage of specialised workforce from the very beginning of the extensive industrialisation process, while Party leadership had to confront the mistakes made earlier in this process, while other forms of dysfunctionalities (e.g. plan mismanagement at enterprise level, raw materials shortages) had started to be officially acknowledged, and while political relations with the Soviet Union had just entered the cold war phase, as Frunză (1999) named it, the personnel decisions were made according to the dogmatic and narrow approach.

All these aspects suggest the existence of a separate network of control, out of the official organisational structures, in charge of personnel management in the Romanian economy. *Serviciul de cadre* decided not only on hiring or promotion issues, but also on expelling students from higher education organisations. As the case presented above shows, these decisions were made against the interests of respective organisations. Some of the respondents – I1 and I4 – suggested that *Serviciul de cadre* was connected better with the Securitate rather than the enterprise manager or Party organisation. This may explain the apparent lack of interest of *Serviciul de cadre* in these organisation's results.

The interviews and the documents identified in Unirea's archive also undoubtedly argue such a characterisation of *Serviciul de cadre*:

- An almost complete lack of knowledge regarding personnel procedures aimed at the development of a competent and efficient industrial workforce;
- A weak interest in enterprise's results, efficiency or objectives;
- A focus on investigation and control of all possible aspects of the personal and professional life of employees, students and probably all citizens.

Consequently, it was not the Party, the unions, or other employees' structures that played the role of gate keeper in Romanian industry. *Serviciul de cadre* was the key element, connected probably with the Securitate, which held all the information and the access keys to upward social mobility. Poorly educated but trustworthy employees decided who deserved to graduate, to be employed and to be promoted in Romanian organisations. According to the respondents, this key role of *Serviciul de cadre* had been constant through the entire communist period. I1 argued that *Serviciul de cadre* always had a very important say in all personnel decisions, it was the director's source of information, and it was suspected that its employees were always likely to be informants or under-cover agents of *Securitate.*

Further evidence of the concentration of all power in managers' hands was also confirmed by the discussions between students and post-1990 managers. Two of the participant managers described the multiple roles played by the directors, under the justification of plan fulfilment: 'All organisations were managed by engineers, everything came from structures above, and they had only to push the production forward' (O7).

The whole society's centralism was replicated at each enterprise's level: 'industry was centralised; each factory had only to produce. In these conditions, the manager had to be the best leader, the best accountant, and the best political and trade union leader' (O7). Every director was a 'little Ceauşescu' in his enterprise, leading a production system rather than an organisation, with the help of two apparently less important departments – *Serviciul de cadre* and *Serviciul Plan.*

In spite of power sharing between the enterprise's manager, the Party secretary, the union leader, and other management structures (*COM, autoconducerea muncitorească*) widely advertised by the official propaganda, the general manager was the central power figure. As it can be observed in

Pangrațiu's case, the Party influence in enterprise decisions was very weak if not completely lacking. This decisional tight centralism explains why *COM* and *autoconducerea muncitorească* largely failed. The managers had been able to undermine any attempt to share the power, and the working class lacked the tradition, power and knowledge to balance managers' power in the organisational structure.

Serviciul Plan: the negotiation ritual

In contrast with the rather marginal position occupied by *Serviciul de cadre* in the organisational structure, *Serviciul Plan* held a much more visible position. In all *Stat de funcțiuni* (D20–D23) documents *Serviciul Plan* was the first one listed immediately after the enterprises' management. According to the documents analysed in the previous chapter, *Serviciul Plan* had played an important role in the official correspondence and negotiation of various plan targets with the ministry. This section is exploring the informal networks of influence in which the department was involved.

Two respondents were particularly important to clarify the negotiation process between the enterprise and the planning authorities: I2 and I4. During discussions with them, a ritual of negotiation of the plan emerged as the reality behind the previously discussed official correspondence.

I2 worked in Unirea for more than 25 years. He was the chief of *Serviciul Plan Dezvoltare* starting with 1974 until 1990. After 1990 he was appointed Unirea's general director.

The respondent I4 had worked for 26 years in the plan department. He started his activity in 1973 in the *Serviciul Plan* of *Unirea*, and from 1980 to 1990, he was the head of *Biroul Plan Dezvoltare* of FMR. Both of them had been deeply involved in the process of setting, modifying, adapting and fulfilling the annual plans. Their testimonies corroborated with the archival documents offer a more clear perspective over the managerial practices deeply embedded in the Romanian command economy. Therefore, the information provided by I2 and I4 is very useful in order to describe the reality behind plan negotiations, the purpose and meaning of the documents previously identified in the archives, the methods, actors and incentives of the negotiation process.

I4 started by defining the process of planning as a 'ritual', with different phases, actors and objectives. The paragraph below describes the ritual, as it resulted from the respondents' answers.

The whole process used to start in the summer of the previous year, when the main plan targets were sent by the plan authorities – the branch ministry until 1973, and from that moment on the *centrala de ramură*. In the early autumn – usually September or October – the employees' structure *Adunarea Generală a Oamenilor Muncii (AGOM)* enthusiastically approved the plan targets, usually promising plan over-fulfilment. Some observations regarding the feasibility of the plan targets were also recorded, but with no specific aim or result at that moment. These observations used to highlight potential limits, dangers or needs which may have affected the plan targets, but also included the employees' commitment to overcome any difficulty.

Immediately after the AGOM meeting, the enterprise's director asked *Serviciul Plan* to begin a very important work – the calculation of the production capacity. This quite laborious work aimed to generate the real production capacity, based on equipment, machines, labour and other resources presumed to be available for the planned year. According to I2 and I4, this was an important, difficult and complex work which used to require all employees of the *Serviciul Plan* for few months.

Once the real figures were computed, the chief of *Serviciul Plan* together with the director had an in-depth analysis and compared the figures with the received targets. I4 recalled numerous situations in which the director asked him to go back and re-compute the figures so the results will be lowered: 'we were asked to mislead the authorities, to change the results we worked intensely for, therefore to support our director strategy with fake results'.

Since the enterprise's final figures resulted from each section, department, or division own figures, re-calculation supposed an internal negotiation process in which the *Serviciul Plan* was asking other departments to reduce the capacities. I3 confirmed that he had to agree such adaptations quite often. Of course, such demands could not be made in official documents therefore the process supposed good personal relations within the enterprise. The chief of *Serviciul Plan* should have been a key element in this organisational structure, in spite of the apparent low level of importance of the department. Officially, *Serviciul Plan* had the role of breaking down the annual plan in quarterly and monthly targets, to record plan completion and to report the results to the central authorities. As it was argued in the previous chapter, *Serviciul Plan* was also in charge with plan negotiations according to enterprise's needs. These findings shows that *Serviciul Plan* was also in charge with the plan negotiations within the enterprise.

After a short period of time, the new results were produced and a detailed documentation was authorised by the enterprise's director. This documentation supported the optimal level of capacity, as the director considered to submit forward. The head of *Serviciul Plan* was in charge with this. Therefore, he had to make a visit to the planning authorities – usually the industrial branch *centrala* – delivering the documentation. Usually this documentation ended up on the shelves, without any comment or feedback. However, I4 recalls that 'many times I was told that "I know you're lying, but I cannot prove this" by the *centrala* chief planner'. When I4 was asked about the purpose of the manipulation of the production capacity, he answered that the main objective was to support the director in his attempts to obtain lower targets using his informal channels of communication with various levels of Party leadership. However I4 also stated that 'finally, the easiest way to get the targets we wanted was to bribe the chief planner of *centrala*'.

I1 also recalls how the general director of Unirea always had a shortcut to discuss with the Party's leaders at local but also at the central level, so Unirea used mostly this method to obtain the targets he considered attainable. But I1 also mentioned that bribery was a usual method to obtain anything from authorities. It must be mentioned here that bribery usually involved gifts, valuable commodities of that period such as whiskey, Western brands of cigarettes (Kent was the most sought after brand, a real currency in the overwhelming shortage of goods) and money, but to a lesser extent. This can be easier explained by the generalised shortage of products, when most people had enough money but not options to use that money. Also, considering the continuous process of negotiating, favours exchange had an important role in the process.

The main objective of all individual involved in this apparently complex process was to make sure that the plan will be fulfilled and over-fulfilled. This was a crucial aspect for of few reasons:

- The enterprise had enough money to pay the salaries. Any plan un-fulfilment potentially affected the salaries funds, so the director would have had to deal with angry workers. O8 recalled the worst experience in his career when few hundreds angry workers cornered him in his office because the salaries were cut. This happened because the enterprise he worked at the moment for did not fulfilled the plan and the management failed to dissimulate the event on due time.
- The managers received financial bonuses and their position in the formal and informal structures was improving. This improvement was very important because it provided more power to negotiate and raised the chances to be promoted.
- The local Party' leaders were happy to have an efficient enterprise in their area of responsibility. Each time an enterprise officially failed to fulfil the plan, the local Party authorities were held responsible and had to act immediately to correct the situation. Improving the ideological level and more political education were the usual methods the Party was supposed to use in order to correct the situation. The plan was considered perfect, and therefore it was the political commitment that led to failure.
- The planning authorities were also happy to report that enterprises fulfilled and over-fulfilled the plan. Any failure was perceived as incapacity to strictly supervise enterprises in the production process. Again, the plan was considered perfect, therefore more administrative measures were required to control plan fulfilment.
- Finally, the Party leaders were delighted to be able to announce every year that the annual plan was over-fulfilled therefore the country was firmly on its path towards communism.

But in the end, the price of this process – a masquerade as I4 called it – was the economic collapse. I4 recalled that six to eight months' worth of production simply did not exist in enterprises' deposits in 1990. In other words, the economic price of plan manipulation, of constantly dissimulating plan fulfilment, and avoiding salary problems demanded wiping out the production for almost an entire year. There is no quantitative evidence which would allow the estimation of the extent of this phenomenon at the scale of the whole economy. But a simple extrapolation of Unirea's experience would suggest that at the end of 1989, 50–70 per cent of the wealth created by the whole country in a year was reported but never produced.

I5 also added that in the last years of the communist regime, at least a third of FMR production was delivered to other enterprises from the same *centrala industrială*. Officially, the aim of these deliveries was to endow the enterprises with the latest available technologies. I5 recalled that FMR had received in the same period machines produced by those enterprises. According to I5 this was a strategy to keep enterprises producing, even if the industry was unable to use those machines.

In addition to resources depletion, the system of permanent dissimulation had affected profoundly the mentality of a newly born working class and it produced an uncertain work environment: 'There were so many people working in uncertainty, who often had to go against the rules in order to make things work' (O5).

Conclusions

The problems examined in this chapter concerning questions relating to personnel, involving the training, selection, promotion or dismissal of employees, reflect at root the failure in communist Romania to create a real working class in a very short period of time. While in quantitative terms there seemed to be a rapid growth of the industrial working class, in reality the trend reflected a large number of peasants tempted by the urban better life to flee rural areas and transform themselves in a formal sense into workers. To a large extent this was convenient for the Party leadership: an amorphous working class was much easier to manipulate not only in ideological terms, but also in physical terms. As a relevant example, this is how thousands of workers were sent by Gheorghiu-Dej to fix the agriculture machines and equipment in 1953. But this is also one of the reasons why later attempts to enhance workers' involvement in enterprise management also largely failed. Another argument supporting this conclusion is the very low level of influence at organisational level of two fundamental structures of the communist regime: the Party organisation and the trade unions. As evidenced in this chapter and Chapter 5, it seems the enterprises were managed by the director with the help of two small but powerful structures: *Serviciul plan* and *Serviciul de cadre*.

The communists used the education system to control society and to create an obedient new working class. In 1949 Gheorghiu-Dej declared that 'the Education Ministry is more important than the Securitate Ministry, because it is about the destruction of our enemy on the cultural field, about training future cadres, about the education of the working class' (Moraru *et al.*, 2003, p. 39). Consequently, the students' social origins and their implication for political activities had an important impact on their access to education and to a job in a better place. However, the same networks of *pile şi relaţii* was used to play the *repartiţia* system. As Ledeneva (1998, p. 40) observed regarding the Russian concept of blat, this meant it was 'a matter of belonging to a circle'. Rather than being just an influencing method, *blat* and its Romanian counterpart *pile şi relaţii*, expressed a kind of favour accessible just to *people of the circle, to one of us*. Furthermore, the documents analysed in this chapter show how the education system, especially the higher education graduate repartition system, was manipulated so employees with *pile şi relaţii* were able to change their workplace and even move in a 'closed city'.

The empirical findings in both this chapter and Chapter 5 have shown how systemic constraints, both the plan and the graduates' repartition systems, were preferred by managers because both saved time and effort for the enterprise, but as well because both were subject of informal arrangements. These informal arrangements – to adapt the plan to the general manager's preference or to hire somebody who was not allocated to the enterprise by the central repartition system, were more than methods of adaptation, but were methods to maintain and enhance the managers' power and positions in such network. The capacity and willingness to help someone else was the one side of the same coin – the other one being the ability to ask for help when needed.

However, in other ways as well, at least in the period for which relevant documents were identified, political criteria significantly dominated over professional performance. The case of Pangraţiu Aurel undoubtedly shows how the enterprise's manager decided to follow the suggestion of *Serviciul de cadre* against the request of the mechanical service. *Red* versus *expert* never was a real dilemma in Romanian communist society, as it results from Pangraţiu case, but as well from Ceauşescu's report: 'our society demands highly skilled managing cadres, with deep political knowledge, unswervingly devoted to the cause of socialism and communism' (Ceauşescu, 1967, p. 77). But in the Romanian case, the meaning of *red* was different than devotion to communism; the real meaning was devotion to the Party leadership and to its real structure. The constant position within *Unirea* of *Serviciul de cadre* until 1989 suggests that its influence had remained un-changed throughout the communist regime.

As has been shown from the documents and from interviews, the secretary of the enterprise's Party organisation was only involved in any kind of decisions to a very limited extent, regarding production problems or regarding personnel problems. While union organisations were just a facade structure, one may expect Party organisation to be deeply involved in the enterprise's problems. But in reality, the Party secretary and the union leader were involved mostly in the formal structures such as the local Party organisation, *autoconducerea muncitorească* or *Consiliul Oamenilor Muncii*. What really mattered was the manager's connection with the higher Party and state authorities. As seen in Chapter 5, good relations with the county's Party secretary and with ministers were far more important in order to manipulate the plan targets or the results. Equally important was the access to the chief planner of the branch industry structure – *centrala de ramură*.

Serviciul de cadre was the real gatekeeper of the communist system. It had more power than other enterprise departments. As the collected evidence suggests, the systems' political constraints were more important than other demands such as development and production targets. It also had decisional power over issues like the expulsion of Pangraţiu in the last year of his studies in spite of his professional performance and mostly based on subjective allegations. *Serviciul de cadre* had not only decisional power but also investigative capabilities, the individual dossier being the product of the service's decision on how references and other personal details should be interpreted. It can be reasonably concluded that after the spheres of influence of the repressive institutions like the *Securitate* or *Miliţia* had been reduced, *Serviciul de cadre* acquired important powers over each person's development and career. According with I1, the power and influence of *Serviciul de cadre* remained unchanged up to the end of the communist regime.

Serviciul Plan was the key piece in the puzzle of complicated negotiations undertaken before the plan was set. *Serviciul Plan* had to supply all technical arguments supporting the manager's objective to get an achievable plan, had to adjust the productive capacities accordingly, and finally had to undertake the official contact with the planning authorities.

The ritual behind the negotiation of both the plan targets and the results suggests that the most important asset for a director was his connections with Party and administrative bureaucrats. The enterprise's planners were supposed to provide all the technical arguments required to support the director's objectives. This network of relations was held together by political and financial advantages, mutual favours and bribes. Behind the apparent rational correspondence between the enterprise and the planning authorities, an invisible network of relations transcending Party and state official structures had facilitated the apparent plan fulfilment, and therefore the apparent economic success.

Note

1 However, as Murgescu (2010) and other authors have argued, in real terms the development gap between Romania and Western economies or even other East European economies increased.

References

Brucan, S. 2012. *Generaţia irosită*. Bucureşti: Editura Teşu.

Ceauşescu, N. 1967. *Report Concerning Measures for Perfecting the Management and Planning of the National Economy and for Improving the Administrative-Territorial Organization of Romania, National Conference of the Romanian Communist Party*. Bucharest: Agerpres.

Direcţia Centrală de Statistică. 1990. *Anuarul Statistic al României*. Bucureşti.

Fotaki, M. 2009. Maintaining the Illusion of a Free Health Care in Post-Socialism: A Lacanian Analysis of Transition from Planned to Market Economy. *Journal of Organizational Change Management*, 22(2).

Frunză, V. 1999. *Istoria comunismului în România*. Bucureşti: EVF.

Gallagher, T. 2005. *Theft of a Nation. Romania since Communism*. London: Hurst.

King, R.R. 1980. *History of the Romanian Communist Party*. Stanford, CA: Hoover Institution Press.

Ledeneva, A.V. 1998. *Russia's Economy of Favours: Blat, Networking and Informal Exchange*. Cambridge: Cambridge University Press.

McGregor, D. 2006. *The Human Side of Enterprise*. New York: McGraw-Hill.

Mercea, G. 1990. *Unirea Cluj-Napoca. 150 de ani. 1840–1990*. Cluj-Napoca.

Moraru, C. and Moraru, C. 2012. *Stenogramele şedinţelor Biroului Politic şi ale Secretariatului Comitetului Central al P.M.R. Vol. V. 1953*. Bucureşti: Institutul Naţional pentru Studiul Totalitarismului.

Moraru, C., Neagu, L., Moraru, C., Neagu, C., Dincă, C. and Zamfir, I. 2003. *Stenogramele şedinţelor Biroului Politic şi ale Secretariatului Comitetului Central al. P.M.R. Vol. II. 1949*. Bucureşti: Arhivele Naţionale ale României.

Murgescu, B. 2010. *România şi Europa. Acumularea decalajelor economice (1500–2010)*. Iaşi: Polirom.

Nelson, D.N. 1988. *Romanian Politics in the Ceauşescu Era*. New York: Gordon and Breach Science Publishers.

Shafir, M. 1985. *Romania: Politics, Economics and Society*. London: Frances Pinter.

Tismăneanu, V., Dobrincu, D. and Vasile C. 2007. *Raport Final al Comisiei Prezidenţiale pentru Analiza Dictaturii Comuniste din România*. Bucureşti: Humanitas.

7 Conclusions

The aim of this book was to examine the main organisational and social characteristics of the Romanian industrial enterprise under communist rule. By employing an interpretive approach, the research explored the complex relations between state planning bodies, enterprises and the managers.

The approach adopted in the research was multi-disciplinary, drawing on industrial management, economics, organisation studies, sociology and political science. The research was also trans-disciplinary because it aimed to create an over-arching perspective on Romania's industrialisation process during the communist regime.

The approach employed in this study was the one labelled by Burrell and Morgan interpretivist. This means that the author's set of assumptions over society and social research lies on the subjective side of the philosophy of science dimension, and is characterised by an integrationist view of society.

The research methods employed were predominantly qualitative, based on interpretation of data collected using interviews and document analysis. Quantitative data was used descriptively to a small extent aiming only to support other findings and conclusions.

The contributions to the current state of knowledge of this book are three-fold. First, the empirical data offer a more accurate image of the practices and actors involved in the management of the planned industry. The practices identified in Romanian communist industry are different to a certain extent from those identified by Berliner in the Soviet enterprise. Definitely these practices had been influenced by the specific characteristics of Romania. This conclusion supports the idea that proper investigation is required to identify the specific characteristics of each communist country. This conclusion also suggests the need for a deeper investigation of each country's communist past in order to understand better its post-communist evolution.

Second, at a meta-theoretical level, a conflict between the ideological orthodoxy and the industrial practices is identified and described. This conflict reflects a competition between two different approaches in managing the whole planned economy between the Party's leadership and the enterprises' managers. In the case or communist Romania, this conflict had undermined the economic performances, led to accumulation of losses, and finally to the collapse of the system.

Third, the potential of the interpretivist approach is revealed from the methodological perspective. Especially in a context with less reliable quantitative data, this sort of research approach could provide very useful data and therefore contribute to a better understanding of the social and economic system.

Empirical findings

The empirical research had three main objectives:

- The formation and key features of Romanian industrial enterprises during the process of industrialisation under the communist regime.
- An in-depth description of the continuous process of negotiation of the plan objectives between enterprises and central state structures.
- The analysis of the human resources processes of the Romanian communist enterprise.

The conclusions of the empirical research are structured based on these initial objectives. The empirical research's contributions help understand better the way Romanian communist enterprise had functioned, the main similarities and differences with the Soviet practices summarised by Berliner, and offer an in-depth description of the plan negotiation and human resources practices. The shortages of various resources had been present from the very beginning of the planned economy, accompanied by significant dysfunctionalities of the planning process, which led to a sophisticated negotiation process of the plan. The negotiation process had aimed to secure the salaries and to keep safe the managers' positions, but also had undermined the feed-back which would have provide reliable data regarding the real economy capabilities. In this way the corrective mechanism, essential especially in a centralised economy, had been almost eliminated.

The predominant qualitative approach, based on interpretation and understanding, provided rich findings relevant for three enterprises – Unirea, FMR and Carbochim. However, there are not enough reasons to argue that all the conclusions are valid for the whole Romanian planned economy. The hyper-centralised structure of the Romanian communist state suggests that the processes identified in these three cases were probably endemic, however, this is an assumption that requires further verification rather than a widely accepted fact. Another research limitation is related with the available documents and former employees. The researcher had very little influence over the selection of archival documents and over the former employees accepting to be interviewed. And while one could expect more archival documents to be available in the future, fewer former employees with long-term first-hand experience of work during the communist regime will likely be available for evident reasons.

The formation and key features of Romanian industrial enterprises during the process of industrialisation under the communist regime

Berliner identified 10 practices that had survived virtually unchanged for almost five decades in Soviet industry. Some of them were also present in the Romanian communist economy. Perhaps the most important similarity regards the constant focus on relating wages to performance. In the Romanian case, this focus took two forms: pressure on the productivity indicator and the implementation of the system *salarizarea în acord global. Pile şi relaţii* – the Romanian version of *blat* – but with a wider and more complex meaning than the one offered by Berliner, was the crucial element in the plan negotiation process. Another similar feature was the lower level of concern regarding quality. Because the plan's focus was almost exclusively oriented towards quantitative indicators, the incentive to improve quality was very weak. The 'ratchet' principle was undoubtedly present in the Romanian planned economy. Romanian enterprises preferred to produce established products, but many employees were enthusiast about the introduction of new technologies and products. Moreover, any new product was an opportunity to negotiate the plan targets and to hoard labour time – a very useful method to secure the salaries fund.

Shortages from the beginning

Resource shortage started to be officially acknowledged in 1960, 10 years after the beginning of the planned economy. While during the first decade, labour was the scarcest resource, in less than 10 years raw materials became the main topic of directives calling for a brutal reduction in consumption. The pressure towards reduction of use of certain raw materials indicates either an unbalanced development exceeding the available resources – a hypothesis which is supported by the memoires of Gaston Marin – or a lack of control over resource consumption at enterprise level. Regardless of the cause of the shortage, the solution envisioned by the Party and implemented by the planning authorities was to reduce radically the consumption of deficit resources with an arbitrarily decided percentage. The reductions required defied any technological principles, and created supra-bureaucratic structures in charge of very detailed aspects of industrial production. In many cases, the resources available in reality were far lower than the resources allocated by the plan. In this situation, there was a critical need to develop informal mechanisms in order to acquire all the resources needed for fulfilling the tasks. The bribes, influence, barter and informal networks were examples of such mechanisms. The whole pursuit to create new and more productive technologies, better and cheaper products failed in less competitive products, old technologies, low level of employees' motivation, loss generating enterprises.

Dysfunctionalities from the beginning

The collected evidence shows that significant dysfunctionalities in the planning process had appeared from the very beginning of the industrialisation process in communist Romania. The evidence also outlines one of the main strategies used by enterprises to avoid or dissimulate indicators of non-fulfilment: the increase of norms for new products, which means labour hoarding strategy, in order to create reserves for further reductions if required.

These dysfunctionalities combined with irrational pressures to increase productivity and decrease material consumption had contributed to a significant extent to the 1980s dramatic crisis. The managers had developed and refined a number of strategies to deal with these problems: plan negotiation, dissimulation, resource hoarding, influence, bribes and even blackmailing the authorities with workers' unrest as consequence of reducing the salaries.

The cumulative effect of these strategies was dramatic: in 1990 Unirea production of six to nine months was simply wiped off the enterprise's records, because it simply did not exist in the enterprise's deposits or in the production flow. This suggests the scale of the economic failure of the Romanian planned economy at the end of 1980s: between 50 per cent and 75 per cent of one year's total production.

Constant loss accumulation

A growing gap between official results and reality had created rising tensions in the financial system. At the beginning of 1970s two attempts were made in order to correct this problem: the recalculation of prices (*reaşezarea preţurilor*) and labour legislation reform. Both attempts had as their main target a better understanding and a better running of the economy. But since prices recalculation ended in failure in less than four years, salary reduction and inflation were the only available valves which could reduce financial tensions in the whole economy. According to Gheţea (2015) printing money was used seven or eight times in the last 22 years of the communist regime. This means that every two or three years of the last two decades of the communist regime, the financial losses were transformed into hidden inflation. Extra money was put into the economy, but no additional products or services were available for the customers. While in the last decade Ceauşescu pushed for an increase in exports at any cost in order to return borrowed money from foreign countries or institutions, the internal market had to bear the consequences of the system. This irrational drive had immediate consequences at enterprise level. While the targets were incessantly increasing, the allocated resources were reduced.

The continuous process of negotiation of the plan objectives between enterprises and central state structures

One of the most relevant findings regarded the continuous negotiation of the plan. This process had been undertaken in two major stages.

The first stage was predominantly informal and took place usually before the beginning of the year. *Serviciul Plan* was the key element in the puzzle of complicated negotiations undertaken before the plan was set. *Serviciul Plan* had to supply all technical arguments supporting the manager's objective to get an achievable plan, had to adjust the productive capacities accordingly, and finally had to contact the planning authorities. The ritual behind the negotiation of both the plan targets and the results suggests that the most important asset for a director was his connections with Party and administrative bureaucrats. The enterprise's planners had to provide all the technical arguments required to support the director's objectives. If necessary they had to adjust the enterprise's capacities according to the manager's desired plan targets.

In the second stage, the plan indicators were systematically changed throughout the whole year. The planning process usually began in the last quarter of the previous year and both parties dispute the values of the indicators. Even in 1951, a period of terror, arrests and deportations, the enterprise seems to have had a significant bargain power with the planning authorities. In the 1960s the enterprise used two main arguments to dispute the plan indicators received. One argument used was the need to assure salaries at promised level. The other argument concerned the burden produced by the investment plan. The enterprise's main objective was to obtain additional funds either as more money for salaries, or as additional funding for the investment plans.

The enterprises seem to have had a strong negotiation power in relation to the planning authorities based on two main advantages: their knowledge regarding the industry, and the control the enterprises had over the working class through salaries.

The network of relations centred on the enterprises' managers was held together by political and material advantages, mutual favours and bribes. Behind the apparent rational correspondence between the enterprise and the planning authorities, an invisible network of relations transcending Party and state structures had facilitated the apparent plan fulfilment, and therefore the apparent economic success.

The human side of the Romanian communist enterprise

While in quantitative terms the Party succeeded in its pursuit to create an industrial working class, in reality a large number of peasants were tempted by the urban better life to leave rural areas and transform themselves into workers. The predominantly rural character of Romania – one of the most visible symptoms of its economic backwardness – provided an almost unlimited source of workforce. But while tempting peasants with an urban life was easy, transforming them into a real working class was difficult, especially in such a short period of time. To a large extent this was convenient for the Party leadership: an amorphous working class was much easier to manipulate not only in ideological terms, but also in physical terms. But this is also one of the reasons why later attempts to enhance workers' involvement in enterprise management also largely failed. As well, the transformation of a largely rural mass of workers into passionate members of Party local organisations or of trade unions had proved to be also difficult. This is why these organisations had a very low level of influence on the enterprise's activity. To a large extent the enterprises were managed by the general manager with the help of two small but powerful structures: *Serviciul plan* and *Serviciul de cadre*. The enterprise's Party organisation and trade union were usually rubber stamping the decisions taken by its manager.

The education system had played a very important role in the process of industrialisation, and of creation of an obedient new working class. The students' social origins and their political involvement had an important impact on their access to education and to a job in a better place. However, the same networks of *pile şi relaţii* was used to play the *repartiţia* system. The graduates' repartition systems were the subject of informal arrangements, of *pile şi relaţii* system. These informal arrangements – to adapt the plan to the general manager's preference or to hire somebody who was not allocated to the enterprise by the central repartition system, were more than methods of adaptation, but were methods to maintain and enhance the managers' power and positions in such network. The capacity and willingness to help someone else was the one side of the same coin – the other one being the ability to ask for help when needed.

The case of Pangraţiu Aurel undoubtedly shows the influence of *Serviciul de cadre* compared with the influence of the technical departments. *Red* versus *expert* never was a real dilemma in Romanian communist society. The meaning of *red* was different than devotion to communism; the real meaning was devotion to the Party leadership and to its real structure. The systems' political constraints were more important than other demands such as development and production targets. *Serviciul de cadre* had investigative capabilities, the individual dossier being the product of the service's decision on how references and other personal details should be interpreted. It also controlled *rezerva de cadre*, the list of persons suitable for promotion. By not including or excluding a person from *rezerva de cadre*, their career evolution could have been cut out. In this way *Serviciul de cadre* controlled not only the present, but also the future of the employees and of the country's elite. *Serviciul de cadre* had had a strong influence throughout the communist regime. It can be concluded that *Serviciul de cadre* was the real gatekeeper of the communist system, not only at the upper echelons of the Communist Party, but in every enterprise.

Serviciul plan had played a crucial role in the process of plan negotiation both before plan setting and after the plan was approved and sent to the enterprise. While *Serviciul de cadre* had played a less visible role, *Serviciul plan* enjoyed a higher status in enterprises' structure. Its official objective was to manage the plan implementation, to transform the enterprise's plan indicators into targets for each section and department, to supervise the plan fulfilment and to report the plan status to the ministry and to other central structures. The research empirical findings reveal the important role *Serviciul plan* had played in the plan negotiations. The negotiation ritual, as one of the respondents called it, suggests that the manager of *Serviciul plan* was also a member of the informal network of connections involved in the process of plan adjustment so the enterprises could report plan fulfilment. *Serviciul plan* had to convince the managers of productive departments to support the technical arguments behind enterprise's demands for lower targets, had to provide extensive documents requesting better plan indicators, and finally its representatives had to convince in various ways ministry's responsible to accept enterprise's demands. During plan implementation, the same *Serviciul plan* had to undertake long correspondence with the ministry arguing for various plan adaptations, so the employees' salaries were not endangered by plan un-fulfilment.

The potential of the interpretivist approach

According to Burrell and Morgan's meta-theoretical framework, the approach employed in this study is interpretivist. This approach is based on a set of assumptions which lies on the subjective side of the philosophy of science dimension, and is characterised by an integrationist view over society. In contract to the dominant functionalist approach, the interpretive paradigm may offer a better understanding of events and evolutions which reveals the systems of meanings, and the structuring and organising processes. According to this paradigm, the organisation is structured by the patterned relationships developed by individuals, these relationships serving as heuristics and symbolic forms. The organisation is not only a rigid, pre-determined structure, based on a set of rules and procedures established elsewhere, but it consists also in a pattern of relationships, more or less formal, with a significant influence over its existence and evolution. The theory-building is more inductive, starting with collection of data that are relevant to the informants, theory-generation being iterative and nonlinear.

There are a few reasons for which the interpretive approach had been used in this research. First, the lack of consistent and reliable statistical data has made very difficult the understanding and forecasting of the communist economies real state and evolution. The second reason is the widespread existence of various types of informal relationships (e.g. blat, *pile şi relaţii*). Third, in spite of the highly irrational constraints imposed by the communist leaders, work conflicts seldom erupted. This suggests that besides the Securitate and Miliţia, the social groups had accommodated to each other to a large extent, and the understanding of the relations between the groups is very important. Finally, the existence of rich archival data, combined with the existence of a significant number of former employees of the communist enterprises, are strong arguments supporting the need of such research approach.

The book's conclusions based on the empirical findings support the potential of the interpretivist approach in the attempt to understand the way in which the enterprises had functioned in the communist regime.

Managers – the grave diggers of the Romanian planned economy?

The hypothesis emerging from the use of the Burrell and Morgan frame was that the ruling group on top of the Communist Party and the enterprises' managers had used different perspectives on the functioning of the industrial system. In order to explore this gap, it is necessary to place the official Marxist-Leninist ideology and the centralised planning system at work in the Burrell and Morgan's frame. Then it may be possible to understand the contradiction between managers and the ruling group in a centralised planned economy.

Apparently, the ruling communist ideology could be placed in the quadrant of radical change theory – aiming for the radical change of society, for new social and work relations and for a continuous struggle with internal and external enemies.

In practice however, this continuous struggle was mostly a survival strategy for the Party's leadership in competition with internal challengers – both from inside the Party and the society, and with external pressures for change. The Romanian communist leaders' reaction manifested a stronger ideological orthodoxy, a tightening control and a focus on industrialisation suggesting that despite its origins in revolutionary Marxism, leaders' approach had become a mode of thinking, a mode of control over society. Therefore, it may be also possible to place the Party's leadership strategy to lead the society and economy in Burrell and Morgan's functionalist quadrant. This quadrant is defined by a tendency to regulate rather than conflict. The objectivist perspective is common for both radical change and functionalist quadrants. This ambiguity worked well for the ruling elite because the pursuit for extensive industrialisation was rooted both in the Marxist-Leninist ideology – the radical change theory, and in science and rationality – a functionalist approach. However, the predominance of the ideology over the rationality was visible in the reaction of the Party's leaders after the 1953 harsh Soviet criticism. They considered the planning committee as the main culprit, but this happened because the leadership neglected to guide CSP properly. Therefore, it can be concluded that a tight ideological dogma, rooted in Marxism but following the leaders' interests, was framing the economic development strategies. This characteristic was present from the top of the leadership down to the enterprises' level.

But this ambiguous mix of dogma and rationalism had created significant problems for the industrial managers who were faced in practice with problems of achieving efficiency and increasing production, while motivating their workforce, implementing effective recruitment and promotion strategies, and salary policies that would be acceptable or at least tolerated by the workforce. The increasingly deterministic, even functionalist character of the planning and development strategies were embedded in a dogmatic Marxist ideology which aimed to conserve the elite domination over the society, but also restricted the possibilities for reaction, adaptation and dynamic improvement of the system of central planning, and failed to offer the managers a framework within which to analyse their problems and devise practical solutions. Instead managers had to innovate informal solutions, based of influence, mutual advantage and personal connections rather than impersonal rules and procedures. These solutions belonged more in the subjective dimension and were more voluntarist in nature, perhaps belonging to the Burrell and Morgan's interpretive perspective over society. While neither scientific nor Marxist in their nature, these solutions had the significant advantage of not challenging the position of the ruling elite. However convenient this behaviour was for the Party's leadership, it also had palpable effects on the real economy. This is why the enterprises' managers were probably the first social category aware of the inevitable collapse of the economy. They were aware of the growing distance between economy's real performances and official statistics. While the Party and administration apparatchiks involved in these networks had less knowledge about the real dimension of dissimulation, the managers knew more precisely the gap between planned targets and the reality in their enterprises. As one of the respondents recalled, in 1990 most of the enterprises simply eliminated from their balances an important quantity of production or stock which was reported but did not exist in reality. In the case of Unirea the production of 6–8 months was simply wiped out of the records because it didn't exist.

To summarise these findings, it can be suggested that a small group composed of the enterprises' managers helped by *Serviciul plan* managers – with technical and informal expertise, and *Serviciul de cadre* – as the system's gatekeepers, well connected with local Party apparatchiks, and other key persons within the ministries or other planning bodies were responsible for the development and perpetuation of this system of informal relations. Of course it may be argued that *pile şi relaţii* was not a characteristic of just the industry, it was a pervasive reality of the entire society. However, the impact of this group actions on the overall economic performance had led to the almost complete failure experienced by the country in the last decade of communism. Going back to the Chapter 2 question, '*Was there a new ruling class?*' this book's answer is '*No, it was no new ruling class*'. It was rather a web of networks of individuals holding different positions, managers of important enterprises and of few departments in these enterprises, bureaucrats in ministries and *centrale industriale*, Party apparatchiks at local or regional level, that were able to manage the economic activity of large industrial sectors, and to manipulate the targets and the industrial output. It wasn't even one or more social groups, because there are no reasons to assume that all enterprises' managers were a part of these networks, or all Party leaders at local levels were involved in these networks. On the other hand, it can't be concluded that the enterprises' managers were the gravediggers of Romanian planned economy. Or, at least, not all of them. But it can be argued that some of them, especially those managing important enterprises, were key participants in the networks described above.

This conclusion is very much in line with Djilas's assessment that communism 'gravediggers are its own more or less doctrinaire pragmatists' (Djilas, 1969, p. 143). In Romanian experience this pragmatism had been limited to a certain extent by a combination of *pile şi relaţii* and narrow ideological fundamentalism.

References

Burrell, G. and Morgan, G. 1979. *Sociological Paradigms and Organisational Analysis*. Aldershot: Ashgate.

Djilas, M. 1969. *The Unperfect Society: Beyond the New Class*. London: Methuen.

Appendix 1

List of archival documents

Doc. no.	*Date*	*Document title*	*Issued by*	*Addressed to*
D1	28 Aug. 1951	Request	Planning Dep., Metallurgical Industry Ministry	Unirea
D2	13 Oct. 1951	Additional labour force request	Unirea	Planning Dep., Metallurgical Industry and Chemical Industry Ministry
D3	15 Dec. 1951	Justification for additional labour force and salaries	Unirea	Planning Dep., Metallurgical Industry and Chemical Industry Ministry
D4	7 Aug. 1952	Ref. inadequate excessive salaries fund	Unirea Chief Planner	Planning Dep., Metallurgical Industry Ministry
D5	17 Nov. 1952	Report on difficulties regarding the labour force plan	Unirea	Planning Dep., Metallurgical Industry Ministry
D6	11 Jan. 1960	Ref. investment plan for 1960	Unspecified	Unirea
D7	29 Oct. 1960	Ref. labour and salaries plan for 1961	Unirea	Heavy Industry Ministry, Planning Department
D8	5 Dec. 1960	Labour and salaries plan for 1961	Unirea	Unspecified
D9	5 Jan. 1961	Request	Heavy Industry Ministry, Planning Department	Unirea
D10	28 Jan. 1961	Salaries fund adjustment for 1961	Heavy Industry Ministry, Planning Department	Unirea
D11	1 Feb. 1961	Salaries fund adjustment for 1961	Heavy Industry Ministry, Planning Department	Unirea
D12	4 Apr. 1961	Order 142	Metallurgy and Machines Building Ministry	General

Doc. no.	*Date*	*Document title*	*Issued by*	*Addressed to*
D13	6 Apr. 1961	Bonus fund award	Metallurgy and Machines Building Ministry	Unirea
D14	17 May 1961	Productivity adjustment	Metallurgy and Machines Building Ministry	Unirea
D15	8 Jun. 1961	Labour force plan	Unirea	Metallurgy and Machines Building Ministry
D16	13 Feb. 1962	Order 21	Metallurgy and Machines Building Ministry	Unirea
D17	16 Feb. 1962	Order 31	Metallurgy and Machines Building Ministry	General
D18	31 Mar. 1961	Request	Heavy Industry Ministry, *Serviciul Personal Învăţământ*	Unirea
D19	3 Apr. 1961	Table with the employees of *Serviciul Cadre*	Unirea	Heavy Industry Ministry, *Serviciul Personal Învăţământ*
D20	1 Jan. 1965	*Stat de Funcţiuni*	Unirea	
D21	1 Oct. 1966	*Stat de Funcţiuni*	Unirea	
D22	1 Mar. 1967	*Stat de Funcţiuni*	Unirea	
D23	1 Nov. 1968	*Stat de Funcţiuni*	Unirea	
D24	22 Feb. 1961	Request	*Serviciul de cadre*. Unirea	*Sfatul Popular* (the local council) of Baraolt
D25	2 Mar. 1961	Request	*Serviciul de cadre*. Unirea	Military Court of Cluj
D26	11 Feb. 1961	*Referat*	*Serviciul de cadre*. Unirea	
D27	24 Apr. 1959	*Referat*	*Serviciul de cadre*. Institutul Politehnic Cluj	
D28	10 Jul. 1959	*Nota de relaţie*	*Serviciul de cadre*. Institutul Politehnic Cluj	
D29	24 Nov. 1959	*Referat*	*Serviciul de cadre*. Institutul Politehnic Cluj	
D30	16 Dec. 1960	*Request*	Pangraţiu Aurel	The Director of Enterprise Unirea
D31	20 Dec. 1960	*Autobiografie*	Pangraţiu Aurel	
D32	21 Dec. 1960	*Nota informativă*	*Serviciul Personal şi Formarea Cadrelor*. Unirea	
D33	21 Dec. 1960		*Serviciul Mecanic Şef şi Investiţii*	The Management of Unirea
D34	22 Dec. 1960		*Serviciul de cadre*. Institutul Politehnic Cluj	

Appendix 2

List of participants

I1 Unirea Chief Engineer until 1989. He graduated in mechanical engineering. This company was his only employer until 1990. After 1990 he went to Bucharest to work in different positions in the Romanian government.

I2 Chief of *Serviciul Plan Dezvoltare* of Unirea starting with 1974 until 1990. After 1990 he was appointed Unirea's general director.

I3 He had worked for 35 years for FMR. He was the chief of *Secţia Prelucrări Mecanice* from 1982 until 1990. In 1994, he was promoted to the position of *Director Producţie*.

I4 He had worked for 26 years in the plan department. He started his activity in 1973 in the *Serviciul Plan* of Unirea, and from 1980 to 1990 he was the head of *Biroul Plan Dezvoltare* of FMR.

I5 He had started his career at FMR in 1979. From 1981 until 1989 he was the head of *Secţia Montaj*. In 1994, he was appointed general director of FMR.

O1 Researcher during the communist regime in the field of economics. Currently university professor of management in Cluj.

O2 General Manager of an industrial organisation UNIMET Cluj, a part of the former Combinatul de Utilaj Greu Cluj. He graduated in 1962 in engineering, and worked in a few industrial organisations. After 1990 he was appointed general manager of UNIMET.

O3 Manager of a producer of industrial equipment for the textile industry – FIMARO Cluj. At the time of the interview the company had 1,100 employees. He had a degree in engineering obtained in 1969.

O4 Manager of an industrial company specialising in railway equipment maintenance. The company was founded in 1869. He graduated in mechanical engineering in 1971.

O5 Manager of a beer producer, URSUS, founded in the eighteenth century. The company was experimentally privatised in 1992. He graduated in electronics engineering. He left the company and at present is a well-known businessman.

O6 Manager of a ceramic wall tiles producer, SANEX Cluj. The company was founded in 1970. In 1996, it was privatised to the employees' association, now it is a part of an important Austrian group and it has 450 employees. He graduated in chemical engineering in 1978.

O7 Manager of communist Romania's biggest shoes producer – Clujana, founded in 1922. The company had an important number of employees and it integrated almost all technological flow. After 2000 it went bankrupt and was closed.

O8 Former chief of planning department at Combinatul de Utilaj Greu Cluj. He has double degree in engineering and economics. Currently he is university professor of management.

Index

Page numbers in **bold** denote tables, those in *italics* denote figures.

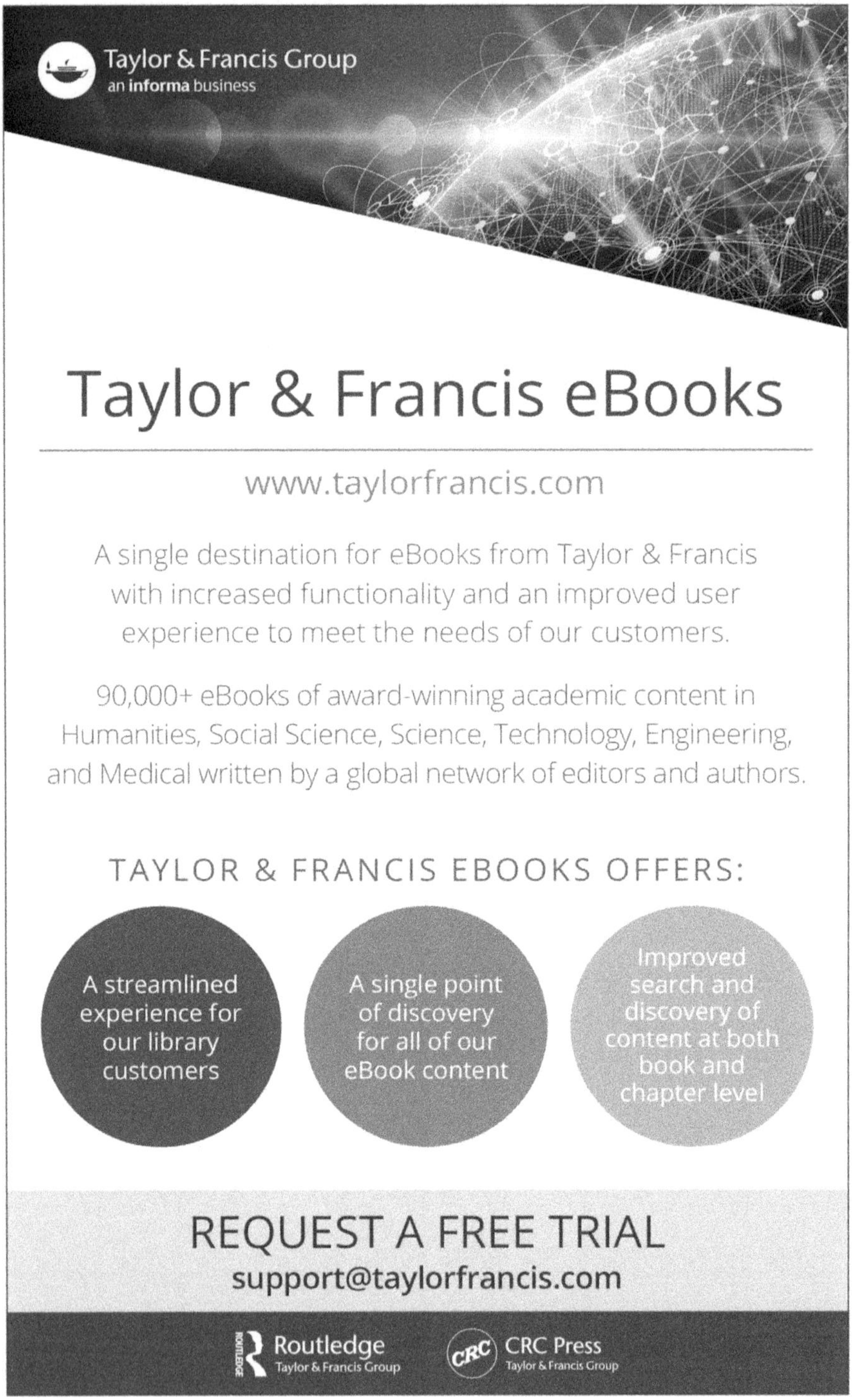

Taylor & Francis Group
an informa business
Taylor & Francis eBooks
www.taylorfrancis.com
A single destination for eBooks from Taylor & Francis with increased functionality and an improved user experience to meet the needs of our customers.
90,000+ eBooks of award-winning academic content in Humanities, Social Science, Science, Technology, Engineering, and Medical written by a global network of editors and authors.
TAYLOR & FRANCIS EBOOKS OFFERS:
A streamlined experience for our library customers
A single point of discovery for all of our eBook content
Improved search and discovery of content at both book and chapter level
REQUEST A FREE TRIAL
support@taylorfrancis.com
Routledge Taylor & Francis Group
CRC Press Taylor & Francis Group

For Product Safety Concerns and Information please contact our EU representative GPSR@taylorandfrancis.com
Taylor & Francis Verlag GmbH, Kaufingerstraße 24, 80331 München, Germany

www.ingramcontent.com/pod-product-compliance
Ingram Content Group UK Ltd.
Pitfield, Milton Keynes, MK11 3LW, UK
UKHW011014180926
475701UK00004B/731
9780367438562